European Yearbook of International Economic Law

Special Issue

The European Yearbook of International Economic Law (EYIEL) is an annual publication in International Economic Law, a field increasingly emancipating itself from Public International Law scholarship and evolving into a fully-fledged academic discipline in its own right. With the yearbook, the editors and publisher intend to make a significant contribution to the development of this "new" discipline and provide an international reference source of the highest possible quality. The EYIEL covers all areas of IEL, in particular WTO Law, External Trade Law for major trading countries, important Regional Economic Integration agreements, International Competition Law, International Investment Regulation, International Monetary Law, International Intellectual Property Protection and International Tax Law. In addition to the regular annual volumes, EYIEL Special Issues routinely address specific current topics in International Economic Law.

More information about this subseries at https://link.springer.com/bookseries/8848

Marc Bungenberg • Andrew Mitchell
Editors

The Australia-European Union Free Trade Agreement

Springer

Editors
Marc Bungenberg
Saarland University
Saarbrücken, Germany

Andrew Mitchell
Monash University
Clayton, Victoria, Australia

ISSN 2364-8392 ISSN 2364-8406 (electronic)
European Yearbook of International Economic Law
ISSN 2510-6880 ISSN 2510-6899 (electronic)
Special Issue
ISBN 978-3-030-91447-9 ISBN 978-3-030-91448-6 (eBook)
https://doi.org/10.1007/978-3-030-91448-6

This Springer imprint is published by the registered company Springer Nature Switzerland AG.
The registered company address is: Gewerbestrasse 11, 6330 Cham, Switzerland

Acknowledgements

The editors wish to express their sincere gratitude to the authors for staying up to date with the ongoing negotiations, updating their chapters prior to the publication of this book to include the most current information, and patiently handling the disrupted publication schedule due to the COVID-19 pandemic. Further, the editors would like to express their appreciation for the collective effort of the team that contributed to the publication of this volume, especially Anna Moskal.

We would also like to thank all the readers for deciding to purchase this book. We trust that you will find inspiring and thought-provoking input in the discussion of future commercial relations between Australia and the EU within this publication and we hope that you will truly enjoy reading it.

Contents

Overview of the Australia–European Union Free Trade Agreement

Marc Bungenberg and Andrew Mitchell

Contents

1 Introduction

Since 18 June 2018, ten rounds of negotiations for an Australia–European Union Free Trade Agreement ('AEUFTA') have been held in a constructive atmosphere, demonstrating a shared commitment between Australia, the European Union ('EU') and its Member states to moving forward with an ambitious and comprehensive agreement. After a lengthy and arduous process disturbed by the United Kingdom's ('UK') withdrawal from the EU, the United States' hesitations regarding the EU's global strategy, and the arrival on global shores of the COVID-19 pandemic, the

M. Bungenberg (✉)
Saarland University, Saarbrücken, Germany
e-mail: bungenberg@europainstitut.de

A. Mitchell
Monash University, Clayton, VIC, Australia
e-mail: andrew.mitchell@monash.edu

M. Bungenberg, A. Mitchell (eds.), *The Australia-European Union Free Trade Agreement*, Special Issue, https://doi.org/10.1007/978-3-030-91448-6_1

negotiations between Australia and the EU finally appear to be nearing completion. Despite challenging times, both parties have demonstrated a shared commitment to a positive trade agenda and the mutual benefits that come with boosting trade, investment, jobs, and economic growth.

This introductory chapter offers a survey of the political and regulatory landscape in which the AEUFTA and its negotiations are now situated. By presenting an overview of the differences and values shared between Australia and the EU, this chapter provides an appropriate background for the analysis in subsequent chapters of the challenges, achievements and missed opportunities that have attended the AEUFTA negotiation process. This background encompasses existing legal and political relations between the EU, its Member States and Australia, as well as each party's trade and investment endeavours with other countries. These relations are shaped by a diverse range of issues, including digital trade, services, intellectual property, trade remedies, investment screening, and dispute settlement mechanisms.

The work presented in this volume will shed light on what will likely be the future shape of commercial relations between Australia and the EU, and the future of those economies' trade and investment negotiations.

2 The European Union and Australian Political Dynamic

Perhaps the most persistent geopolitical issue now dominating Australia-EU relations is climate policy. Even after the EU has passed its much-anticipated Carbon Border Adjustment Mechanism, Australia continues its policy of "technology not taxes"[1] approach to lowering emissions—for which it has been criticised heavily both at home and abroad.[2] In 2021, the Australian Government dedicated $1.2 billion under its national Budget to developing an Australian hydrogen industry. Roughly half is to fund hydrogen and carbon capture and storage hubs, while the other half is to be invested in establishing international partnerships and low emissions projects.[3] In April, Australia opened its $50 million Carbon Capture, Use and Storage Development Fund for more significant investment in carbon recycling, negative

[1] Angus Taylor, 'Keeping our export markets free, open and tax free' (Media Release, 4 August 2021) <https://www.minister.industry.gov.au/ministers/taylor/opinion-piece/keeping-our-export-markets-free-open-and-tax-free>.

[2] Michael Mazengarb, 'Time to stop flirting with "blue" hydrogen and go green, experts say' (*Renew Economy*, 14 May 2021) <https://reneweconomy.com.au/time-to-stop-flirting-with-blue-hydrogen-and-go-green-experts-say/>.

[3] Commonwealth of Australia, Budget Paper No. 1: Budget Strategy and Outlook 2021–22 (11 May 2021) 28.

emissions/direct air capture, and carbon capture and storage technologies in collaboration with economies like Japan, Singapore, and Korea.[4]

But European countries also hope to benefit and partake in Australia's hydrogen strategy. Australia has since entered into partnership agreements with Germany[5] and the UK.[6] Trade missions and diplomacy efforts continue between Australia and EU countries.[7] Trade delegates from Australia and European countries, including Australia's key partner France,[8] continue to discuss and review opportunities in Australian renewable energy and hydrogen production and agriculture and their shared interests in secure and reliable critical mineral supply chains.[9] All of this comes as the EU seeks to impose its climate policies on other countries like Australia, showing an unwillingness to engage in climate issues at the same level as its UNFCC counterparts.

Similarly, the liberalisation of agriculture markets agreed to under the in-principle accord between Australia and the UK may act as a warning bell for the EU, which is committed to protecting its subsidised agricultural markets and maintaining its grip on its agriculture regulatory environment. Similar political tensions caused rifts between UK trade and agriculture departments.[10] Meanwhile, the expansion of Australia's agriculture sector, particularly in industries where it has long sought market access (e.g. beef, sugar, seafood, wheat and dairy),[11] is occurring as Australia's emerging battery and critical minerals industries continue to create European export and investment opportunities.[12] As the EU (along with its UK

---

[4] Christian Porter and Angus Taylor, 'Building Australia's hydrogen industry through research collaborations' (Joint Media Release, 6 July 2021) <https://www.minister.industry.gov.au/ministers/porter/media-releases/building-australias-hydrogen-industry-through-research-collaborations>.

[5] Angus Taylor, 'Australia and Germany partner on hydrogen initiatives' (Media Release, 13 June) <https://www.minister.industry.gov.au/ministers/taylor/media-releases/australia-and-germany-partner-hydrogen-initiatives>.

[6] Angus Taylor, 'Australia-UK partnership to drive low emissions solutions' (Media Release, 29 July 2021) <https://www.minister.industry.gov.au/ministers/taylor/media-releases/australia-uk-partnership-drive-low-emissions-solutions>.

[7] See e.g. Steven Marshall, 'Bonjour, SA! Paris Trade Office to drive SA export growth in Europe' (Media Release, 16 June 2021) <https://www.premier.sa.gov.au/news/media-releases/news/bonjour,-sa!-paris-trade-office-to-drive-south-australian-export-growth-in-europe>.

[8] Bröhmer (this volume).

[9] Dan Tehan, 'France-Australia Joint Statement on visit to Paris' (22 April 2021) <https://www.trademinister.gov.au/minister/dan-tehan/media-release/france-australia-joint-statement-visit-paris>.

[10] Peter Foster and George Parker, 'UK government split over Australia trade deal' (*Australian Financial Review*, 18 May 2021) <https://www.afr.com/world/europe/uk-government-split-over-australia-trade-deal-20210518-p57stt>.

[11] See Department of Agriculture, Water and the Environment, 'Agricultural Trade and Market Access Cooperation (ATMAC) Program' (20 August 2021) <https://www.agriculture.gov.au/market-access-trade/atmac>.

[12] Australian Trade and Investment Commission, *Unlocking Australia-India Critical Minerals Potential* (Report, July 2021) 21.

and Asian competitors) continues to dominate the electric vehicle market,[13] and Australia seeks to diversify its export markets beyond China, these developments bring Australia and Europe into even closer alignment in the international arena.[14]

These developments reveal a nuanced political and economic relationship between Australia and the EU. The United Kingdom's withdrawal from the EU has also created new dynamics in the realignment of international relations. Jürgen Bröhmer argues that relationships of varying intensity do not only exist between Australia and the UK, but also between Australia and the member states of the EU, and with the EU itself. On the back of discussion around intellectual property and data exclusivity protection for pharmaceuticals, this realignment and 'the significant EU reform agenda and other emerging global changes' were most recently cited by Australia's Therapeutic Goods Administration ('TGA') as important considerations in the reform of the TGA's International Engagement Strategy.[15]

As Bröhmer's chapter reveals, behind binding legal instruments between Australia and EU, there are both unique historical ties and emerging economic and political dynamics that will remain highly relevant to the development of the Australia-Europe relationship.

3 Dispute Resolution Procedures in the AEUFTA

Both Australia and the EU have spoken repeatedly of the rules-based international order's importance. In May 2021, the Australian Government said that the "multilateral rules-based trading system, with the World Trade Organization . . . at its core . . . is critical to Australia's economic recovery and prosperity".[16] Both economies have not paid mere lip service to these ideals but continue to rely on dispute settlement procedures within the multilateral trade regime and under Free Trade Agreements ('FTAs'). The EU is the second biggest litigator at the WTO after the United States,[17] and Australia has looked to the WTO on numerous occasions in

---

[13] McKinsey & Company 'McKinsey Electric Vehicle Index: Europe cushions a global plunge in EV sales' (17 July 2020) <https://www.mckinsey.com/industries/automotive-and-assembly/our-insights/mckinsey-electric-vehicle-index-europe-cushions-a-global-plunge-in-ev-sales>.

[14] Australia Government, Australian Government Response to the Joint Standing Committee on Trade and Investment Growth Report: "Pivot: Diversifying Australia's Trade and Investment Profile" (July 2021) 2–3.

[15] Therapeutic Goods Administration, *International Engagement Strategy 2021-2025* (26 July 2021) 4. The TGA states that its 'alignment with European regulations for medical devices, whilst taking into account the significant reforms being implemented the by the European Commission, is . . . informed by identifying the most appropriate regulatory settings for Australia': 5.

[16] 'Supporting our region, advancing our interests and investing in trade and tourism to secure Australia's recovery' (Joint Media Release, 11 May 2021) <https://www.foreignminister.gov.au/minister/marise-payne/media-release/supporting-our-region-advancing-our-interests-and-investing-trade-and-tourism-secure-australias-recovery>.

[17] World Trade Organization, 'Disputes by Member' (*World Trade Organization*) <https://www.wto.org/english/tratop_e/dispu_e/dispu_by_country_e.htm#eec>.

recent months. In 2021, a panel was established to hear Australia's complaints over Chinese tariffs on Australian barley.[18] Meanwhile, Australia requested bilateral consultations with China over its anti-dumping duties on Australian wine,[19] while China requested consultations with Australia over its duties on Chinese deep drawn stainless steel sinks, windmill towers and railway wheels.[20]

Therefore, securing a means of ensuring compliance with treaty rules remains of utmost importance to the EU and Australia in both defending and litigating claims.[21] The Department of Foreign Affairs and Trade has stated that Australia and the EU "have common approaches to many [dispute resolution] issues, particularly in relation to enhanced transparency of proceedings" and that not all obligations will be subject to dispute mechanisms.[22]

The EU Proposed Text and the report on the negotiations released by the EU and Australia indicate that the negotiations on state-to-state dispute settlement clauses may have reached the final stages, with potentially only minor issues to be resolved.[23] State-to-state dispute settlement procedures may need to be carefully negotiated with a view to preventing procedural hurdles in future proceedings.[24] Angshuman Hazarika's chapter identifies potential procedural hurdles that remain within the AEUFTA negotiations and provides practical suggestions for streamlining the treaty so that these barriers can be addressed.

4 Australia and Europe in the Bilateral Arena

As Australia continues its negotiations with the EU, its trade representatives throw themselves at the negotiating tables of other existing and potential trade partners. The crisscrossing of bilateral ties between each AEUFTA party and the rest of the

[18] China—Anti-Dumping and Countervailing Duty Measures on Barley from Australia—Constitution of the Panel established at the request of Australia—Note by the Secretariat, WTO Doc WT/DS598/6 (6 September 2021).

[19] China—Anti-Dumping and Countervailing Duty Measures on Wine from Australia, Request for Consultations by Australia, WTO Doc WT/DS602/1, G/L/1390 G/ADP/D137/1, G/SCM/D132/1 (28 June 2021).

[20] Australia—Anti-Dumping and Countervailing Duty Measures on Certain Products from China, Request for Consultations by China, WTO Doc WT/DS603/1, G/L/1391 G/ADP/D138/1, G/SCM/D133/1 (29 June 2021).

[21] European Parliament, 'Motion for a European Parliament Resolution: towards a WTO-compatible EU carbon border adjustment mechanism' (2020/2043(INI)) A9-0019/2021 (15 February 2021).

[22] Department of Foreign Affairs and Trade, 'Australia – EU Free Trade Agreement Summary of negotiating aims and approach' <https://www.dfat.gov.au/sites/default/files/a-eufta-summary-of-negotiating-aims-and-approach.pdf>.

[23] Hazarika (this volume).

[24] Hazarika (this volume).

world's key players means that Australia and Europe must keep track of each other as they seek to connect within the "spaghetti bowl" of international economic agreements.[25]

Notwithstanding that the Comprehensive and Progressive Agreement for Trans-Pacific Partnership ('CPTPP') membership already boasts a moderately long list of treaty parties, Australia seems poised to accept others to the party as well, with its Joint Standing Committee on Foreign Affairs, Defence and Trade undertaking an inquiry into whether CPTPP membership should be expanded to countries like the UK.[26] As Australia's relationship with China continues on a downward path, Australia has been beckoned by Taiwan to effectively abandon its official stance on China's 'one China policy' by renewing negotiations for a trade pact.[27] Meanwhile, the EU continues to negotiate with countries in the global south, including China, Indonesia, New Zealand, and the Philippines.[28]

Michael Hahn examines both the legal and political framework of bilateral trade agreements.[29] His chapter reveals what the advent of FTAs means for the fragmentation of regulation about global issues such as digital trade. Hahn notes that preferential trade agreements would be incompatible with membership in the WTO, were it not for Article XXIV GATT and its sister provision in the GATS. Hahn shows—through his thorough and systematic analysis of these treaty provisions—that, despite the abrupt and radical change concerning the compatibility of the multilateral trading system with FTAs, "the limitations established by Article XXIV GATT are more pronounced than is often appreciated."[30] However, whatever uncertain legal basis underpins the AEUFTA and the EU's negotiations with New Zealand, these agreements will allow their respective signatories to show the global North that they share a unique and close economic partnership.

[25] Bhagwati J (1998) A stream of windows: unsettling reflections on trade, immigration, and democracy. The MIT Press, pp 290–291.

[26] Parliament of Australia, 'Terms of Reference, Inquiry into expanding membership of the Comprehensive and Progressive Agreement for Trans-Pacific Partnership' <https://www.aph.gov.au/Parliamentary_Business/Committees/Joint/Foreign_Affairs_Defence_and_Trade/CPTPPMembership/Terms_of_Reference>. See also Dan Tehan 'Japan-Australia Ministerial Economic Dialogue' (Media Release, 15 July 2021) <https://www.trademinister.gov.au/minister/dan-tehan/media-release/japan-australia-ministerial-economic-dialogue>.

[27] Joyce Cheng, Dong Xing and Erin Handley, 'Taiwan is seeking free trade deals with the US and Australia as China's Xi Jinping vows 'peaceful reunification'' (*ABC News*, 7 July 2021) <https://www.abc.net.au/news/2021-07-07/taiwan-us-free-trade-agreement-xi-jinping-speech-australia/100269014>; Angelica Oung, 'Taiwan, Australia discuss hydrogen technology, trade' (*Taipei Times*, 30 July 2021) <https://www.taipeitimes.com/News/biz/archives/2021/07/30/2003761691>.

[28] European Commission, 'Negotiations and agreements' (22 January 2021) <https://ec.europa.eu/trade/policy/countries-and-regions/negotiations-and-agreements/#_being-negotiated>.

[29] Hahn (this volume).

[30] Hahn (this volume).

5 Investment and Market Access in the AEUFTA

Both Australia and the EU have expressed their desire to increase investment market access liberalisation.[31] However, a clear view of Australia's approach to investment is perhaps impaired by its soured relationship with China. On the one hand, Australia has demonstrated—through its FTA negotiations with the UK—its partiality toward investment screening cap increases. The result is less UK firms becoming subject to the Foreign Investment Review Board's processes. On the other hand, the federal Parliament in 2020 enacted the Foreign Arrangements Scheme, a legislative framework giving the Commonwealth effective veto power over State investment MOUs with foreign nations.[32] The Government has already cancelled a raft of memoranda between State governments and Chinese firms, including under China's Belt and Road Initiative ('BRI').[33] The BRI is intended to open trade routes between China and other nations through global infrastructure projects. These moves—one made almost exclusively in the political sphere and the other in the context of trade agreement brokerage—reveal Australia's careful and multifaceted approach to foreign investment liberalisation.

At the same time, the EU has released a draft text of its EU-China Investment Agreement following 8 years of negotiation and an eventual announcement of the in-principle agreement in December 2020.[34] The agreement is heavily liberalisation-focused and also includes provisions on subsidies, state-owned enterprises and technology transfer. It shows the EU's keen interest in expanding the market access of European investors abroad,[35] notwithstanding the political barriers potentially standing in the way of its ratification.[36]

Jarrod Hepburn examines investment screencaps and investment market access as two potential entryways, or barriers, to greater two-way Australia-European investment.[37] Hepburn provides an overview of the general purpose of the envisaged

[31] Australian Government, Department of Foreign Affairs and Trade (2018) Australia-European Union Free Trade Agreement: Objectives <www.dfat.gov.au/trade/agreements/negotiations/aeufta/Pages/australia-european-union-fta-objectives>; Council of the European Union (2018) Negotiating Directives for a Free Trade Agreement with Australia <www.consilium.europa.eu/media/35794/st07663-ad01dc01-en18.pdf>.

[32] *Australia's Foreign Relations (State and Territory Arrangements) Act 2020* (Cth).

[33] Ben Westcott, 'Australian government tears up Victoria's Belt and Road agreement with China, angering Beijing' (*CNN Business*, 22 April 2021) <https://edition.cnn.com/2021/04/22/business/australia-china-belt-and-road-initiative-intl-hnk/index.html>.

[34] European Commission, 'EU-China investment negotiations' (22 January 2021) <https://trade.ec.europa.eu/doclib/docs/2021/january/tradoc_159343.pdf>.

[35] Gisela Grieger, 'EU-China Comprehensive Agreement on Investment: Levelling the playing field with China' (European Parliament, Briefing, International Agreements in Progress, March 2021).

[36] Jakob Hanke Vela, Merkel: China must make 'significant progress' on forced labor before EU ratifies trade deal (*Politico*, 13 June 2021) <https://www.politico.eu/article/germany-chancellor-angela-merkel-eu-china-trade-investment-deal-labor-rights/>.

[37] Hepburn (this volume).

provisions on investment screening and investment market access in the AEUFTA and an assessment of the particular value of these provisions in the Australia-EU relationship. Although the AEUFTA could potentially address both issues, offering enhanced market access in particular sectors and/or offering higher screening thresholds, evidence remains unclear on whether higher screening thresholds play a significant role in encouraging more investment. In light of current economic and political uncertainties, AEUFTA negotiators may also be tempted to include broad negative list reservations to their market access commitments, preserving their flexibility to meet future policy challenges. Both Australia and Europe have recently demonstrated such a predisposition toward greater controls over foreign investment.

6 Digital Trade

With the multilateral regime lagging behind,[38] digital trade is now dominating the bilateral and regional trade agreement environment, with many countries opting to go beyond their commitments in existing agreements, either by entering into new digital trade treaties or reforming old ones to adapt them to the new data economy. Australia's run of digital-focused agreements over the past few years, particularly with Asian countries, culminated in the Australia-Singapore Digital Economy Agreement (DEA), an amendment of the existing Singapore–Australia Free Trade Agreement.[39] A second version of the Thailand–Australia Free Trade Agreement is likely to feature a similar addition.[40] But now Australia is discussing the potential for regional digital trade agreements with the likes of the United States,[41] a key forebearer of the CPTPP's e-commerce chapter, an agreement from which the United States later withdrew. Australia's undertakings in the CPTPP reveal that Australia is open to clear prohibitions on data localization, provided there are exceptions to match.[42] The Singapore-Australia DEA shows Australia is moving forward with personal information protection, protections for cryptography, source

[38] However, see World Trade Organization, 'Co-convenors of e-commerce negotiations: We are heartened by progress made so far' (*World Trade Organization*, 16 March 2021) <https://www.wto.org/english/news_e/news21_e/ecom_16mar21_e.htm> and World Trade Organization, 'Further progress cited in e-commerce negotiations' (*World Trade Organization*, 22 July 2021) <https://www.wto.org/english/news_e/news21_e/jsec_22jul21_e.htm>.

[39] *Singapore – Australia Free Trade Agreement* [2003] ATS 16 (signed 17 February 2003, entered into force 28 July 2003) as amended by *Australia – Singapore Digital Economy Agreement* [2020] ATS 13 (signed 6 August 2020, entered into force 8 December 2020).

[40] Phusadee Arunmas, 'Thailand, Australia mull economic deal' (*Bangkok Post*, 6 August 2021) <https://www.bangkokpost.com/business/2160723/thailand-australia-mull-economic-deal>.

[41] James Riley, 'Australia-US in talks on digital trade pact' (*InnovationAus*, 7 June 2021) <https://www.innovationaus.com/australia-us-in-talks-on-digital-trade-pact/>.

[42] *Comprehensive and Progressive Agreement for Trans-Pacific Partnership* (signed 8 March 2018) ('CPTPP') incorporating the *Trans-Pacific Partnership Agreement* (signed 4 February 2016) arts 14.11, 14.13.

code and open government information, and soft commitments on artificial intelligence, amongst other things. But things like the EU's data protection regimes are likely to raise additional sticking points.

Neha Mishra assesses the significance of the Digital Trade chapter of the AEUFTA and focuses on the disciplines necessary to boost digital trade.[43] In the author's view, the EU and Australia are likely to agree upon conventional digital trade disciplines, as well as provisions on online consumer trust and spam, and more contemporary disciplines on source code disclosure and data localisation. Although these disciplines can undoubtedly contribute to boosting digital trade between Australia and the EU, data flows and data protection will remain more contentious in the ongoing negotiations, given the differences in the negotiating parties' data protection laws, and "the EU's exceptionally defensive approach to data protection."[44]

Mishra emphasises that the negotiations provide an opportunity for adopting more profound disciplines on digital trade facilitation that would have significant implications for start-ups and regulatory cooperation in more insipient areas such as artificial intelligence and open government data.

7 The Demise of Investment Protection?

Australia has a long and inconsistent history with investment protection. The Australia–United States FTA and the Australia–Malaysia FTA both lack an investor-state dispute settlement ('ISDS') mechanism,[45] the latter omission reflecting Australia's former ISDS policy encapsulated within the former Labor Prime Minister Julia Gillard's statement that:

> the Government does not support provisions that would confer greater legal rights on foreign businesses than those available to domestic businesses ... In the past, Australian Governments have sought the inclusion of [ISDS] procedures in trade agreements with developing countries at the behest of Australian businesses. The Gillard Government will discontinue this practice ...[46]

Australia's approach has since been adjusted. Now the national Liberal government, in power since 2013, takes a case-by-case approach.[47] That approach is demonstrated in Australia's in-principle agreement with the UK, who shares

---

[43] Mishra (this volume).

[44] Mishra (this volume).

[45] *Australia-United States Free Trade Agreement*, signed 18 May 2004, [2005] ATS 1 (entered into force 1 January 2005) ('AUSFTA'); *Malaysia–Australia Free Trade Agreement*, signed 22 May 2012 (entered into force 1 January 2013) ('MAFTA').

[46] Department of Foreign Affairs and Trade, Gillard Government Trade Policy Statement: Trading our way to more jobs and prosperity (April 2011) 14.

[47] Julie Bishop, 'Free Trade Focus' (28 March 2013).

Australia's approach to ISDS negotiation.[48] The agreement outline reveals that the final version of the trade treaty will not include provisions for ISDS.[49]

The European story is perhaps more unique and linear. The EU was the first to propose a revised system of investment protection that centres around strengthened transparency requirements and a more permanent investment court. It first did so when it attempted to negotiate for such a system in the Transatlantic Trade and Investment Partnership.[50] The EU's reforms were later incorporated into the EU--Canada Comprehensive Economic and Trade Agreement ('CETA') and other agreements.[51] It involves strengthened transparency requirements and a more permanent investment court, including an appeals mechanism and the use of impartial tribunal members.[52]

The AEUFTA seems to go further than just excluding ISDS by resorting exclusively to state-to-state provisions. Instead, it takes a liberalisation-focused approach to investment flows. Esmé Shirlow introduces the contours of the bilateral investment relationship between the EU and Australia in this context, to situate the FTA's relevance to the investment flows between these parties.[53] She examines why the FTA adopts an exclusively liberalisation-focused approach to address whether the exclusion of investment protection and ISDS mechanism from the scope of the FTA is a strategic omission on the part of one or both parties.[54] She considers whether such omission is a missed opportunity, and in particular what focus the investment-related provisions of the treaty will adopt and what impact the FTA is likely to have vis-à-vis investors and existing investment treaties.

---

[48] UK Government, 'The United Kingdom's exit from and new partnership with the European Union' (Policy Paper, 2 February 2017) 35.

[49] Department of Foreign Affairs and Trade, 'Australia-UK FTA negotiations: agreement in principle' (16 June 2021) <https://www.dfat.gov.au/trade/agreements/negotiations/aukfta/australia-uk-fta-negotiations-agreement-principle#dispute>.

[50] European Commission, Concept Paper: Investment in TTIP and Beyond—The Path for Reform (May 2015) 4.

[51] See Comprehensive Economic and Trade Agreement (CETA) between Canada, of the one part, and the European Union and its Member States, of the other part, Canada-European Union, OJ L 11/23 (entered into force provisionally on 21 September 2017) Chapter 8, Section F ('CETA'); *Free Trade Agreement between the European Union and the Socialist Republic of Viet Nam* [2020] OJ L 11/23 (entered into force 1 August 2020) Chapter 3, Section A and Chapter 8.

[52] Dickson-Smith K (2016) Does the European Union have new clothes? Understanding the EU's new investment treaty model. J World Invest Trade 17(5):773, 799–810.

[53] Shirlow (this volume).

[54] Shirlow (this volume).

8 Services

Given that services trade represents a third of Australia's two-way trade relationship with the EU,[55] it perhaps comes as no surprise that trade in services has emerged as one of the most discussed areas in the AEUFTA negotiations. However, at the time of publication of this book, the outcomes of the negotiations for this area remain unknown. Australia's recent in-principle agreement with the UK may foreshadow the deal struck between Australia and the EU regarding professional and education services liberalization.[56] Charlotte Sieber-Gasser offers unique insights into trade in services within the context of the AEUFTA, from the conflicting standpoints of both parties.[57] Sieber-Gasser explains that while we can expect substantial liberalisation in professional and education services, along with temporary movement of persons, the currently proposed regulatory structure of the AEUFTA service chapter otherwise suggests limited regulatory innovation. Ultimately, the chapter itself does not aim to deliver substantial and particularly progressive rules with regard to services trade liberalisation. However, as individual schedules of commitments in services trade liberalisation in AEUFTA are expected to be identical to the offers submitted by both sides in the 2016 Trade in Services Agreement ('TiSA') negotiations, Sieber-Gasser expects the services chapter to have a role in re-enforcing each parties' commitment to engage at the plurilateral level in modernising and deepening international trade in services regulation.

9 Subsidies

The issue of subsidies has perhaps been thrown into greater contention than ever before by the COVID-19 pandemic, with many governments resorting to grants and subsidies to boost domestic industries. China imposed anti-dumping duties on Australian barley out of fears that Australian grain subsidies risk undercutting local Chinese industry.[58] Within the AEUFTA context, Australian potato growers in 2020 attempted to lobby the government to launch anti-dumping measures against the EU over fears the European Commission's subsidies on European potatoes as

[55] Department of Foreign Affairs and Trade, 'Australia – EU Free Trade Agreement Summary of negotiating aims and approach' <https://www.dfat.gov.au/sites/default/files/a-eufta-summary-of-negotiating-aims-and-approach.pdf>.

[56] Department of Foreign Affairs and Trade, 'Australia-UK FTA negotiations: agreement in principle' (16 June 2021) <https://www.dfat.gov.au/trade/agreements/negotiations/aukfta/australia-uk-fta-negotiations-agreement-principle#dispute>.

[57] Sieber-Gasser (this volume).

[58] *China—Anti-Dumping and Countervailing Duty Measures on Barley from Australia*—Request for Consultations by Australia, WTO Doc WT/DS598/1, G/L/1382 G/ADP/D135/1, G/SCM/D130/1 (21 December 2020).

part of its COVID-19 relief package would flood the Australia market with cheap French fries.[59]

The pandemic has thrown into doubt the circumstances in which governments can directly subsidise domestic industries at risk of being materially affected or otherwise apply emergency safeguard tariffs to particular goods. Philipp Reinhold examines the regulation of subsidies within the context of European trade policy and considers what can we expect from the AEUFTA. Although the subsidy rules are only one element of comprehensive negotiations and are not at the forefront of EU-Australia trade, they will continue to form an important part of international trade rules in the future, and thus both countries should not pass over the opportunity to engage in the further development of international subsidy law.[60] Rheinhold notes that, on the one hand, subsidy rules can serve as a template for further agreements and as a political signal with regard to multilateral reforms of WTO subsidy law. On the other hand, Australia can use the opportunity to negotiate provisions that make it easier for Australian companies to deal with a new EU subsidy regime.[61]

10 Competition

Even though competition is not a classic trade-related area, it is becoming increasingly popular and is taken into account in almost all modern trade agreements. Competition aspects play a crucial role for companies worldwide and the distortion of competition does not only affect the trade flows between countries but also the national welfare. Although there are no international rules against the restriction of competition, numerous countries try to regulate cooperation and coordination in the field of competition regulation either by including rules in FTAs or in so called dedicated competition agreements. Mareike Fröhlich examines future approaches in the AUSFTA and points out possible regulatory gaps.[62] She draws a comparison with similar agreements of the EU and Australia, such as with the United Kingdom or Canada, which deal with cooperation possibilities in the international fight against restraint of competition and international merger control, respectively. This contribution concludes, that a new starting point could be the Multilateral Mutual Assistance and Cooperation Framework for Competition Authorities, which was concluded in 2020 at the executive level and to which Canada, the United Kingdom and the USA have also signed, in addition to Australia.

[59] Brad Thompson, 'Potato growers spitting chips over European dumping threat' (*Australian Financial Review*, 21 May 2021) <https://www.afr.com/companies/agriculture/potato-growers-spitting-chips-over-european-dumping-threat-20200521-p54v5z>.

[60] Reinhold (this volume).

[61] Reinhold (this volume).

[62] Fröhlich (this volume).

11 Conclusion

Together, these insightful and thought-provoking chapters contribute to the passionate discussion on the future of commercial relations between the European Union and Australia. This publication makes not only a relevant academic contribution, but also supports the progress of the ongoing AEUFTA negotiations. At the time of publication, negotiation outcomes for some areas, like trade services, are unknown. Other areas, about which we can maker firmer conclusions, may continue to be reconsidered or reshaped before an agreement is finalised.

However, the negotiation process's uncertainty is perhaps a reflection of the uncertain legal, political and economic global atmosphere to which the treaty parties themselves continue to contribute.

References

Bröhmer J (this volume) Existing political and legal relations between the EU, its Member States and Australia. In: Bungenberg M, Mitchell A (eds) The Australia-European Union Free Trade Agreement. Springer, Cham

Fröhlich M (this volume) The competition chapter in the EU-Australia FTA. In: Bungenberg M, Mitchell A (eds) The Australia-European Union Free Trade Agreement. Springer, Cham

Hahn M (this volume) The framework of bilateral trade agreements. In: Bungenberg M, Mitchell A (eds) The Australia-European Union Free Trade Agreement. Springer, Cham

Hazarika A (this volume) Panel procedures under the proposed EU-Australia FTA. In: Bungenberg M, Mitchell A (eds) The Australia-European Union Free Trade Agreement. Springer, Cham

Hepburn J (this volume) Investment screening and market access in the AEUFTA. In: Bungenberg M, Mitchell A (eds) The Australia-European Union Free Trade Agreement. Springer, Cham

Mishra N (this volume) Digital trade in the Australia – EU FTA: a future-forward perspective. In: Bungenberg M, Mitchell A (eds) The Australia-European Union Free Trade Agreement. Springer, Cham

Reinhold P (this volume) European trade policy and the regulation of subsidies: what can we expect from the EU-Australia FTA? In: Bungenberg M, Mitchell A (eds) The Australia-European Union Free Trade Agreement. Springer, Cham

Shirlow E (this volume) Investment protection in the AEUFTA: missed opportunities or strategic exclusions? In: Bungenberg M, Mitchell A (eds) The Australia-European Union Free Trade Agreement. Springer, Cham

Sieber-Gasser C (this volume) Services trade liberalisation in the Australia – EU FTA: progress but no Quantum-Leap. In: Bungenberg M, Mitchell A (eds) The Australia-European Union Free Trade Agreement. Springer, Cham

Marc Bungenberg is Director of the Europa-Institut and a professor of public law, European law, public international law and international economic law and Jean Monnet Chair for the EU Constitutional Framework of International Dispute Settlement and the Rule of Law at Saarland University in Germany (since 2015), as well as visiting professor at the University of Lausanne/ Switzerland (since 2011). He has taught at inter alia Sydney, Geneva, Lucerne, Lausanne, Tashkent, Copenhagen, Hamburg, and Munich. He is the recipient of multiple research grants. He received his doctorate in law from the University of Hannover and wrote his habilitation treatise at the Friedrich-Schiller-University Jena. He holds an LL.M. from Lausanne University. His main fields of research are European (Common Commercial Policy, public procurement and state aid law) and international economic law, particularly international investment and WTO law.

Andrew Mitchell is Associate Dean (Research) and Professor at the Faculty of Law, Monash University, and a member of the Indicative List of Panelists to hear WTO disputes. He has previously practised law with Allens Arthur Robinson (now Allens Linklaters) and consults for States, international organisations and the private sector. Andrew has taught law in Australia, Canada, Indonesia, Singapore, and the US. He is the recipient of six major grants from the Australian Research Council (including a Future Fellowship), the Australian National Preventive Health Agency and the National Health and Medical Research Council. Andrew has published over 150 academic books and journal articles, and is an Editor of Edward Elgar's International Economic Law Series, an Editorial Board Member of the Journal of International Economic Law and the Journal of International Dispute Settlement. He has law degrees from Melbourne, Harvard and Cambridge and is a Barrister and Solicitor of the Supreme Court of Victoria.

Existing Legal and Political Relations Between the EU, Its Member States, and Australia

Jürgen Bröhmer

Contents

Abstract The relationship between Australia, the European Union and member states of the European Union have a long history based on shared values, democratic political systems, and a strong foundation in the rule of law. Historically, the ties to the United Kingdom have been and remain special, not least because Australia was and, albeit to a much lesser degree, can still be understood as a (now) fully sovereign partial reflection of the UK in the southern hemisphere, which whom it shares a language, a legal history based on the common law, a colonial past and, not least, a head of state. But there are close ties with other countries as well. France is a power with substantial interests in the greater area around Australia. France is also a close

J. Bröhmer (✉)
Murdoch University, School of Law, Perth, Western Australia
e-mail: j.brohmer@murdoch.edu.au

M. Bungenberg, A. Mitchell (eds.), *The Australia-European Union Free Trade Agreement*, Special Issue, https://doi.org/10.1007/978-3-030-91448-6_2

strategic security partner. The relationship with the EU has been problematic in the past because of profound differences of opinion concerning agriculture. UK membership in the EU initially jeopardized Australia's trade relationship with the UK. Brexit is seen to create new opportunities albeit at a much smaller scale than the concerns raised by the UK's joining the EEC/EU. Relative to Australia's primary natural resources of iron ore and coal and relative to the growth of China as a market for Australia's natural resources, including agricultural products, the UK, and the EU, play a significantly smaller role today. This paper attempts to present an overview of the various bi- and multilateral relationships that are the foundation for the envisaged AU-EU FTA.

1 Introduction

The United Kingdom's exit from the European Union[1] has created new dynamics in the realignment of international relations. After 40 years of membership in the EU with its exclusive jurisdiction over external trade (in goods), the UK must negotiate trade agreements with other partners to replace what was previously provided by the EU. Conversely, states outside the EU must now reassess their relationships both to the UK (and, to a lesser degree, to the EU). They cannot rely exclusively on dealing with the EU to cover any special (trade) interest they may have regarding the UK. Given the historically founded special relationship between Australia and the UK, it is not surprising that the Brexit process has been followed closely in Australia. The 2017 Foreign Policy White Paper of Australia refers to the United Kingdom as one of Australia's most important partners and stipulates that Brexit will "change the framework of our engagement."[2]

Relationships of varying intensity do not only exist between Australia and the UK; they also exist between Australia and the member states of the EU and with the EU itself. This paper attempts to provide an overview of the existing framework of relations between the EU, its member states, and Australia. Whereas the emphasis is on legal instruments, the legal perspective is not exclusive as there are unique historical ties that have remained impactful in the development of these relationships. Australia's ongoing negotiations concerning FTAs with both the UK and the EU will also be briefly presented.

[1] Henceforth referred to as UK and EU.

[2] Australian Government, 2017 Foreign Policy White Paper, p. 80, https://www.dfat.gov.au/publications/minisite/2017-foreign-policy-white-paper/fpwhitepaper/pdf/2017-foreign-policy-white-paper.pdf (last accessed 9 September 2021).

2 The Scope of (Existing) Australia-EU Relations

Australia is geographically not a European country in the sense of Article 49 TEU and hence could not, even if it wanted to, become a member state of the EU. However, if one were to measure Australia against the so-called Copenhagen criteria for membership as formulated at the 1993 European Council in Copenhagen,[3] it is evident that Australia's performance against these criteria would be very strong indeed. Australia has strong credentials on democracy, human rights, the rule of law, and a solid and competitive market economy.[4] Given the—still—very close cultural links to Europe and the UK, and the similarities of the economic, legal, and political systems, this is hardly surprising. Australia established diplomatic relations with what was then still the European Economic Community (EEC) already in March 1962, almost 60 years ago.[5]

2.1 *The Agriculture Problem*

However, the overall relationship has had its share of problems. The UK's accession to the EEC had profound effects on Australia, not least because of the detrimental features of the EU's agricultural policy, which not only protected the EU home market from external competition in a sector important for and in Australia, but which also subsidized EU agricultural exports and turned the EU into an artificially boosted competitor on the world markets. Together with the loss of the special relationship Australia had enjoyed as part of the British Commonwealth, including

[3]European Council in Copenhagen, 21–22 June 1993, Conclusions of the Presidency, http://www.consilium.europa.eu/ueDocs/cms_Data/docs/pressData/en/ec/72921.pdf, p. 13 (last accessed 9 September 2021): "Membership requires that the candidate country has achieved stability of institutions guaranteeing democracy, the rule of law, human rights and respect for and protection of minorities, the existence of a functioning market economy as well as the capacity to cope with competitive pressure and market forces within the Union. Membership presupposes the candidate's ability to take on the obligations of membership including adherence to the aims of political, economic and monetary union."

[4]Prime Minister John Howard in 1997 underscored the success of Liberal Party fiscal policy by pointing to the fact that Australia and Luxembourg were, at the time, the only countries fulfilling the Maastricht criteria for membership in the common currency (emphasizing the nature of his comparison as a mere example for fiscal success, but that there is no such interest of joining the Euro), see J Howard, Address to the South Australian Division of the Liberal Party State Council, Adelaide, 23 August 1997, https://pmtranscripts.pmc.gov.au/release/transcript-10454 (last accessed 9 September 2021).

[5]The origins of the EU's diplomatic relations go back to the European Coal and Steel Community (ECSC) and the establishment of an "Information Office" in Washington, D.C. in 1954 after the US had already established a permanent representative already in 1952. See Pajtinka (2020), p. 456.

being a prime supplier of agricultural products to the UK, this development had a profound impact on Australia.[6]

The disagreements between the EU and Australia regarding trade in agriculture became a significant liability in the relationship between the two entities.[7] The depth of the problem is perhaps reflected by a speech given by the then Prime Minister of Australia, John Howard, in Tasmania on 22 August 1997 and his choice of words to describe the relationship:

> (...) I have spent a large part of my political life denigrating, quite rightly and with some passion, the rotten anti-Australian policies of the European Economic Union, that have done immense damage to the agricultural industries of Australia and represent one of the high watermarks of world trading hypocrisy. If ever a group of nations has preached the theory of free trade but practiced protection to demented lengths, it's the European Union.[8]

Whereas the differences in this area were never resolved, the impact has been greatly diminished by several factors. One such factor is the rise of Asian countries and, most of all, China as trading partners of Australia both in non-agricultural areas, especially iron ore and coal, and in the agricultural sector.[9] The relative significance of trade in agricultural products with the EU has shrunk at the same time as China and other Asian countries became more relevant as agriculture markets and as destinations for non-agricultural products. This development has been highlighted by the recent developments in the relationship between Australia and China and the latter's—presumably punitive—measures regarding Australian exports of barley or wine.[10]

---

[6]See Yencken (2018), pp. 586–587.

[7]See Matera and Murray (2018), pp. 179 et seq.

[8]J Howard, Address at the Tasmanian Liberal Party State Council Dinner, Country Club Casino, Launceston, 22 August 1997, https://pmtranscripts.pmc.gov.au/release/transcript-10452 (last accessed 9 September 2021).

[9]Australia's exports in agriculture, forestry and fisheries grew from about AUD 30 billion in 2007–2008 to AUD 52.2 billion in 2017–2018. In the same decade, minerals and fuels exports more than doubled and grew from under AUD 90 billion in 2007–2008 to almost AUD 190 billion in 2017–2018, with iron ore and coal each alone exceeding AUD 60 billion and thus eclipsing the whole of agriculture and with natural gas on a steep rise as well. See Department of Foreign Affairs and Trade, Trade and Investment at a Glance 2019, https://www.dfat.gov.au/sites/default/files/trade-and-investment-at-a-glance-2019.pdf (last accessed 9 September 2021). China is also the largest trading partner of Australia in agricultural trade. Volumes of Australian exports have grown from roughly AUD 4 billion to 16 billion in the past decade, with growth being aided by the China-Australia Free Trade Agreement (ChAFTA), which became effective in December 2015. See Wilson and King (2020), p. 4 (last accessed 9 September 2021).

[10]With regard to barley, the matter has now gone to dispute settlement under the DSU of the WTO, see DS598: China—Anti-dumping and countervailing duty measures on barley from Australia, China, https://www.wto.org/english/tratop_e/dispu_e/cases_e/ds598_e.htm (last accessed 9 September 2021). With regard to wine, on 27 November 2020, the Chinese government announced "preliminary duties and tariffs" on Australian wine exports of "up to 212%", see Press Conference on 27 November 2020 by the (now) Minister for Finance (and Minister for Trade, Tourism and Investment until 22 December 2020), Simon Birmingham, https://www.senatorbirmingham.com.au/press-conference-adelaide-9/ (last accessed 9 September 2021). For an

The second factor lies in profound changes in the Common Agricultural Policy (CAP) of the EU. Especially the CAP's subsidy regime has undergone profound changes for the better commencing with Agricultural Commissioner Ray McSharry's reforms of 1992. The internal interventions to secure farmers reasonable prices for their products by, in essence, buying up agricultural products not sellable into the market at high intervention prices (price support) creating large and expensive surpluses gave way to direct payment to farmers that were largely decoupled from production volumes and which in turn looked at farmers not only as agricultural supply factors but also as custodians of the land they were looking after and farming on.[11] In 2015 the external subsidy pillar was reformed, and the EU ceased paying export subsidies[12] by finally agreeing to and implementing the prohibition of the use of such subsidies at the WTO Nairobi Ministerial Council,[13] essentially bringing an end to a long period of multilateral pressure to abolish this devastating policy. Under the export subsidy regime, the EU paid farmers the price difference between the intervention price and the lower world market price, in effect dumping their surplus production on the world market with significant adverse effects, of which the unfair competition with Australian farmers on third country export markets was not the worst. Australia played an important role in the continued application of multilateral pressure, not least through the so-called Cairns Group, a coalition of 19 agricultural exporting countries.[14] Under the "Producer Support Estimate" (PSE) of the OECD, which measures the percentage of gross farm income provided by subsidies, the EU has come down from just over 38% in 1986 to 19% in 2019 and hence close to the OECD average of 19%. That is still considerably higher than Australia's PSE, which has decreased from 12.8% in 1986 to a mere 1.9% in 2019.[15]

A third factor lies in a change of priorities within Australia that is likely connected to the two developments mentioned previously. Australia is a highly urbanized

overview of Chinese measures up to July 2020, see Wilson and King (2020), p. 7 (last accessed 9 September 2021). For a recent overview, see J Scott, Why China Is Falling Out With Australia, 11 January 2021, Bloomberg, https://www.bloomberg.com/news/articles/2021-01-10/why-china-is-falling-out-with-australia-and-allies-quicktake (last accessed 9 September 2021).

[11] For an instructive current overview of CAP cf. Hristov et al. (2020), pp. 718 et seq.; OECD, Evaluation of Agricultural Policy Reforms in the European Union, 2011, DOI: https://doi.org/10.1787/9789264112124-en, pp. 47 et seq. See also Matthews and Soldi (2019) (last accessed 9 September 2021).

[12] Matthews and Soldi (2019), p. 7 (last accessed 9 September 2021).

[13] Ministerial Decision of 19 December 2015, WT/MIN(15)/45, WT/L/980, https://www.wto.org/english/thewto_e/minist_e/mc10_e/l980_e.htm (last accessed 9 September 2021).

[14] Members of the Group are Argentina, Australia, Brazil, Canada, Chile, Colombia, Costa Rica, Guatemala, Indonesia, Malaysia, New Zealand, Pakistan, Paraguay, Peru, the Philippines, South Africa, Thailand, Uruguay and Vietnam. Ukraine is an observer of the Group. See https://www.cairnsgroup.org/Pages/Introduction.aspx (last accessed 9 September 2021).

[15] OECD data, Agricultural Support, Producer support (PSE), % of gross farm receipts, 1986–2019, https://data.oecd.org/agrpolicy/agricultural-support.htm (last accessed 9 September 2021). The US has decreased its PSE from 22.9% in 1986 to 12.1% in 2019.

country, and non-urban, rural interests face an uphill struggle for recognition. The political reflection of this lies in the existence of the National Party, which is aligned with the main conservative Liberal Party but with the intention to represent the specific interests of the more remote areas, which, in Australia, more or less constitutes everything beyond a perimeter around the five major metropolitan areas.[16] Unsurprisingly, that is where the agricultural interests are mainly based, notwithstanding the fact that Australian agriculture tends to be large scale and is often owned by national or even international corporate interests.[17]

However, the permanent coalition of a more rural-based and a more urban-based conservative party has not pushed agricultural issues as much as one might have expected. Business interests in general and perhaps manufacturing and the so-called tech sector appear to have taken a more centre stage and facilitated the agreement of recent FTAs concluded with China, Japan, and Korea.[18]

That said, agriculture remains an important topic for mainly two reasons. Agricultural products make up a significant part of Australia's export activities because Australia's agriculture industry is highly productive and, as evidenced by the low levels of subsidy support, able to convert on existing comparative advantages. Secondly, the COVID-19 pandemic has placed increasing emphasis on strategic supply chain considerations in many sectors, including agriculture and food security. The challenges are complex and reach from labour shortages caused by illness or travel restrictions, logistical problems such as getting products and customers to markets, availability of fertilizers and seeds to price increases, food shortages, and

[16] Sydney, Melbourne, Brisbane/Gold Coast, Adelaide, Perth. The Australian Bureau of Statistics (ABS) also includes the smaller capital cities of Darwin and Hobart, and of course, Canberra and tallies the joint population of these capital cities at just over 17 million, with the total population currently sitting at just over 25 million. However, the share of the population in urban conglomerates is even larger if one is willing to cast the net just a little bit further, for example, to include Wollongong and perhaps even Newcastle (and the coastal areas in between) into the Sydney conglomerate or extend the reach of Melbourne to Geelong and that of Brisbane to the Gold Coast. For current numbers, see ABS, Capital Cities (at 30 June 2019), https://www.abs.gov.au/statistics/people/population/regional-population/latest-release. As of 30 June 2020, the total population of Australia was determined to be 25,687,041 people, https://www.abs.gov.au/statistics/people/population (both last accessed 9 September 2021).

[17] The fourth report of the Register of Foreign Ownership of Agricultural Land as of 30 June 2019 was released on 19 June 2020, https://firb.gov.au/sites/firb.gov.au/files/2020-06/2019-rfo-agriculturalland.pdf (last accessed 9 September 2021) states that that the total area of Australian agricultural land with a level of foreign ownership is just over 52 million hectares (13.8%, considerably more than the 36 million hectares that make up Germany). According to media reports, there are more than 20 individuals or corporate groups with agricultural holdings of more than 1 million hectares (=10,000 km^2), see Australia's biggest private landowners revealed, https://www.lovemoney.com/gallerylist/72694/australias-biggest-private-landowners-revealed, 11 December 2019 (lovemoney.com describes itself as a personal finance site that provides expert help, intelligent discussion areas and market-leading comparison tools and published by the Love Incorporated Group). The largest private landowner in Australia is mining (and property) magnate Gina Rinehart, who is reported to own almost 10 million hectares, which is larger than Bavaria.

[18] McKenzie (2018), p. 263 points to policy changes favouring more negotiation flexibility in agricultural matters to increase chances of concluding agreements in the first place.

worse.[19] Whereas the pandemic led to disruptions in Australia as well[20] and whereas the impact of factors such as climate change remains hard to assess in exact scope, extent, and timeline, it is nonetheless safe to assume that, for the time being, Australia will hopefully be able to continue to play a significant role as a global provider of agricultural products and thus help to stabilize food security. One important factor for this to remain possible is continued trade liberalization and facilitation for capital products (e.g., machinery) and other products to maintain productivity, from spare parts to fertilizers, and the ability to open borders so that products can be harvested and brought to market.

2.2 *The Joint Declaration 1997*

The first formal document reflecting the close ties was the "Joint Declaration on Relations between the European Union and Australia" of 26 June 1997.[21] The Declaration in its Preamble makes amble reference to the "close historical, political, economic and cultural ties" serving as its foundations. The Preamble also mentions, as another pillar of the relationship, "shared commitments to the respect and promotion of human rights, fundamental freedoms, democracy and the rule of law." Those shared commitments notwithstanding, the original intention to conclude the Joint Declaration as a treaty failed because the EU insisted on a human rights conditionality clause.[22] Such conditionality clauses have gained prominence in recent years.[23] The failed attempt to achieve such a clause with Australia despite the fact that Australia, notwithstanding that matters can always be improved, is certainly not a human rights pariah, might give rise to the question of why such clauses could become stumbling blocks between entities such as the EU and Australia. Research on similar human rights conditionality clauses in the Canada-EU FTA[24] suggests that such clauses are introduced primarily for internal political

---

[19] Cf. The World Bank, Food Security and COVID-19, last updated 5 February 2021, https://www.worldbank.org/en/topic/agriculture/brief/food-security-and-covid-19 (last accessed 9 September 2021). See also Bartlett (2020), p. 422.

[20] Whelan et al. (2021), p. 417.

[21] http://eeas.europa.eu/archives/delegations/australia/documents/eu_australia/1997_joint_declaration_en.pdf (last accessed 9 September 2021).

[22] Murray and Benvenuti (2014), p. 444.

[23] Meissner and McKenzie (2018), (last accessed 9 September 2021). For policy background (and quasi-legal basis), see Resolution on the Communication from the Commission on the inclusion of respect for democratic principles and human rights in agreements between the Community and third countries (COM (95)0216—C4-0197/95), OJ C 320/261 (28 October 1996), https://eur-lex.europa.eu/legal-content/EN/TXT/?uri=CELEX:51996IP0212 (last accessed 9 September 2021).

[24] Comprehensive Economic and Trade Agreement (CETA), available at https://trade.ec.europa.eu/doclib/docs/2014/september/tradoc_152806.pdf and https://ec.europa.eu/trade/policy/in-focus/ceta/ceta-chapter-by-chapter/. In this regard, CETA must be read in the light of the Strategic Partnership Agreement between Canada and the EU (SPA), http://www.international.gc.ca/

("strategic") reasons and not so much to pursue real human rights improvement goals.[25]

The Joint Declaration is a classic piece of "soft law" containing no legal obligations in the narrow sense and limited to general consultation and information and cooperation goals in various areas ranging from trade to human rights. In the light of the harsh characterization of the EU by then Prime Minister John Howard reproduced above not even 2 months after the signing of the Joined Declaration, one could be surprised that agriculture does not figure more prominently in the Declaration. Instead, all that is contained is a "lukewarm" clause stating that the partners will

> promote contacts and cooperation on agriculture and fisheries, and examine in a spirit of cooperation and goodwill the opportunities in our trade-in agricultural and fisheries products; (. . .).

At least to some degree, the Prime Minister's language in the speech quoted above stands in contrast to the content of the document. Perhaps this reflected a level of frustration as a result of not achieving the treaty originally envisaged and not making any progress on the trade in agricultural goods issue.

2.3 *EU-Australia Partnership Framework 2008*

The Joint Declaration was expanded into and replaced by the European Union—Australia Partnership Framework of 2008.[26] The terror attacks in the US on 11 September 2011 can safely be regarded as the major event prompting renewed emphasis on mutual relations.[27] The document was given a much more dynamic form and described as a "living document"[28] with ongoing reviews and "immediate action" items. However, the content remained limited to "soft" consultation, collaboration, and cooperation" intentions in the areas of foreign policy and security, international trade, development assistance, climate change and energy, science and research, innovation and technology, education, and culture.[29] That said, the

europe/assets/pdfs/can-eu-spa-text-eng.pdf (last accessed 9 September 2021), and especially Articles 28.3 and 28.7 thereof. See also the "denial of benefits"-clause in Article 8.16 CETA and the Joint Declaration on Articles 8.16, 9.7 and 29.6 CETA, which allows a party to deny benefits to an investor of the other party in the context of the maintenance of international peace and security including human rights.

[25] Meissner and McKenzie (2018), pp. 10 et seq. (last accessed 9 September 2021).

[26] Available at https://eeas.europa.eu/sites/default/files/partnership_framework2009eu_en.pdf (last accessed 9 September 2021).

[27] Cf. Murray and Benvenuti (2014), p. 444.

[28] Then Australian Foreign Minister Stephen Smith in his foreword, http://eeas.europa.eu/sites/eeas/files/partnership_framework2009eu_en.pdf, p. 3 (last accessed 9 September 2021).

[29] See Markovic (2009).

shared political objectives between the two parties in trying to uphold and develop the UN-based system of international law are a trademark of the document and the common denominator spanning across the policy goals of security and anti-terrorism, to the rules-based international trade and investment system, to climate change, international criminal law, human rights, development and a whole array of other objectives, large and small.

2.4 The 2017 Framework Agreement

Progress since 2008 has been slow. It was not until 2017 that both parties developed the 2008 Framework into a full treaty in 2017, the Framework Agreement between the European Union and its Member States and Australia.[30] The FA-2017 goes back to the Prime Ministership of Julia Gillard, who visited the EU in Brussels and return visits in Canberra by her EU counterparts, then EU High Representative for Foreign Affairs and Security Policy, Catherine Ashton, and European Commission President, Jose Manuel Barroso. Negotiations commenced under Prime Minister Rudd in 2011. The fact that it took 6 years to sign a text coupled with the fact that this text has not yet been ratified is a testament either to continuing difficulties in the relationship or to a relative lack of perceived (political) necessity for such a document, or both. The urgency of ratification is somewhat diminished by the fact that as of 4 October 2018, the FA-2017 has been elevated into a state of "provisional application" of selected provisions as provided for in Article 61.2 FA-2017.[31] However, the provisional application applies only to Article 3 ("political dialogue"), Article 10 ("cooperation in regional and international organizations"), and Article 56 ("Joint Committee").[32] The bulk of the agreement is not applicable and remains relegated to informal cooperation outside the scope of a formal treaty. That applies to, for example, human rights, crisis management, weapons of mass destruction and arms control generally (Articles 4 et seq.), global development and humanitarian aid (Articles 12, 13), collaboration in trade matters (Articles 14–31), justice, freedom, and security (Articles 32–40), research, education, and culture (Articles 41–44) and sustainable development, energy and transport (Articles 45–54). This brief overview illustrates that the partners are aiming to put their relationship on a broad foundation,

[30] Framework Agreement between the European Union and its Member States, of the one part, and Australia, of the other part, OJ L 237/7 (15 September 2017) of 7 August 2017, https://eur-lex.europa.eu/legal-content/EN/TXT/?toc=OJ:L:2017:237:TOC&uri=uriserv:OJ.L_.2017.237.01.0007.01.ENG (last accessed 9 September 2021), henceforth referred to as FA-2017.

[31] Notice concerning the provisional application of the Framework Agreement between the European Union and its Member States, of the one part, and Australia, of the other part, OJ L 313/1 (10 December 2018), https://eur-lex.europa.eu/legal-content/EN/TXT/?uri=uriserv:OJ.L_.2018.313.01.0001.01.ENG (last accessed 9 September 2021).

[32] Article 56.3 points (g) and (h) are also excluded from provisional application.

but the overview also amply demonstrates that the lack of ratification leaves a considerable gap that cannot be filled by the agreement's provisional application. Until ratification, the lower level, MoU-like framework document from 2008 is still today the basis for EU-Australian relations.

The FA-2017, if and when ratified, will elevate the relationship between the two entities to treaty level. The "National Interest Analysis" provided by the Australian Department of Foreign Affairs and Trade (DFAT)[33] states that "the proposed Agreement will establish a legally binding framework for cooperation."[34] The gist is on the creation of formal dialogue and cooperation processes to address an almost comprehensive range of policy fields where the parties see benefit in working together.

The collaboration is institutionally supported by the creation of a Joint Committee (Article 56), through which much of the practical implementation of the agreement is channelled. The Joint Committee operates by consensus and can set up sub-committees and working groups (Article 56.4). Interestingly the FA-2017 is silent on the exact composition of the Joint Committee other than stating that it will generally meet once a year on a senior official level, with ministerial-level meetings being an option (Article 56.5). The exact composition will have to be part of the adoption of the Committee's rules of procedure (Article 56.4).

The Joint Committee will also serve as a dispute settlement body (Articles 56 (g), 57). The dispute settlement approach is more of a political nature and not comparable to the quasi-judicial approach that is the trademark of the WTO-DSU. In the event of differences arising in the context of the implementation of the agreement, the parties undertake to consult as quickly as possible with the option of subsequently, or, in the case of "special urgency", immediately (Article 57.3), referring the matter to the Joint Committee (Article 57.2), commencing on senior official level under a tight timeline for resolution of a maximum of 30 days. If there is still no resolution, the Joint Committee will have another 15 days to resolve the matter sitting on a ministerial level. Failing that, parties can then resort to substantiated and proportional countermeasures (Articles 57.4, 57.5).

---

[33] Under the Commonwealth Constitution, the Commonwealth Parliament has no formal role in the conclusion of international treaties as this is a matter of executive prerogative under Section 61. However, in order to improve the openness and transparency of the treaty-making process in Australia, the procedure was reformed on a sub-constitutional level in 1996. In particular, a Joint Standing Committee on Treaties would be set up by way of a resolution of both Houses of Parliament and the government resolved to table treaties for scrutiny—but not for approval—at least 15 days before taking definitive action on the treaty together with a "National Interest Analysis" (NIA). See the Parliament of the Commonwealth of Australia, A History of the Joint Standing Committee on Treaties: 20 Years, Report 160, March 2016, para. 2.35 (p. 15) https://www.aph.gov.au/-/media/02_Parliamentary_Business/24_Committees/244_Joint_Committees/JSCT/2016/Seminar/PDF/Report160/FinalReport.pdf (last accessed 9 September 2021).

[34] National Interest Analysis (2018) ATNIA 2, with attachment on consultation, Framework Agreement Between Australia, of the one part and the European Union and its Member States, of the other part (Manila, 7 August 2017), http://www.austlii.edu.au/au/other/dfat/nia/2018/2.html (last accessed 9 September 2021), p. 2.

At the time of writing, the Joint Committee has met three times, with the last meeting having taken place on 19 October 2020 and thus in the middle of the Sars-Covid-2 pandemic and consequently by video conference. The joint press release reporting on the meeting illustrates that the main impetus of the FA-2017 is communication and exchange of views and that the legal obligations in the FA-2017 as such are more of a procedural nature and do not extend in any way to substantive policy. Important agenda points were, unsurprisingly, the Covid-19 response of the EU and Australia with an emphasis on both parties lauding themselves for their various financial contributions to worldwide efforts in combatting the pandemic. It is, however, interesting that the EU allocates significant amounts of money in the Pacific region, which is of prime importance for Australia and where such activities by the EU will indirectly benefit Australia, if only because it allows a more focused concentration of Australia's efforts. In other policy areas mentioned, such as security, trade, or climate change, the meeting only took note of the current status of affairs together with expressions of a political will to continue the work.[35]

Another noteworthy element of the FA-2017 is the care taken to ensure that nothing contained therein will negatively prejudice any other agreement between the parties, including a future trade agreement if one were concluded. The starting point is that any such further agreement will form part of the bilateral relationship and insofar falls within the ambit of the FA-2017 (Article 55.1). However, the interpretation and application of such other agreements are to remain autonomous, and that is especially the case regarding dispute settlement provisions of other agreements (Article 55.2). In other words, the FA-2017 is quite clear that it is to be regarded as a *lex generalis* and subject to *lex specialis* arrangements in other agreements. As far as the policy area of trade and investment is concerned, Article 15.5 adds to this by clarifying the obvious, i.e., that the FA-2017 "neither requires nor precludes the negotiation and conclusion of an FTA between the Parties in the future to complement and extend the economic provisions in this Agreement.". The level of detail and care spent on language designed to avoid even the appearance of anything in the FA-2017 that could hinder any additional efforts the parties may wish to undertake between themselves borders on the humorous. There is certainly no discernible legal reason for this kind of language. It is not conceivable that the absence of these clauses could lead to a legal argument that, for example, the FA-2017 precludes the parties from, or, conversely, compels the parties to negotiate and conclude an FTA

[35] See DFAT, Joint press release EU-Australia Joint Committee, 19 October 2020, https://www.dfat.gov.au/news/media-release/joint-press-release-eu-australia-joint-committee.The pandemic also serves as a basis for what one might refer to as Covid-diplomacy. On 16 February 2021, the website of the Delegation of the EU to Australia celebrated the fact that "Australia receive(d) its first Covid-19 vaccines from the European Union" and the EU's Ambassador to Australia, Michael Pulch apparently did "a sweep of media interviews" letting everybody know "that the first vaccines to be rolled out in Australia were from Europe", https://eeas.europa.eu/delegations/australia/93203/australia-receives-its-first-covid-19-vaccines-european-union_en (all last accessed 9 September 2021).

between themselves. Similarly, the *lex specialis derogat legi generali* conflict rule would also not require the level of attention afforded to it in the FA-2017.

3 The Implications of Brexit on the EU-AU Relationship

The most obvious ramification of Brexit for Australia lies in the area of trade. That is simply because foreign trade constitutes an exclusive competence of the EU.[36] Leaving the EU, therefore, means that the UK must reassume jurisdiction and responsibility of the whole policy field of international trade. Third countries, such as Australia, now have an additional significant potential partner to engage with. Whereas trade is certainly not the only area of relevance in this regard, given its cross-sectional aspects, for example, into the area of agriculture,[37] it is probably one with the highest significance. That said, collaboration in other areas such as climate change or international security will also be affected, albeit to a lesser degree, as policies in that area were already more or less nationally determined, and Brexit, therefore, does not have quite the same impact intensity.

As far as trade is concerned, one must, however, take account of the fact that even from Australia's perspective, the UK is a relatively small partner despite its ranking in fifth place in the latest league table of Australia's two-way trading partners in goods and services.[38] The reason for this lies in the dominating role of China, Japan, and the USA as the top three trading partners for Australia and in the dominant role of the resources sector and the main commodities of iron ore, coal, natural gas, and gold, which make up more than half of Australia's trade.[39]

In 2019 the total value of two-way trade in goods and services with the UK came to AUD 38.5 billion, a significant increase over the 2018 figure of AUD 27 billion. However, that number pales in the light of the AUD 252 billion of trade value vis-à-vis China. And even Japan and the USA, ranked two and three respectively, more than double that figure individually. The UK now sits slightly larger as a trading partner than New Zealand or Singapore and somewhat smaller than South

[36] Articles 3.1(e), 207.1 and 207.2 TFEU. Hahn (2016), (inter alia) paragraphs 1, 22, 56.

[37] Agriculture is another policy area where the EU has broad, although not exclusive, jurisdiction (Article 4.2(d) TFEU). Trade and access to the EU market is a key concern of Australia.

[38] DFAT, Trade Statistics, Australia's Trade in Goods and Services 2019, Australia's goods and services trade by top 15 partners 2019, https://www.dfat.gov.au/sites/default/files/australias_goods_and_services_by_top_15_partners_2019.pdf (last accessed 9 September 2021).

[39] Of Australia's top 25 exports, the "big four commodities" (iron ore, coal, natural gas, and gold make up over 47% of the total; the commodities' share rises to over 54% if one includes aluminium, crude oil, copper, and other ores. The non-resource part of trade is quite diverse, with the top items (out of 25 overall) such as education-related travel services, personal travel, professional, financial, and technical services and pharmaceuticals making up the bulk of the remainder. See DFAT, Trade Statistics, Australia's Trade in Goods and Services 2019, Australia's goods and services by top 25 exports 2019, https://www.dfat.gov.au/sites/default/files/australias_goods_and_services_by_top_15_partners_2019.pdf (last accessed 9 September 2021).

Korea, which is the fourth-ranked trading partner. That comes to an overall share of 4.2% for the UK, compared to 9.2% for the EU. As an export market alone, the UK represents 4.3% of the total for Australia; the EU has a slightly smaller share at 4.2%. From the point of view of the UK, trade with Australia is borderline neglectable. Trade with all Commonwealth countries amounted to only 9.1% of the UK's total trade in 2019. Of that volume, 14.4% accounts for trade between the UK and Australia. In other words, from the UK's perspective, Australia's weight as a trading partner is a relatively minute 1.3%.[40]

Beyond the sheer statistics, a lot will depend on policy decisions in the wake of Brexit. Brexit will have an impact on many business decisions ranging from where to open subsidiaries to supply chain consideration to the outcome of negotiations of possible FTAs between Australia and the EU and bilaterally with the UK. One area relevant for Australia is the future ease of access for Australians who wish to work in the UK, given that immigration restrictions were a central theme for Brexiteers and given that Australia itself is rather restrictive when it comes to free movement.[41]

4 Bilateral Relationships Between Australia and EU-Member States

4.1 Australia–UK

The relationship between the UK and Australia is a very special one. It is fair to say that the UK is in many ways the "mother country", notwithstanding that Australia as

[40] Ward (2020), p. 3 (last accessed 9 September 2021).

[41] According to media reports, Australia rejected a visa-free travel proposal from London in 2020. Overall, however, the reaction to free movement was rather reserved. Tarde Minister Simon Birmingham was quoted as saying that "(f)irst and foremost, this is a trade deal, and our number one priority will be to improve market access and boost export opportunities for Australian farmers, businesses and investors," but "(w)here there are opportunities for more flexibility around work rights and the movement of people, particularly youth, we are open to exploring them", L Parsons, Australians will be able to live and work in the UK for more than 2 years under visa changes being considered as part of a trade deal—and the Poms will be able to stay here longer too, Daily Mail Australia, 22 October 2020, https://www.dailymail.co.uk/news/article-8867789/Australians-able-live-work-UK-longer-visa-changes.html (last accessed 9 September 2021). Earlier media reports state that Australia would not accept full free movement because it could "cause an exodus of highly trained workers to the UK and an influx of unskilled British workers to Sydney and Melbourne", A McCulloch, Australia rejects visa-free immigration deal with UK, in Personnel Today, 6 January 2020. However, it should be noted that Australia cannot do much against feared "brain drain" to the UK because the UK control their own immigration policy and giving more access is an entirely domestic affair. Only if movement became a transactional issue could Australia gain traction. What Australia can do is limit any influx from the UK and thus, presumably, force the UK to withhold free movement rights for Australians. Brain drain scenarios, however, are not transactional because they always benefit one side at the expense of the other. Australia would therefore have to pay a price for this fear elsewhere in the deal or find ways to restrict Australians from emigrating to the UK.

a country has profoundly changed over the decades, not least regarding immigration and the people who make up what Australia is today. As mentioned at the beginning of this paper, the relationship has been affected by the UK's membership in the EU after 1973, and it appears to be affected by the UK's departure from the EU, as well as the bilateral partnership will be intensified.

Australia joined the international community of states when the six original colonies federated into the Commonwealth of Australia in 1901. Whereas the Commonwealth Constitution was the result of lengthy discussions stretching over more than a decade, of several constitutional conventions and referenda in all six constituting colonies (with a delay in Western Australia), the federal Constitution of the Commonwealth of Australia is an act of the Westminster Parliament in London.[42] The creation of the Australian Federation through this constitutional process in 1901 was only the first step towards the development of a fully sovereign nation and a number of subsequent steps over the coming decades incrementally and eventually led to the cutting of all remaining constitutional ties to the United Kingdom.[43] This process was not completed until the passage of the Australia Act of 1986.[44]

It is therefore not surprising that many in the UK and Australia are looking at Brexit as an opportunity to re-intensify the bilateral relationship. Politicians in the UK and Australia have been quick to speak about the potential benefits this new landscape presents. That is especially true for those politicians who looked at Brexit as a positive development, as obviously is the case especially (but not only) for the current UK government under Prime Minister Boris Johnson. Openly pro-Brexit positions were also espoused here in Australia, perhaps most prominently by the former Prime Minister Tony Abbott.[45] It is, therefore, no coincidence that the former Australian Prime Minister was appointed as an Advisor to the UK Board of Trade in

[42] Commonwealth of Australia Constitution Act 1900, https://www.legislation.gov.uk/ukpga/Vict/63-64/12/contents/enacted; see also the most recent compilation with (only eight) amendments that have been made since 1901: Commonwealth of Australia Constitution Act, https://www.legislation.gov.au/Details/C2013Q00005 (both last accessed 9 September 2021).

[43] For more detail Bröhmer (2012), pp. 689 et seq.

[44] Australia Act 1986, No. 142, 1985, An Act to bring constitutional arrangements affecting the Commonwealth and the States into conformity with the status of the Commonwealth of Australia as a sovereign, independent and federal nation, https://www.legislation.gov.au/Details/C2004A03181 (last accessed 9 September 2021).

[45] See, for example, a comment originally published in The Spectator UK (27 October 2018), available at https://tonyabbott.com.au/2018/10/how-to-save-brexit/. See also Van Leeuwen, Hans (Europe Correspondent of the Australian Financial Review-AFR), Tony Abbott beats the Brexit drum with abandon, AFR 3 September 2019, https://www.afr.com/world/europe/tony-abbott-beats-the-brexit-drum-with-abandon-20190902-p52na3 (all last accessed 9 September 2021). However, it should also be noted that in stark contrast to the UK joining what was then the EEC, the intention to leave was met with reservation by many in Australia's political elite. The Australian government supported the remain position before the referendum; both then Prime Minister Malcolm Turnbull and then opposition leader Bill Shorten voiced positions in favour of remain, Allison-Reumann et al. (2018), p. 288.

September 2020.[46] One of Australia's foremost op-ed commentators in foreign policy, Greg Sheridan of the daily broadsheet The Australian, consistently wrote in favour of Brexit and only recently referred to the EU as being "essentially the work of the Devil".[47]

In a speech at the UK-Australia Chamber of Commerce on 4 June 2019, Australian Prime Minister Scott Morrison evoked the "special bonds of history" and laid a path from the constitutional principles inherited from the motherland via World War II and the Normandy D-Day operation directly to the importance of (WTO-) multilateralism in trade and directly to the potential FTA to be negotiated and concluded between Australia and the UK immediately after Brexit becomes effective,[48] which in the meantime it has as of 1 February 2020.

In that same speech, the Prime Minister also referred to another important aspect of the relationship between European countries and Australia, the defence industry. In his speech, the PM mentioned a joint venture with BAE-Systems around the construction of nine navy frigates. However, the flagship project, literally, in this regard, would the agreement with the French Naval Group for the joint construction (in Australia) of 12 Attack Class submarines with an estimated minimum cost of AUD 50 billion. Experience suggests that this number will likely increase. The total value of the acquisition of the submarines and the full sustainability costs of the system until 2080 is estimated to be around over AUD 220 billion in "out-turned" dollars.[49] Of course, defence transcends just the trading aspect as it points to foundational strategic common interests and, at least often and certainly in the context of the EU/Europe-Australian relationship, to shared political and values. Again, the special relationship to the UK, historically, constitutionally, legally, and culturally plays a role so significant that it is hard to overestimate. After World War II and the demise of the UK's ability to guarantee security against external threats, the United States has taken over that role, and Australia looks to the US as its main ally strategically. The common language, legal tradition, and, essentially, political value system supports this alliance. The fact that China is Australia's leading trading partner and the significance of that trade for the economic well-being of Australia

---

[46] https://www.gov.uk/government/news/government-announces-new-board-of-trade (last accessed 9 September 2021). The Board of Trade "engages with the whole of the UK on the UK's global trade and investment agenda. The board and its advisers take a collaborative approach, focused on promoting the UK regions as destinations to trade and do business with", https://www.gov.uk/government/groups/board-of-trade#advisers-to-the-board-september-2020 (last accessed 9 September 2021). Mr. Abbott appears to be the only "advisor" (formally, membership to the Board is open only to Privy Councillors) not fully based in the UK.

[47] In a TV appearance on Sky News and in the context of carbon border adjustment measures which might put levies on Australian products, see https://www.skynews.com.au/details/_6241183266001 (last accessed 9 September 2021). Greg Sheridan self-proclaims as religious and is the author of the 2018 book "God is Good for You: a Defense of Christianity in Troubled Times". It is unlikely that the comparison is a mere slip of the tongue.

[48] PM Scott Morrison, Australia-UK Chamber of Commerce, Speech, 4 September 2019, London, https://www.pm.gov.au/media/australia-uk-chamber-commerce (last accessed 9 September 2021).

[49] Brangwin (2020).

creates significant policy tensions for Australia but, at the same time, demonstrates the necessity for strategic partnerships in order to secure Australia's security into the future. This should provide opportunities to develop a strategic relationship with the EU as well.

It should be noted that Brexit might have impacts in this regard as well. The UK and the EU will also have to redefine their security partnership. NATO is under increasing pressure, and the policies of the Trump administration in the US complicated matters. It is perhaps no coincidence that the "anglosphere" is back in the headlines. The British historian Andrew Roberts published a call "to form a new superpower union with Canada, Australia and NZ and the US" in two leading conservative newspapers.[50] The creation of such a "superpower" may not be the official policy of Australia, but such ideas do resonate considerably. The so-called "Five Eyes Intelligence Partnership" provides more illustration for "the anglosphere" collaborating in core strategic and sensitive areas.[51]

4.2 Australia–France

The relationship between Australia and France is in many ways exceptional. There are historical ties that reach back into the first half of the nineteenth century. World War I, which figures extremely prominently in Australia as a core nation and identity-building event and is to this day commemorated with the most important national holiday in the calendar, ANZAC Day.[52] It was in France (and Belgium)

[50] Roberts, Andrew, It's Time to Revive the Anglosphere—The U.K. should form a new union with Canada, Australia and New Zealand to work as a global partner of the U.S., The Wall Street Journal, 8 August 2020, https://www.wsj.com/articles/its-time-to-revive-the-anglosphere-11596859260 (last accessed 9 September 2021). Also published under the title "Now is the time to revive the anglosphere" in: The Australian, 9 August 2020, https://www.theaustralian.com.au/business/the-wall-street-journal/its-time-to-revive-the-anglosphere/news-story/8f91ee95ea369ddcf755521758989646 (last accessed 9 September 2021).

[51] For more information on this intelligence partnership, see the website of the Five Eyes Intelligence Oversight and Review Council (FIORC), https://www.dni.gov/index.php/ncsc-how-we-work/217-about/organization/icig-pages/2660-icig-fiorc (last accessed 9 September 2021).

[52] Arguably that national holiday is not Australia Day, which commemorates the arrival of the First Fleet under Captain Arthur Phillip on 26 January 1788, and which became a national holiday in 1946. Rather it is ANZAC-Day which is observed on 25 April each year and commemorates in a narrower sense the contribution of the Australian and New Zealand Army Corps (ANZAC) in a bloody campaign in Gallipoli, Turkey, in the context of World War I but which, in a broader sense commemorates all servicemen and -women who served in all of Australia's armed conflicts and in that sense is the Australian version of the US Veteran's Day. However, there is a strong emphasis on World War I in which Australia lost more than 60,000 soldiers (of a total population of less than five million at the time; another 156,000 were wounded, gassed, or taken prisoner), see Australian War Memorial, First World War 1914–18, https://www.awm.gov.au/articles/atwar/first-world-war (numbers vary slightly depending on the source). In his article 'Casualties of War', also published

where Australia suffered by far the most casualties from its involvement in World War I.[53]

There are currently 32 bilateral agreements that form the general legal framework of the relationship between France and Australia. Among those bilateral treaties is the Agreement on Maritime Delimitation between the Government of Australia and the Government of the French Republic concerning the maritime boundaries between Australia and New Caledonia and between the Heard and McDonald Islands and Kerguelen Island.[54] The recitals of this agreement point to the intention to "strengthen(ing) the bonds of neighbourliness and friendship between the two countries", which brings to the fore the fact of France's vast maritime interests in the Indian and Pacific Oceans; the latter forms the most significant part of France's about 11 million km^2 of maritime area.[55] A strategy paper by the French Defense Department states that "France is a nation of the Indo-Pacific",[56] highlighting the significance of this area for France and thus for French-Australian relations.[57] During his visit to Australia in 2018, French President Emmanuel Macron suggested a strategic "Indo-Pacific axis" with Australia and India at its core, and he left no doubt that this

on the website of the Australian war memorial, Craig Tibbitts cites the number 60,00 as well but also uses the number 54,000 as "battle casualties", see https://www.awm.gov.au/wartime/article2.

[53] Many battles in which Australians took place in World War I were in France and Belgium and most Australian lives, 46,000, were lost on the western front. Some of the battles and battle locations, e.g. the river Somme (Battle of the Somme), are household names in Australia. See Australian Government—Department of Veterans Affairs, A Guide to Australian Memorials on the Western Front in France and Belgium—April 1916-November 1918, https://www.dva.gov.au/sites/default/files/files/publications/commemorations-war-graves/westernfront.pdf (last accessed 9 September 2021).

[54] (1983) ATS 3, https://info.dfat.gov.au/Info/Treaties/treaties.nsf/AllDocIDs/4CE7E4CF395D3E3DCA256AF00002CA4B (last accessed 9 September 2021).

[55] République Française, Premier Ministre, National strategy for the security of maritime areas, Adopted by the inter-ministerial sea committee on 22 October 2015, https://www.gouvernement.fr/sites/default/files/contenu/piece-jointe/2016/01/strategie_nationale_de_surete_des_espaces_maritimes_en_national_strategy_for_the_security_of_maritime_areas.pdf, p.3 (last accessed 9 September 2021).

[56] Ministère des Armées, France's Defence Strategy in the Indo-Pacific, https://apcss.org/wp-content/uploads/2020/02/France-Defence_Strategy_in_the_Indo-Pacific_2019.pdf, p. 5; see also Ministère des Armées, France and Security in the Indo-Pacific, May 2019, Foreword by the Minister of the Armed Forces Florence Parly, https://www.defense.gouv.fr/layout/set/print/content/download/532754/9176250/version/3/file/France+and+Security+in+the+Indo-Pacific+-+2019.pdf (both last accessed 9 September 2021).

[57] The term "Indo-Pacific" is relatively new and the concept behind it is still developing, see, for example, He and Feng (2020), p. 149. Critical A. Gyngell, To Each Their Own 'Indo-Pacific', EastAsiaForum, 23 May 2018, https://www.eastasiaforum.org/2018/05/23/to-each-their-own-indo-pacific/?utm_source=newsletter&utm_medium=email&utm_campaign=newsletter2018-05-27 (last accessed 9 September 2021).

strategy is in no small part prompted by the new Chinese assertiveness in this region.[58] Other bilateral treaties of note include an extradition treaty,[59] a double taxation convention,[60] and agreements concerning the transfer and processing of nuclear material.[61]

The significance of this relationship has become most visible in recent years with the signing of an AUD 50 billion agreement with the French Naval Group[62] for the provisions of 12 Attack class submarines for the Australian Navy as a central pillar of Australia's maritime defence.[63] The French Naval Group prevailed against intense competition from German and Japanese consortia. Anecdotal experience suggests that it is highly likely that the total financial volume of this agreement will grow considerably due to cost increases.[64] But even at the communicated sum of AUD 50 billion, the program is significantly larger than the 2020–21 consolidated funding for the Department of Defense (including the Australian Signals Directorate) of AUD 42.746 billion.[65] This particular aspect of French-Australian relations is currently governed by the Framework Agreement between Australia and France

[58] Elysée, Discours à Garden Island, base navale de Sydney, 3 May 2018, https://www.elysee.fr/emmanuel-macron/2018/05/03/discours-a-garden-island-base-navale-de-sydney (video only, last accessed 9 September 2021).

[59] Treaty of Extradition with the Government of the Republic of France, (1989) ATS 27, https://info.dfat.gov.au/Info/Treaties/treaties.nsf/AllDocIDs/6C3144882DDF7F9ACA256B99000CD67D (last accessed 9 September 2021).

[60] Convention with the Government of the French Republic for the avoidance of double taxation with respect to taxes on income and the prevention of fiscal evasion, and Protocol, (2009) ATS 13, https://info.dfat.gov.au/Info/Treaties/treaties.nsf/AllDocIDs/01E5CA84E5D80AA7CA2571A0001DA0D9 (last accessed 9 September 2021).

[61] Agreement between the Government of Australia and the Government of the French Republic concerning Nuclear Transfers between Australia and an Associated Exchange of Letters, (1981) ATS 23; Agreement between the Government of Australia and the Government of the French Republic Concerning the Reprocessing in France of Australian Irradiated Nuclear Fuel Elements, (2018) ATS 13.

[62] See https://www.naval-group.com.au/who-we-are/about (last accessed 9 September 2021).

[63] For details see Brangwin (2020), (last accessed 9 September 2021).

[64] In November 2019, Australian Rear Admiral Sammut advised the Senate that the acquisition cost of the Future Submarine was 'in the order of $80 billion out-turned', with an estimated sustainment cost of $145 billion out-turned to 2080, see Australian National Audit Office (ANAO), Future Submarine Program—Transition to Design, 14 January 2020, at 3.29, https://www.anao.gov.au/work/performance-audit/future-submarine-program-transition-to-design; see also Senate Foreign Affairs, Defence and Trade Legislation Committee, 29 November 2019, Testimony of Rear Admiral Sammut, https://www.aph.gov.au/Parliamentary_Business/Hansard/Hansard_Display?bid=committees/estimate/70150859-b9a2-4ed6-bcc6-e235ccee8bb3/&sid=0000 (last accessed 9 September 2021).

[65] Australian Strategic Policy Institute (ASPI), Defense & Strategy Program, The Cost of defence 2020–2021, Part 2: ASPI 2020–2021 Defence Budget Brief, https://www.aspi.org.au/report/cost-defence-2020-2021-part-2-aspi-defence-budget-brief (last accessed 9 September 2021). The Australian government attempts to provide longer-term certainty on funding arrangements for defence and has states that the total funding for Defence to be provided in the decade ending 2029–2030 will be AUD 575 billion. See Australian Government—Department of Defence, 2020

"Concerning Cooperation on the Future Submarine Program".[66] The primary function of this agreement is to, for example, ensure the transfer of technology and information, the streamlining of export controls, to secure the security of the supply chain into the future, and to maintain industry cooperation so as to enable Australia actually to maintain this future submarine capability in a self-reliant way.[67] There are several other defence-related bilateral instruments in place between the two countries ranging from mutual logistics support to the exchange and protection of classified material.[68]

From an overarching perspective, the French-Australian Relationship currently rests on the Joint Statement of Enhanced Strategic Partnership signed in March 2017.[69] The Statement spans the major political areas, including defence, security, and intelligence cooperation. Economic cooperation is kept fairly general with an emphasis on information exchange. Both parties also agree (E.1.) to cooperate "in efforts towards a balanced and mutually beneficial Australia-European Union Free Trade Agreement." This formulation is somewhat odd. France is part of the EU, and in line with Article 207.3 TFEU the EU's free trade negotiations are mandated by the EU member states via the Council and conducted by the Commission, however, in consultation with a very influential Council Committee.[70] In one sense, it is therefore not incorrect to speak of the matter as if France and Australia were equally distant third parties envisaging an FTA with the EU. That said, France is a member of the EU and under Article 4.3 TEU has specific solidarity commitments to the EU, which disallow measures "which could jeopardize the attainment of the Union's objectives." The clause, therefore, cannot be interpreted as France agreeing to look after the Australian interest in the FTA negotiations. Any concluded FTA is inherently a

Defence Strategic Update, https://www1.defence.gov.au/sites/default/files/2020-11/2020_Defence_Strategic_Update.pdf (last accessed 9 September 2021), p. 53.

[66] (2017) ATS (7), http://www.austlii.edu.au/au/other/dfat/treaties/ATS/2017/7.html (last accessed 9 September 2021).

[67] Cf. National Interest Analysis with attachment on consultation—Framework Agreement between the Government of Australia and the Government of the French Republic concerning Cooperation on the Future Submarine Program (Adelaide, 20 December 2016), (2017) ATNIF 4, http://www.austlii.edu.au/au/other/dfat/ATNIA/2017/4.html (last accessed 9 September 2021).

[68] See Agreement between the Government of Australia and the Government of the French Republic regarding the Provision of Mutual Logistics Support between the Australian Defence Force and the French Armed Forces (2019) ATS 12; Agreement between the Government of Australia and the Government of the French Republic regarding Defence Cooperation and Status of Forces (2009) ATS 18; Agreement between the Government of Australia and the Government of The Republic of France concerning Collaboration in Defence Research and Technology (1990) ATS 42.

[69] Signed on 3 March 2017, https://www.dfat.gov.au/geo/france/Pages/joint-statement-of-enhanced-strategic-partnership-between-australia-and-france (last accessed 9 September 2021).

[70] See Hahn (2016), paras. 95 et seq.

mutually beneficial agreement because otherwise, the parties would not have signed and ratified it. It is in that sense that the clause calls on both France and Australia to pursue such an outcome in good faith. The Joint Statement also emphasizes cooperation in the Pacific and Indian Oceans, where both countries are heavily invested as regional powers.[71] As indicated above, the common shared history of World War I is also prominently reflected in the document.[72]

4.3 Australia's Relations with Other European Countries: Brief Overview

Australia and the various member states of the European Union are connected by varying numbers of bilateral agreements between them. Some of these reflect matters of particular relevance between the participating states. Then there are some agreement types that are common to many of these bilateral relationships: double taxation, extradition, and social security agreements.

The Australian-German relationship is but one example. It is not based on any formal instrument dealing with the matter from a general, overarching perspective. There are currently 20 bilateral agreements in force between the two countries covering various matters, including the ones mentioned above, extradition[73] or double taxation.[74] The social security agreement between Australia and Germany (and many other European partners) facilitates the entitlement to benefits under the respective public pension schemes of both countries.[75] These agreements can be a significant factor in avoiding disadvantages for nationals of the one country who spent time working in the respective other country. In some cases, such as Belgium

[71] See Joint Statement of Enhanced Strategic Partnership, signed on 3 March 2017, https://www.dfat.gov.au/geo/france/Pages/joint-statement-of-enhanced-strategic-partnership-between-australia-and-france (last accessed 9 September 2021), as part of Defence Cooperation (B.) in the chapeau and, in particular, in B.7, B.8 and under its own heading (C.).

[72] Joint Statement of Enhanced Strategic Partnership, signed on 3 March 2017, https://www.dfat.gov.au/geo/france/Pages/joint-statement-of-enhanced-strategic-partnership-between-australia-and-france (last accessed 9 September 2021), J. and in the chapeau of B.

[73] Treaty between Australia and the Federal Republic of Germany concerning Extradition, (1990) ATS 21.

[74] Agreement between Australia and the Federal Republic of Germany for the Elimination of Double Taxation with Respect to Taxes on Income and on Capital and the Prevention of Fiscal Evasion and Avoidance, (2016) ATS 23.

[75] Agreement on Social Security with the Federal Republic of Germany, and Concluding Protocol, (2003) ATS 7; see also Agreement with the Federal Republic of Germany on Social Security to Govern Persons Temporarily Employed in the Territory of the Other State ("Supplementary Agreement"), Concluding Protocol and Implementation Arrangement (2008) ATS 13.

and the Netherlands, there are also agreements with Australia concerning benefits under their respective health care insurance schemes.[76]

The Netherlands is an example of a partner state with which Australia has also concluded some more specialized arrangements. Overall, there are 24 bilateral agreements between the two countries, and that qualifies the Dutch-Australian partnership as one of the more intensive ones. One of the special agreements between these two countries is a bilateral agreement concerning customs law and customs offences.[77] In the energy sector, the Netherlands and Australia have also agreed that Australia can fulfil its obligations of maintaining a 90-day strategic oil reserve under the Agreement on an International Energy Program by holding oil stocks in the territory of the Netherlands under commercial oil stocks contracts.[78] Of note is also a recent agreement that arose from the tragedy of the shooting down of the Malaysia Airlines Flight MH17 over the Ukraine in which many nationals from both countries were killed.[79]

Relations between Australia and Italy are also not based on an overarching framework instrument. Given that there are considerable ties through the immigration history of Italians coming to Australia, particularly after World War II, this may seem a little surprising. To this day, Italians are the strongest contingent of immigrants from Europe into Australia, second only to the UK.[80] This history might explain why a legal instrument in the form of an exchange of letters came into effect in 2004 to circumvent difficulties for Australians wishing to marry in Italy while being unable to fulfil documentary requirements set by Italian law.[81]

Obviously, there are also countries that only have a few bilateral agreements in force with Australia. For example, there are only two recent bilateral treaties between Luxembourg and Australia concerning extradition and mutual assistance in criminal

[76] Agreement between Australia and the Kingdom of Belgium on Health Care Insurance, (2009) ATS 21; Agreement with the Kingdom of the Netherlands concerning the Provision of Medical Treatment, (1992) ATS 3; Exchange of Notes constituting an Agreement to amend the Agreement between Australia and the Netherlands concerning the Provision of Medical Treatment of 5 April 1991, (2010) ATS 20.

[77] Agreement with the Kingdom of the Netherlands on Mutual Administrative Assistance for the Proper Application of Customs Law and for the Prevention, Investigation and Combating of Customs Offences, (2003) ATS 20.

[78] Agreement between the Government of Australia and the Government of the Kingdom of the Netherlands concerning Oil Stocks Contracts, (2018) ATS 21. See also Agreement on an International Energy Program, (1979) ATS 7.

[79] Treaty between Australia and the Kingdom of the Netherlands on the Ongoing Presence of Australian Personnel in the Netherlands for the Purpose of Responding to the Downing of Malaysia Airlines Flight MH17, (2019) ATS 14.

[80] Australian Bureau of Statistics, Migration, Australia Statistics on Australia's international migration, internal migration (interstate and intrastate), and the population by country of birth, Reference period 2018–19 financial year (Released 28 April 2020), https://www.abs.gov.au/statistics/people/population/migration-australia/latest-release (last accessed 9 September 2021).

[81] An Exchange of Letters between Australia and Italy concerning Australian Citizens wishing to marry in Italy, (2004) ATS 20.

matters.[82] There are no bilateral agreements between Croatia and Australia. The existing instruments go back to the 1970s and beyond and were concluded with what was then Yugoslavia. There is only an air services agreement between Australia and Serbia.[83] Whereas both are relatively small countries, there are about 270,000 Australian residents who were either born there or claim Serbian or Croatian ancestry.[84] Ireland is another country where immigration ties are significant because one in ten Australians claim Irish descent.[85] This notwithstanding, the relationship as measured against the eight bilateral agreements in force consists mainly of the relatively standard presence of extradition, double taxation, and social security agreements. The relationships to Hungary and Poland run along similar lines as well.

5 Current Negotiations for a Free Trade Agreement of Australia with the EU and with the UK

5.1 Australia–EU FTA (AEUFTA)

The creation of a free trade agreement between Australia and the EU (AEUFTA) would constitute a natural extension of the FA-2017. As explained above, the parties went through noticeable length to communicate in the FA-2017 that nothing in that agreement would in any way prejudice the envisaged FTA. Negotiations on the AEUFTA began in 2018; the ninth round of negotiation was concluded in December 2020, the tenth round on 19 March 2021 and the next round of talks is scheduled for June 2021. There are several sticking points beyond the traditional issues of FTAs. Perhaps among the more difficult ones are issues around market access, in particular for agricultural products and, in particular, the protection sought by the EU for geographical indication names. The EU has provided a lengthy list of such

[82] Treaty on Extradition between Australia and The Grand duchy of Luxembourg, (1988) ATS 16; Treaty with the Grand Duchy of Luxembourg on Mutual Assistance in Criminal Matters, (1994) ATS 14.

[83] Air Services Agreement between the Government of Australia and the Government of the Republic of Serbia, (2014) ATS 11.

[84] 2016 census data as reported by DFAT in the respective country briefs, see Serbia country brief, https://www.dfat.gov.au/geo/serbia/Pages/serbia-country-brief and Croatia country brief, https://www.dfat.gov.au/geo/croatia/Pages/croatia-country-brief (both last accessed 9 September 2021).

[85] See https://www.dfat.gov.au/geo/ireland/Pages/ireland-country-brief (last accessed 9 September 2021).

geographical indications that will have to be worked through during the negotiations.[86] DFAT's report[87] on the latest round is scarce in detail but does state that some preliminary text has been finalized or brought close to finalization, for example, in the area of government procurement. The chapter on customs and trade facilitation was provisionally finalized. Significant progress was also claimed in the services and investment sector, including temporary entry of natural persons and in dispute settlement and the trade remedies area. In other areas, the formulations chosen in the report point to more difficulties in finding common ground. This appears to be the case in the area of competition and subsidies, state-owned enterprises, energy and raw materials or SPS and animal welfare.

In July 2020, the EU tabled a discussion draft document containing language around institutional provisions of the AEUFTA. This draft envisages the creation of a Trade Committee with representatives from both parties and co-chaired by the respective trade minister/commissioner. This Trade Committee will function as the body responsible for supervising and facilitating the AEUFTA and is also linked via a duty to inform the Joint Committee established under the Framework Agreement. Its powers are not insignificant. It includes the power to establish and dissolve specialized Committees, to recommend amendments to the FTA and even "to adopt decisions to amend this Agreement (AEUFTA) in enumerated instances, such as annexes containing concrete application lists of substantive provisions of the AEUFTA and rules and codes of procedure relevant in the dispute settlement context (Article X.2.2.d). The Committee will also have the power to adopt interpretations of the provisions of the AEUFTA (Article X.2.2.e). Article X.3 even envisages a kind of implied powers authority and stipulates that the Committee shall have the power to take decisions where provided for in this Agreement if that is necessary to attain the objectives of this Agreement. Article X.7 aims at the inclusion and balanced representation of independent civil society organizations, so-called "domestic advisory groups" (Article X.6.3), employers, unions. Here as in other policy fields, it is becoming increasingly important to seek ways to open up the traditionally highly technocratic governance in matters of trade and seek transparency and participation of society as a whole. The institutional provisions draft is at this stage just that, a mere draft and what will become of it remains to be seen.

[86] See DFAT, List of EU's requested Geographical Indications—Level of GI protection requested by the EU, https://www.dfat.gov.au/trade/agreements/negotiations/aeufta/geographical-indications/list-of-eu-requested-geographic-indications-gis; see also European Commission, eAmbrosia—the EU geographical indications register, https://ec.europa.eu/info/food-farming-fisheries/food-safety-and-quality/certification/quality-labels/geographical-indications-register/ (both last accessed 9 September 2021).

[87] DFAT, Australia-EU FTA—Report on Negotiating Round Ten, 9–19 March 2021, https://www.dfat.gov.au/trade/agreements/negotiations/aeufta/news/australia-eu-fta-report-negotiating-round-ten-9-19-march-2021 (last accessed 9 September 2021).

5.2 *Australia–UK FTA*

Australia commenced negotiations with the UK on an FTA in June 2020.[88] The Agreement was signed on 17 December 2021, when this article was already in the final proofing stages. Whereas the parties had been talking about seeking an "ambitious and comprehensive" FTA,[89] in actual fact, the goals and the outcomes are more modest.[90] The FTA is in many ways a very classical FTA concentrating on the more or less full abolition of tariffs between the two countries and creating improvements for certain services, for example, financial services and certain professions. "Behind the border" issues are not dealt with in this agreement. There is, for example, no realization of any form of mutual recognition of each other's standards. For example, Art. 22.3 of the FTA specifically provides that both parties retain the "sovereign right to establish [their] own levels of domestic environmental protection and [their] own priorities relating to the environment, including climate change, and to establish, adopt or modify [their] environmental laws and policies." Both countries are the second-largest source of foreign direct investment for each other and that translated into investment liberalization so that, for example, most UK investments in Australia are no longer subject to review by the Australian Foreign Investment Review Board. One goal was to make the free movement of people easier and some modest improvements were achieved for professionals and young people seeking to temporarily work in Australia. There are some improvements in the fintech and digital area, where both countries regard themselves as being at the forefront of developments. For example, the FTA in its chapter 14 contains language around data localization and data protection or about electronic contracts. However, the language is rather generic and nothing strikes the reader as particularly forthcoming.

6 Closing Observations

The four years of the Trump presidency, while not being the sole cause or even the beginning of the difficulties, have amply demonstrated the fragility of what is often referred to as the rules-based international order. More bluntly, one should perhaps speak of the fragility of international law and, by extension, the rule of law rather

[88] DFAT, Australia-United Kingdom Free Trade Agreement, https://www.dfat.gov.au/trade/agreements/negotiations/aukfta (last accessed 9 September 2021).

[89] DFAT, Australia-UK FTA negotiating aims and approach https://www.dfat.gov.au/trade/agreements/negotiations/aukfta/negotiating-aims-and-approach (last accessed 9 September 2021).

[90] All content information and the current status of the negotiations were obtained from a BDO Webinar: UK-Australia Free Trade Negotiations presented on 16 March 2021. The main speakers were Joanne Freeman, Director of Trade Australia (UK), Vivian Life, Director Asia, and Australasia Negotiations (UK) and chief negotiator for the UK and James Manning (UK), lead negotiator for investment. A recording of the webinar is available at https://youtu.be/G6EwrdvxIaE (last accessed 9 September 2021).

than hiding behind a technocratic term. The rule of law will remain under pressure if only because superpowers will always at least be tempted to use their influence to bend others to their will rather than have their own will tamed by multilaterally created legal rules. The powerless and less powerful have more to gain from the rule of law than superpowers such as China or the US. At least one could have the impression that this kind of thinking is on the rise. Such thinking can be short-sighted even for superpowers. Challenges ranging from climate change to pandemics, from local and regional conflicts to food security and refugees illustrate on a daily basis that a heavy price is to be paid now or later for transnational governance deficits arising from a profound misunderstanding of the concept of the "national interest". Herein lies the real tragedy of Brexit—it weakens two major proponents of the rule of law. Third parties such as Australia might now be speculating on gaining advantages they otherwise might not have had. However, it is questionable whether Australia or other third states, for that matter, will really be able to gain. There will be two FTAs where otherwise will have been one. There are no indications that the quality of those two will be in any way better than the one would have been. The bureaucracy and administrative costs of these complex FTAs will be high. The "spaghetti bowl" of FTAs around the globe has reached a point where more does not mean better anymore.

The EU, its member states and Australia are champions of the rules-based international order. It is to be hoped, and there are encouraging signs that the two parties are aware of this and willing to work together to promote this agenda. Whereas Australia is a much smaller entity in all aspects, it is a considerable economic and political power in the Asia-Pacific region operating on a relatively strong foreign policy consensus and currently torn between its natural allies in the US and Europe and the strong cultural, historical and political ties in that direction and an ever more assertive and nationalistic China, which already is a regional superpower and whose economic development finances much of the wealth in Australia. The EU is much larger and faces a number of challenges to step up and fulfil an international role commensurate with its economic and soft-power status but has to do so burdened by inherent internal struggles between its own institutions and its member states, which, in the area of foreign policy in the broader sense, jealously guard their own power and influence and sometimes compete with each other. In this context, projects such as the AEUFTA, although in the scope of things and by itself only a small element in the world of international trade, will be a test for the ability of like-minded entities to pool their interests in a mutually beneficial way.

References

Allison-Reumann L, Matera M, Murray P (2018) Assessing Australia's options in the context of Brexit: engaging with the UK and the European Union. Aust J Int Aff 72(3):287–303

Bartlett CB (2020) Overcoming global food security challenges through science and solidarity. Am J Agric Econ 103(2):422–447. https://doi.org/10.1111/ajae.12160

Brangwin N (2020) Managing SEA 1000: Australia's Attack Class Submarines, Parliament of Australia, Research Paper Series, 2019–20. https://parlinfo.aph.gov.au/parlInfo/download/library/prspub/7206909/upload_binary/7206909.pdf

Bröhmer J (2012) Grundlegende Entwicklungen des australischen Verfassungsrechts. Jahrbuch des öffentlichen Rechts der Gegenwart 60:689–729

Hahn M (2016) Artikel 207. In: Calliess C, Ruffert M (eds) EUV/AEUV Kommentar. Beck, München

He K, Feng H (2020) The institutionalization of the Indo-Pacific: problems and prospects. Int Aff 96(1):149

Hristov J, Clough Y, Sahlin U, Smith HG, Stjernman M, Olsson O, Sahrbacher A, Brady MV (2020) Impacts of the EU's Common Agricultural Policy "Greening" reform on agricultural development. Biodiversity Ecosyst Serv Appl Econ Perspect Policy 42(4):716–738

Markovic N (2009) Courted by Europe? Advancing Australia's relations with the European Union in the new security environment, research paper no. 1 2009–10 (Foreign Affairs, Defence and Security Section, 14 July 2009). https://www.aph.gov.au/About_Parliament/Parliamentary_Departments/Parliamentary_Library/pubs/rp/rp0910/10rp01

Matera M, Murray P (2018) Australia's relationship with the European Union: from conflict to cooperation. Aust J Int Aff 72(3):179–193

Matthews A, Soldi R (2019) Evaluation of the impact of the current CAP on the agriculture of developing countries, European Committee of the Regions Commission for Natural Resources. https://op.europa.eu/s/oMJO

McKenzie L (2018) Overcoming legacies of foreign policy (dis)interests in the negotiations of the European Union-Australia Free Trade Agreement. Aust J Int Aff 72(3):255–271

Meissner KL, McKenzie L (2018) The paradox of human rights conditionality in EU trade policy: when strategic interests drive policy outcomes. J Eur Publ Policy 26(9):1273–1291

Murray P, Benvenuti A (2014) EU-Australia relations at fifty: reassessing a troubled relationship. Aust J Polit Hist 60(3):431–448

Pajtinka E (2020) The beginnings of the European Diplomatic Service from the 1950s to the 1980s. Teorija in Praksa 57(2):455–470

Ward M (2020) Statistics on UK trade with the Commonwealth, House of Commons Library, Briefing paper number CBP 8282, 2 December 2020. https://researchbriefings.files.parliament.uk/documents/CBP-8282/CBP-8282.pdf

Whelan J, Brown AD, Coller L, Strugnell C, Allender S, Alston L, Hayward J, Brimblecombe J, Bell C (2021) The impact of COVID-19 on rural food supply and demand in Australia: utilizing group model building to identify retailer and customer perspectives. Nutrients 13(2):417. https://doi.org/10.3390/nu13020417

Wilson J, King G (2020) Political risks for the Australia-China agriculture trade, Perth USAsia Centre, Indo-Pacific Analysis Briefs 11. https://perthusasia.edu.au/our-work/political-risks-for-the-australia-china-agricultur

Yencken E (2018) From the common agricultural policy to the Eurozone crisis: bilateral disputes in the Australia–EU relationship, The Round Table – The Commonwealth. J Int Aff 107(5): 585–600

Jürgen Bröhmer is Professor of Law at the Law School of Murdoch University in Perth, Western Australia. He joined Murdoch University at the beginning of 2012 as Dean of the Law School and Professor of Law and served in that function until the creation of the new College of Arts, Business, Law and Social Sciences (ABLSS) of Murdoch University in 2019. Before joining Murdoch University, he worked at the University of New England, in Armidale, NSW, Australia, having commenced there in 2006 and leading that Law School from 2007 to 2011. Professor Bröhmer received his law degree from Mannheim University in Germany and his doctorate and post-doctoral habilitation from Saarland University in Saarbrücken, Germany where worked at the Europa-Institute of Saarland University from 1992 to 2006. Professor Bröhmer is a fellow of the Australian Academy of Law.

The Framework of Bilateral Trade Agreements

Michael Hahn

Contents

Abstract Preferential trade relationships—regardless whether their legal fundament would be a Free Trade Agreement (FTA) or a Customs Union—would be incompatible with membership in the WTO, were it not for Article XXIV GATT and its sister provision in GATS. The generous exception for FTAs only came to be as a consequence of the US wanting to accommodate a close ally which would have been rendered impossible on the basis of the long-held US position. Despite the abrupt and radical change concerning the compatibility of the multilateral trading system with FTAs, the limitations established by Article XXIV GATT are more pronounced than is often appreciated. This may become particularly relevant in a new trading landscape centred around (meta-)regional hubs. Article XXIV may have a second lease of life ensuring that the trend toward regional integrations does not eliminate the floor for inter-regional cooperation that may become a central task for the WTO.

M. Hahn (✉)
Institute of European and International Economic Law, World Trade Institute, University of Bern, Bern, Switzerland
e-mail: michael.hahn@iew.unibe.ch

M. Bungenberg, A. Mitchell (eds.), *The Australia-European Union Free Trade Agreement*, Special Issue, https://doi.org/10.1007/978-3-030-91448-6_3

1 Introduction

These days, all the action and the fun of international economic law is associated with Free Trade Agreements (FTAs). This volume and the following chapters would seem to support that view: old concepts are being advanced and refined, new approaches are being developed and, one would hope, submitted to many decades of endurance testing. In contrast, the World Trade Organization, once a beacon of hope that herbivores like the EU could advance reciprocally beneficial and advantageous trade relations with Asian dragons, North American eagles and other jungle creatures, has been put in an induced coma, and us bystanders can only hope that *she'll be fine*, eventually.

That positivity associated with FTAs—be it as laboratory of ideas[1]or as an acceptable second-best solution for managing trade relations worldwide—was not a given until weeks before the current text of the predecessor provision of Article XXIV GATT became the new normal. During the early phases of the negotiations eventually leading to GATT, it was received wisdom in many pro-trade circles—and the firmly held position of the US Government until the 11th hour[2]—that there was "no place in a world of order and peace for arrangements under which certain countries discriminate against other members of the world community of nations."[3] Nevertheless, Article XXIV GATT now does contain language that explicitly addresses both customs unions (CUs) and Free Trade Areas (FTAs).[4]

In the following, this paper will have a quick look at the history of how the provision on FTAs found its way into the GATT and why it happened (Sect. 2). Secondly, readers will be reminded of the legal status quo and the relationship between the multilateral system and Free Trade Agreements (Sect. 3). Lastly, the chapter will conclude with highlighting the dual interests states may have in pursuing the conclusion of FTAs (Sect. 4).

---

[1]Cf. the dissent by Justice Brandeis in *State Ice Co. v. Liebmann*, 285 US 262 (1932) where he characterizes the federal system as a laboratory in which "novel social and economic experiments without risk to the rest of the" system may be tried.

[2]Chase (2006), pp. 1–30.

[3][US] National Foreign Trade Council, Position of the National Foreign Trade Council with Respect to the Havana Character for an International Trade Organization, New York, 1950, 65 et seq.; Chase (2006), Fn. 9.

[4]See Irwin et al. (2008), pp. 165 et seq; see also Matsushita et al. (2015), pp. 507 et seq.

2 The Relevance of (Geo-)Political Considerations for Internalizing an FTA Exception Into GATT

For a considerable time, the rather generous insulation of FTAs and CUs from the wrath of MFN violations[5] had been seen as one of the last successes of British diplomacy to protect the trade benefits of the moribund British Empire.[6] The reason for this perception had been the intense advocacy for a comprehensive MFN-based regime by the US starting with the "Suggested Charter for an International Trade Organization" (ITO) 16 months or so after VE day.[7] Apart from certain colonial preferences that were supposed to be kept upon request of the UK, only "unions for customs purposes" were supposed to be exempt from that strict legal command. One of the main reasons for this exemption was that the formation of a customs union was seen as the destined path for (continental) Europe to overcome the destruction (not only of economic life) after two world wars originating there.[8] Historically, customs unions had either failed or led to (Federal) statehood, e.g. in Switzerland or Germany during the nineteenth century, and before that, of course, in France and elsewhere. Not standing in the way of European integration and unification was perceived an essential building block for the *Pax Americana*. In contrast, FTAs were not supposed to enjoy the same benevolent treatment. They would have been outlawed as a violation of the MFN obligation. And the US position, paraphrased in the cited passage above, was reflective of the US view that trade discrimination, and be it as a consequence of preferential trade agreements, "bred political conflict" and was "morally repugnant".[9] This stance, developed between 1921 and 1933 in the Framework of the League of Nations, then internalized by US Reciprocal Trade Agreements Act was a central point of the Suggested Charter[10] and was kept in the London Draft (November 1946), the New York Draft (February 1947) and the Geneva Draft (October 1947). However, in Article 44 of the *Havana Charter*, the former nemesis of MFN, the Free Trade Area, was suddenly on par with the protected species that had been the customs union, and the customs union only.

How did that change of fortune happen? After the Christmas break 1947, the Lebanese and Syrian representatives tabled a proposal for an amendment to exempt from MFN rules regional groups that eliminated restrictions on mutual trade without establishing a common customs system.[11] France suggested modifications, further negotiations ensued with the participation of the Western leading power, the US, and

---

[5]Curzon (1965), p. 64.

[6]See Odell and Eichengreen (1998), p. 183.

[7]Chase (2006), p. 4.

[8]Bhagwati (1991), p. 65; Odell and Eichengreen (1998), p. 183.

[9]Chase (2006), p. 3.

[10]"Suggested Charter for an International Trade Organization of the United Nations," State Department Publication No. 2598, September 1946.

[11]Chase (2006), p. 14.

on 23 March 1948, the Havana Charter was signed containing the following Article 44, placed just before the General Exception of Article 45:

> 1. Members recognize the desirability of increasing freedom of trade by the development, through voluntary agreements, of closer integration between the economies of the countries parties to such agreements. They also recognize that the purpose of a customs union or free-trade area should be to facilitate trade between the parties and not to raise barriers to the trade of other Member countries with such parties.
>
> 2. Accordingly, the provisions of this Chapter shall not prevent, as between the territories of Members, the formation of a customs union or of a free-trade area or the adoption of an interim agreement necessary for the formation of a customs union or of a free-trade area; *Provided* that:
>
> (a) with respect to a customs union, or an interim agreement leading to the formation of a customs union, the duties and other regulations of commerce imposed at the institution of any such union or interim agreement in respect of trade with Member countries not parties to such union or agreement shall not on the whole be higher or more restrictive than the general incidence of the duties and regulations of commerce applicable in the constituent territories prior to the formation of such union or the adoption of such interim agreement, as the case may be;
>
> (b) with respect to a free-trade area, or an interim agreement leading to the formation of a free-trade area, the duties and other regulations of commerce maintained in each of the constituent territories and applicable at the formation of such free-trade area, the duties and other regulations of commerce maintained in each of the constituent territories and applicable at the formation of such free-trade area or the adoption of such interim agreement to the trade of Member countries not included in such area or not parties to such agreement shall not be higher or more restrictive than the corresponding duties and other regulations of commerce existing in the same constituent territories prior to the formation of the free-trade area, or interim agreement, as the case may be; [. . .]
>
> 3. (a) Any Member deciding to enter into a customs union or free-trade area, or an interim agreement leading to the formation of such a union or area, shall promptly notify the Organization and shall make available to it such information regarding the proposed union or area as will enable the Organization to make such reports and recommendations to Members as it may deem appropriate. [. . .]
>
> 4. For the purposes of this Charter:
>
> (a) a customs union shall be understood to mean the substitution of a single customs territory for two or more customs territories [. . .]
>
> (b) a free-trade area shall be understood to mean a group of two or more customs territories in which the duties and other restrictive regulations of commerce (except, where necessary, those permitted under Section B of Chapter IV and under Article 45) are eliminated on substantially all the trade between the constituent territories in products originating in such territories. [. . .]

As many readers of this book will immediately realize, the vast majority of Article 44 of the Havana Charter is still good law, as Article XXIV GATT is to a large extent a *verbatim* copy of the quoted provision.

We know today that this was not a success of Levantine or French diplomacy. Rather, the reason for the US retreat from its previously held position had geopolitical reasons, namely to respond to an urgent economic need of an important ally in distress. Between October 1947 and March 1948, the idea of creating an FTA between Canada and the US had advanced to the point that the US government saw fit to give up the well-entrenched support for strict and consistent MFN supremacy for every Member, with the only exception for those who were prepared to enter into a very close union that in itself merited support by the post-war world order.

That about-face had begun with the request by the Canadian government to its Southern neighbour to grant free listings in the US tariff code to certain key exports to the US.[12] For obvious reasons of political economy, the US government was unable to grant that demand. However, being keen to be seen as a good neighbour and reliable partner in difficult times, the US suggested entering into a customs union.[13] But Canada was neither Germany nor twice-destroyed France; it was a victorious power, having fought alongside US troops in the European and Asian theatres. Entering a union with its giant neighbour was out of the question for Canada, as the unavoidable loss of competencies (and therefore potentially diminished sovereignty) attached to entering into such a CU would have met unsurmountable political headwinds. Thus, the only realistic option to get both Canada and the US what they wanted was a preferential trade agreement. This, however, was incompatible with the US position on preferential trade agreements in general. Something had to give, and it was not the reliability of the US having Canada's back.[14] The Syrian and Lebanese amendment proposals, somewhat adapted to the needs of the US, thus became the law of GATT until today.

It is a law which has not been kindly reviewed by academic authors. It has been labelled an "absurdity",[15] "a failure, if not a fiasco"[16] and "full of holes".[17] Given that (perceived) regulatory failure of the drafters, it comes as no surprise that the provision has lent itself to being abused, "and those abuses are amongst the least noted".[18]

To some extent, the criticism of state practice may seem exaggerated: after all, as will be seen below in *sub* 3., there are guardrails which would seem more robust than is generally acknowledged. But it is interesting to note that from the very beginning of the multilateral trading system, the thorny issue of FTAs had a geopolitical dimension. Geopolitical considerations—*in casu* taking care of the northern neighbour—trumped a just and fair world order, nothing less, as trade discrimination had been recognized by Cordell Hull as "handmaiden of armed aggression".[19]

---

[12] Chase (2006), p. 12.

[13] Chase (2006), p. 13.

[14] Chase (2006), pp. 14 et seq.

[15] Haight (1972), p. 398.

[16] Dam (1970), p. 275.

[17] Bhagwati (1993), p. 44.

[18] WTO (1995), p. 63.

[19] Gardner (1956), p. 8; see also Chase (2006), p. 10.

Past may be prologue in this context. Today's FTA discussions also have very much a political dimension, as they very often are a reaction not just to the changing landscape of international trade, but also to altered international relations in general, e.g., the Australia—US FTA had more to do with rewarding an ally for the Gulf-related sacrifice in blood and treasure than economic considerations; the race between the antipodean cousins for concluding an FTA with China was fuelled as much by general political considerations as by economic interest. Recently, the whiff of lawlessness that entered US politics in January 2017 (and which became a stench on 6 January 2021) had immediate consequences in the FTA arena. As the 45th US president openly sabotaged the US-centred multilateral order, blocking (against the clear obligation of the DSU) the appointment of Appellate Body Members,[20] taking WTO-incompatible protectionist measures masqueraded as national security measures (covered by Article XXI GATT)[21] and committing other clear and manifest breaches of WTO law, the world reacted with a flurry of activity: important trading nations started negotiating and concluding FTAs when they had not planned to do so before.

For example, it does not seem outlandish to posit that the fact that the current contracting parties of the Comprehensive and Progressive Agreement for Trans-Pacific Partnership (CPTPP) did proceed with entering into that agreement, despite the US government's unconventional extraction from the process that President Obama had initiated, was more than just a commitment to improve terms of trade for the parties. Rather, it was a signal both to the US and to the rest of the world that the heterogenous group of participants that have sometimes only the proximity to the Pacific Rim in common, was prepared to proceed even in the absence of either of the two Great Pacific Powers.

In a similar fashion, not without pertinence for this volume, the European Union also adapted its external economic policy, the so-called *Common Commercial Policy*[22] to the new challenge. Firstly, Europe started to review and then strengthen its arsenal of unilateral trade measures in order to achieve better preparedness for responding to abuses and coercive measures by trade partners.[23] Secondly, though,

---

[20] Members do not have a political choice to fill or not fill the roster of the Appellate Body. Article 17 (2) DSU unequivocally states that they shall.

[21] See: US – Certain Measures on Steel and Aluminium Products, WT/DS548, https://www.wto.org/english/tratop_e/dispu_e/cases_e/ds548_e.htm (last accessed 9 September 2021).

[22] See Hahn and Van Der Loo (2020).

[23] Cf. Communication from the Commission to the European Parliament, the Council, the European Economic and Social Committee and the Committee of the Regions: Trade Policy Review—An Open, Sustainable and Assertive Trade Policy, COM/2021/66 final; see also Charles Michel, President of the European Council, "A stronger and more autonomous European Union powering a fairer world", speech at the UN General Assembly, 25 September 2020, https://www.consilium.europa.eu/de/press/press-releases/2020/09/25/a-stronger-and-more-autonomous-european-union-powering-a-fairer-world-speech-by-president-charles-michel-at-the-un-general-assembly/ (last accessed 9 September 2021). As things take time in the multi-level governance structure of the European Union, these efforts have come to fruition very late during the 45th US presidency. The Anti-Coercion instrument will only be formally proposed late 2021/early 2022; see Joint

the Union strengthened its investment in FTAs, as the following three examples may illustrate. Firstly, the Union started to awake the *sleeping beauties* that were the dispute settlement mechanisms (DSMs) of EU FTAs.[24] Initiating within a year for proceedings, where in the decades before there had been none, is no coincidence. The two completed disputes concern two particularly ambitious agreements: the first concerns the FTA with Korea, and more specifically the novel labour right provisions;[25] the second concerned the "deep and comprehensive" FTA with Ukraine that basically projects the rules of the Single Market beyond its borders.[26] While at first sight one may be inclined to perceive such an inflationary use of DSMs as an indication of problematic relationships, it would seem that the targeted use of the bilateral DSMs was supposed to affirm relevance and viability.[27] Secondly, Japan and the EU concluded (after what felt like decades of negotiations) a bilateral FTA,[28] and even celebrated the agreement more than a year before it really happened,[29] just

---

Declaration of the Commission, the Council and the European Parliament on an instrument to deter and counteract coercive actions by third countries, OJ 2021 C 49/1. Cf. Hindelang and Morberg (2020), pp. 1427 et seq.

[24] Cf. European Commission, "Disputes under bilateral trade agreements", <https://ec.europa.eu/trade/policy/accessing-markets/dispute-settlement/bilateral-disputes/> (last accessed 9 September 2021).

[25] Panel of experts proceeding constituted under article 13.15 of the EU-Korea Free Trade Agreement. Report of the panel of experts of January 20, 2021, https://trade.ec.europa.eu/doclib/docs/2021/january/tradoc_159358.pdf (last accessed 9 September 2021). Central to the dispute was Art. 13.4.3 of. the Agreement, pursuant to which "in accordance with the obligations deriving from membership of the ILO and the ILO Declaration on Fundamental Principles and Rights at Work [...] [the contracting parties] commit to respecting, promoting and realising, in their laws and practices, the principles concerning the fundamental rights, namely: a. freedom of association and the effective recognition of the right to collective bargaining; b. the elimination of all forms of forced or compulsory labour; c. the effective abolition of child labour; and d. the elimination of discrimination in respect of employment and occupation. The Parties reaffirm the commitment to effectively implementing the ILO Conventions that Korea and the Member States of the European Union have ratified respectively. The Parties will make continued and sustained efforts towards ratifying the fundamental ILO Conventions as well as the other Conventions that are classified as 'up-to-date' by the ILO."

[26] Restrictions applied by Ukraine on exports of certain wood products to the European Union, Final Report of the Arbitration Panel, 11 December 2020, https://trade.ec.europa.eu/doclib/docs/2020/december/tradoc_159181.pdf (last accessed 9 September 2021).

[27] See for the strategy of the EU its "Non paper of the Commission services, Feedback and way forward on improving the implementation and enforcement of Trade and Sustainable Development chapters in EU Free Trade Agreements", 26 February 2018, <https://trade.ec.europa.eu/doclib/docs/2018/february/tradoc_156618.pdf> (last accessed 9 September 2021).

[28] Agreement between the European Union and Japan for an Economic Partnership, OJ 2018 L 330/3, https://eur-lex.europa.eu/legal-content/EN/TXT/?uri=celex:22018A1227%2801%29 (last accessed 9 September 2021).

[29] Joint Statement by the President of the European Commission Jean-Claude Juncker and the Prime Minister of Japan Shinzo Abe, 8 December 2017, https://trade.ec.europa.eu/doclib/press/index.cfm?id=1768&title=Joint-Statement-by-the-President-of-the-European-Commission-Jean-Claude-Juncker-and-the-Prime-Minister-of-Japan-Shinzo-Abe (last accessed 9 September 2021).

to send a signal to both the White house and the rest of the world that the first and third G 7 trading powers were still believing in rules-based trade relations, not in *Scarface*-informed practices.[30] Lastly, the EU added the two antipodean democracies to the list of nations with which it would be desirable to conclude FTAs. Despite the reciprocal benefit that will, without doubt, ensue from a successful conclusion, there were at least two additional reasons to enter into negotiations with Australia and New Zealand. Firstly, the expression of a shared commitment to rules-based trade relations, even if for the EU, bilateral relations remain, as a matter of principle, only the second-best solution. Secondly, the FTA was supposed to send a message to the rest of the world that Europe remained attached to its South Pacific partners and was, if welcome, not prepared to leave their markets to other Northern hemisphere powers.

3 The Legal Status Quo

While the sudden acceptance of FTAs rendered it possible for GATT contracting parties—and now WTO members—to conclude FTAs, the extent and scope of the exception is, pursuant to both the wording of the provision and its reading by the Appellate Body, not as generous and forgiving as some would like to (make) believe. Article XXIV is not a broad "get-out-of-jail"-card for each and any WTO-incompatible measure that a Member may want to implement in the context of setting up an FTA or CU and eventually managing and developing it.

3.1 Article XXIV GATT as Interface Between WTO Law and FTA

Of course, concluding and implementing an FTA would be a violation of a WTO Member's obligation (Article XVI (4) DSU) and trigger its responsibility (Article 41 VCLT[31]), were it not for Article XXIV GATT (and its sister provision, Article V GATS). Article XXIV GATT 1994 and Article V GATS (in the following reference will mostly be made to the Article XXIV GATT exception) allow WTO Members to depart from their general WTO obligations when they establish FTAs, CUs or (with regard to services) agreements liberalizing trade in services. While not pertinent for this volume, it should be added that developing countries have, in addition to Article

[30] *Colorandi causa*: https://www.rottentomatoes.com/m/scarface/quotes/ (last accessed 9 September 2021).

[31] Odendahl (2012); Cottier and Foltea (2006); Dörr and Schmalenbach (2012).

XXIV GATT/V GATS, the Enabling Clause[32] as a possible WTO fundament for their endeavor.[33] In one of its more recent summaries of the current state of WTO jurisprudence with regard to FTAs the Appellate Body explained:[34]

> 5.112. [. . .] Article XXIV of the GATT 1994 specifically permits departures from certain WTO rules in FTAs. However, Article XXIV conditions such departures on the fulfilment of the rule that the level of duties and other regulations of commerce, applicable in each of the FTA members to the trade of non-FTA members, shall not be higher or more restrictive than those applicable prior to the formation of the FTA.
>
> 5.113. In the light of the above, we consider that the proper routes to assess whether a provision in an FTA that may depart from certain WTO rules is nevertheless consistent with the covered agreements are the WTO provisions that permit the formation of regional trade agreements - namely: Article XXIV of the GATT 1994, or the Enabling Clause as far as agreements between developing countries are concerned, in respect of trade in goods; and Article V of the General Agreement on Trade in Services (GATS) in respect of trade in services. [. . .]
>
> 5.115. In *Turkey – Textiles*,[35] the Appellate Body considered that Article XXIV of the GATT 1994 may provide justification for measures that are inconsistent with certain other GATT 1994 provisions, *provided that two cumulative conditions are fulfilled*: (i) the party claiming the benefit of this defense must demonstrate that the measure at issue is introduced upon the formation of a customs union or FTA that fully meets the requirements of Article XXIV; and (ii) that party must demonstrate that the formation of that customs union or FTA would be prevented if it were not allowed to introduce the measure at issue.
>
> 5.116. In setting out the above cited conditions for a GATT 1994-inconsistent measure to be justified as part of a customs union or FTA under paragraph 5 of Article XXIV of the GATT 1994, in *Turkey - Textiles*, the Appellate Body relied also on paragraph 4 of this provision, which states that the purpose of a customs union or FTA is "to facilitate trade" between the constituent members and "not to raise barriers to the trade" with third countries. We further note that paragraph 4 qualifies customs unions or FTAs as "agreements, of *closer* integration between the economies of the countries parties to such agreements". In our view, the references in paragraph 4 to facilitating trade and closer integration are not consistent with an interpretation of Article XXIV as a broad defense for measures in FTAs that roll back on Members' rights and obligations under the WTO covered agreements.

[32] Decision on Differential and More Favourable Treatment, Reciprocity and Fuller Participation (Enabling Clause), adopted by the GATT CONTRACTING PARTIES in 1979, L/4903, https://www.wto.org/english/docs_e/legal_e/enabling1979_e.htm (last accessed 9 September 2021).

[33] The Agreement Establishing the African Continental Free Trade Area (https://au.int/en/treaties/agreement-establishing-african-continental-free-trade-area (last accessed 9 September 2021).) refers to the WTO-Agreement and not to a specific provision.

[34] *Peru — Additional Duty on Imports of Certain Agricultural Products*, WT/DS45, 20 July 2015 (adopted on 31 July 2015), https://www.wto.org/english/tratop_e/dispu_e/cases_e/ds457_e.htm (last accessed 9 September 2021), (footnotes omitted, emphasis added).

[35] [Footnote not in the original]: Appellate Body Report, *Turkey – Restrictions on Imports of Textile and Clothing Products*, WT/DS34/AB/R, 22 October 1999 (adopted on 19 November 1999), https://www.wto.org/english/tratop_e/dispu_e/cases_e/ds34_e.htm (last accessed 9 September 2021).

The 5-year-old quote restates the 1999 report on *Turkey—Textiles*.[36] There, the Appellate Body first established that the provision of Article XXIV (4) was the *chapeau* of the operational provisions, meaning that it may be the loadstar for the following three paragraphs 5–8, but does not contain actionable language itself. Article XXIV (4) reads:

> The contracting parties recognize the desirability of increasing freedom of trade by the development, through voluntary agreements, of closer integration between the economies of the countries parties to such agreements. They also recognize that the purpose of a customs union or of a free-trade area should be to facilitate trade between the constituent territories and not to raise barriers to the trade of other contracting parties with such territories.

Thus, that provision "informs"[37] the following three paragraphs,[38] which define the conditions under which CU/FTA participants may justifiably take WTO-incompatible measures because they do so for the benefit of a purpose accepted by the WTO-system in Article XXIV GATT (and its sister provision). In the following we will only address the law of Article XXIV GATT as it pertains to FTAs, given the focus of this volume.

[36] *Turkey – Restrictions on Imports of Textile and Clothing Products*, WT/DS34/AB/R.

[37] Language of the Appellate Body regarding Art. III (1) GATT: Appellate Body report: *Japan – Taxes on Alcoholic Beverages*, WT/DS8/AB/R, 4 October 1996 (adopted on 1 November 1996), https://www.wto.org/english/tratop_e/dispu_e/cases_e/ds8_e.htm (last accessed 9 September 2021), p. 18.

[38] Which read in pertinent parts: "5. Accordingly, the provisions of this Agreement shall not prevent, as between the territories of contracting parties, the formation of a customs union or of a free-trade area or the adoption of an interim agreement necessary for the formation of a customs union or of a free-trade area; *Provided* that:

(a) with respect to a customs union, or an interim agreement leading to a formation of a customs union, the duties and other regulations of commerce imposed at the institution of any such union or interim agreement in respect of trade with contracting parties not parties to such union or agreement shall not on the whole be higher or more restrictive than the general incidence of the duties and regulations of commerce applicable in the constituent territories prior to the formation of such union or the adoption of such interim agreement, as the case may be;

(b) with respect to a free-trade area, or an interim agreement leading to the formation of a free-trade area, the duties and other regulations of commerce maintained in each of the constituent territories and applicable at the formation of such free-trade area or the adoption of such interim agreement to the trade of contracting parties not included in such area or not parties to such agreement shall not be higher or more restrictive than the corresponding duties and other regulations of commerce existing in the same constituent territories prior to the formation of the free-trade area, or interim agreement as the case may be [. . .]

3.2 *The* Internal Requirements *an FTA has to Meet in Order for Article XXIV to Apply*

Pursuant to Article XXIV (5) GATT only arrangements that meet the standard that Article XXIV (8) sets up for FTAs may benefit from GATT's pertinent exception. Article XXIV (8) GATT has been exceedingly well explored by the literature, not the least by the seminal piece of one of the editors of this volume.[39] While the Appellate Body has left certain questions open, there is a rather good sense of what are clear and obvious cases of compatibility and non-compatibility. Article XXIV (8) reads in pertinent parts (i.e. to the extent that it applies to FTAs) as follows:

> [...] A free-trade area shall be understood to mean a group of two or more customs territories in which the duties and other restrictive regulations of commerce (except, [...] those permitted under Articles XI, XII, XIII, XIV, XV and XX) are eliminated on substantially all the trade between the constituent territories in products originating in such territories.

Thus, duties and other restrictive regulations of commerce (Sect. 3.2.1) need to be eliminated on substantially all the trade between the constituent territories (Sect. 3.2.2) in order to make GATT FTA justification for violating the non-discrimination principle of Article I GATT available.

3.2.1 Duties and Other Restrictive Regulations of Commerce

The term *duties and other restrictive regulations of commerce* defines the type of regulatory impediments that need to be abolished by the parties of an FTA in order to qualify under Article XXIV GATT. Contrary to a possible reading of *restrictive regulations of commerce* that would be in parallel with the ECJ's famous *Dassonville* formula[40] and would encompass *all* regulations that directly or indirectly, actually or potentially affect intra-FTA trade, it would seem that the correct interpretation would only capture the type of measures that were already identified in the 1940s as prototypical regulations of (international) commerce: this would include all border measures and also discriminatory internal measures, but not capture other laws and regulations that somewhat burden and impede international commerce. The *Understanding on the Interpretation of Article XXIV* would seem to confirm this view as it focusses on the border measures and fails to address internal measures as such.

If one would follow the *Dassonville* approach, only fully integrated FTAs with harmonized FTA law would benefit from Article XXIV: that was obviously not what the drafters of the GATT—and the negotiators of the WTO agreement!—wanted.

---

[39] Lockhart and Mitchell (2005).

[40] CJEU, case C-8/74, *Dassonville*, ECLI:EU:C:1974:82, para. 5: "All trading rules enacted by Member States which are capable of hindering, directly or indirectly, actually or potentially, intra-Community trade are to be considered as measures having an effect equivalent to quantitative restrictions."

The state practice regarding FTAs focusses on the elimination of custom duties and their substitutes, and of discriminatory internal measures. Of course, modern FTAs do deal with internal regulations that have proved to be too burdensome, as this volume illustrates. But such ambition is not a condition for meeting the standard of Article XXIV (8) GATT.

3.2.2 Substantially All the Trade Between the Constituent Territories

Neither the drafters of the GATT or the WTO negotiators,[41] nor the WTO adjudicative bodies have clearly defined what "substantially all the trade between the constituent territories in products originating in such territories" means. In an almost cheeky fashion, the Appellate Body in *Turkey—Textiles*[42] stated:

> It is clear, though, that "substantially all the trade" is not the same as *all* the trade, and also that "substantially all the trade" is something considerably more than merely *some* of the trade. We note also that the terms of sub-paragraph 8(a)(i) provide that members of a customs union may maintain, where necessary, in their internal trade, certain restrictive regulations of commerce that are otherwise permitted under Articles XI through XV and under Article XX of the GATT 1994. Thus, we agree with the Panel that the terms of sub-paragraph 8(a)(i) offer "some flexibility" to the constituent members of a customs union when liberalizing their internal trade in accordance with this sub-paragraph. Yet we caution that the degree of "flexibility" that sub-paragraph 8(a)(i) allows is limited by the requirement that "duties and other restrictive regulations of commerce" be "eliminated with respect to substantially all" internal trade.

In state practice and academic writing two basic approaches have materialized as good practice: a qualitative approach and a quantitative approach. The former would require the elimination of restrictions with respect to *all* major sectors of the economies of FTA participants, as determined by economic and trade statistics. The latter would require a certain threshold of all the trade—say, 90 or 95%—to be liberated from restrictions. The difference between these approaches is easily explained when looking at FTAs between OECD countries in the Northern hemisphere: there, the value of agricultural trade tends to be comparatively low, so much that even with their quasi-exclusion from liberalizing efforts, a 90% of trade coverage would normally be met. In light of the Appellate Body's embrace of flexibility, any of these approaches will do. Percentage-wise, 90% would seem to realistically eliminate any legal risk with regard to meeting the threshold of "substantially all the trade".

[41] Lockhart and Mitchell (2005), p. 232.

[42] *Turkey – Restrictions on Imports of Textile and Clothing Products*, WT/DS34/AB/R, para. 48.

3.3 Two Substantive Conditions for WTO Compatibility

The Appellate Body focusses[43] on the wording in para. 5 pursuant to which the provisions of the GATT 1994 shall not prevent "the *formation* of a customs union/ free-trade area". From that wording the Appellate Body derives that

> Article XXIV can justify the adoption of a measure which is inconsistent with certain other GATT provisions only if the measure is introduced *upon the formation* [of a CU/FTA], and only to the extent that the formation of the customs union would be prevented if the introduction of the measure were not allowed.

If this is to be taken *verbatim*, any WTO-incompatible measure based on an FTA will only be justifiable if the measure's legal basis is present at the FTA's creation. The opposite view would be that a CU or FTA may mature over time, leading only many years or decades later to an interest in rendering market access for third countries undesirable from the FTA/CU's perspective.

An example for such a possibility is currently playing out in the EU's squeezing out of Switzerland from the European electricity grid that was set up originally by Switzerland, France and Germany, not the least because shortly after WW II the two former enemies were not quite prepared to have direct interconnectors.

In the last years, the Union has increased legislative activity to create a truly pan-European electricity grid. Physically, the Swiss grid remains at its heart, connecting the energy-poor South with the energy-rich Northern and Western parts, along the EU's growth corridor that stretches from Rotterdam to Milan. Market integration in the field of electricity requires further technical integration to adapt to new challenges posed, inter alia, by renewable energies. Due to their opportunistic production (only when the sun shines, only when the winds blow, etc.) grids need to be managed more tightly to avoid instability and net insecurity. EU legislation aims to do that, but also to restrict market access for Switzerland. Pertinent laws expressly state that if a currently blocked framework agreement proposal that would put the mutually highly beneficial (but complicated) relations between those two trading partners on a new basis, Switzerland's squeezing-out would be reversed.

Such a (partial) elimination of a fellow WTO member from the EU market for reasons inherently linked to the third country's not being a member of the FTA, with the goal to exercise pressure on the third country to join the FTA/CU or conclude an agreement addressing all outstanding issues between the FTA/CU and the third country would seem difficult to reconcile with the *Turkey-Textile* quote above: the violation of WTO rights and obligations is only justifiable if the measure *is introduced upon the formation* [of a CU/FTA]. In the case at hand, the measure was not taken *upon the formation* of an FTA, but rather decades after its formation and

[43] *Turkey – Restrictions on Imports of Textile and Clothing Products*, WT/DS34/AB/R, para. 46.

pursuant to secondary legislation that aims at advancing the EU Internal Market. It would thus not be justifiable pursuant to Article XXIV.[44]

The Appellate Body's text-centered analysis is supported by para. 6. It reads:

> If, in fulfilling the requirements of subparagraph 5 (*a*), a contracting party proposes to increase any rate of duty inconsistently with the provisions of Article II, the procedure set forth in Article XXVIII shall apply. In providing for compensatory adjustment, due account shall be taken of the compensation already afforded by the reduction brought about in the corresponding duty of the other constituents of the union.

This paragraph is the only part of Article XXIV GATT that addresses new measures introduced by a participant in an FTA/CU, i.e. *not* introduced *upon the formation* of the FTA. It was important for the US in late 1947, as it ensured the necessary regulatory space for the intended US-Canada FTA (that was not to be), as Congress would not have accepted being unable to raise tariffs in the future. But the reference to the general provisions of Article XXVIII renders clear that this would have been possible, albeit for a price. It would seem that by explicitly regulating one case in which parties to the agreement can deviate due to circumstances developing not *upon the formation* of the FTA, but rather afterwards, would indicate that the Appellate Body's reading of the provision and the distillation of a first condition for a successful invocation of Article XXIV GATT—that "the party claiming the benefit of this defense must demonstrate that the measure at issue is introduced upon the formation of a customs union that fully meets the requirements of sub-paragraphs 8 (a) and 5(a) of Article XXIV"—is the correct one. The Appellate Body then adds another condition:[45]

> [S]econd, that party must demonstrate that the formation of that customs union would be prevented if it were not allowed to introduce the measure at issue. [...] [B]*oth* these conditions must be met to have the benefit of the defense under Article XXIV. (emphasis in the original)

The requirement that the state invoking Article XXIV GATT must show that the formation of the FTA would have been *prevented* is a high threshold, but one that is explicitly stated in Article XXIV (5) GATT. This condition will typically not be met by new measures of an FTA/CU, taken long after the formation is completed. In the case of the squeezing out of Switzerland from the governance and use of the European grid, of which it is a founder and physically an integral part of, the EU would not meet that condition, taking new measures, destined to exercise pressure on a partner, some 70 years after the formation. Clearly, the formation of the EU did not depend on excluding the Swiss network provider from different trading platforms.

---

[44] Hahn (2021), p. 100.

[45] *Turkey – Restrictions on Imports of Textile and Clothing Products*, WT/DS34/AB/R, para. 58.

3.4 One Formal Conditions for WTO Compatibility

Pursuant to Article XXIV (7) GATT, further concretized by the *Understanding on the Interpretation of Article XXIV,* any contracting party deciding to enter into an FTA "shall promptly notify the CONTRACTING PARTIES", i.e. today the WTO,[46] so that the membership is capable to "make such reports and recommendations [. . .] as they may deem appropriate". While this obligation to notify ensures transparency and allows trading partners to consider voicing their concerns or even lodge a formal complaint to initiate a formal dispute settlement procedure, it is noteworthy that neither Article XXIV nor the *1994 Understanding* make the formation of an FTA dependent on the approval of the membership. Rather, the Committee on Regional Trade Agreements (CRTA) will examine the agreements establishing the FTA in light of Art XXIV GATT, and also consider compatibility with *all* other WTO-agreements on trade in goods (Annex 1A to the WTO-Agreement).[47] However, the conclusions will only address the compatibility with Article XXIV GATT,[48] and only for the purposes of deliberation and discussion, not as a basis for grating or rejecting permission to enter into an FTA/CU.

While the wording of Article XXIV (7) GATT is rather clear as to the obligation to notify *before* the conclusion, state practice has developed otherwise, no doubt because this breach of a clear obligation has no consequences due to consent of the membership not being necessary for the conclusion of a WTO-compatible agreement. Nevertheless, this nonchalance reflects the probably increasing attitude that concluding FTAs is a sovereign choice which will be notified to others once consumed, but not for advice or consent ex ante.

4 Conclusion

The interest to accommodate an important ally and partner was the reason why all the principled rejection of preferential trade agreements was given up during the negotiations for the Havana Charter. Without such US *realpolitik*, Article XXIV would have only allowed CUs such as the European Union or the one between Liechtenstein and Switzerland, i.e. models of integration that create an integrated common market. It is, of course, impossible to know what would have happened, if

[46]The notification is to be made to the Council for Trade in Goods which adopts the terms of reference and then transfers the agreement to the Committee on Regional Trade Agreements (CRTA) which was set up in 1996; see the pertinent General Council decision WT/GC/M/10, 6 March 1996, para. 11.

[47]Beginning with the 1995 Working Party on the Enlargement of the European Communities, Accession of Austria, Finland and Sweden, Terms of Reference and Membership, WT/REG3/1, this has become the standard practice in the WTO.

[48]Tevini (2011), p. 643.

FTAs would not have been permitted: but it is more likely than not that the number of FTAs, and in particular of rather shallow FTAs, would have been much smaller than is the case today.

The multilateral trading system was supposed to be an integral part of a New World Order, with the United Nations and its Security Council at its helm, thereby ensuring that the atrocities of the first part of the twentieth century would not repeat itself. This idea was dead on arrival when the Charter was ratified in October 1945, given it was by then impossible to overlook the iron curtain that had come down separating Western democracies from the Soviet sphere of influence. In the absence of a fair, free and efficient world governance—which does not seem to come about any time soon—allowing bilateral or "plurilateral" integration seemed a sensible solution then, and would seem reasonable today. Thus, it would seem an unhelpful and wrong perception that the American concerns for their Northern neighbour constituted a poisoning of a hereto pure well of non-political economic reason put in law.

The establishment of the WTO, some 40 years after the failure of the ITO, was in certain ways a repeat effort, albeit on a more modest level, limiting itself to global *economic* governance. But the explosion of the number of concluded FTAs coinciding with the establishment of the WTO may indicate the need for specific regional fora or vessels for like-minded partners.

Systemic global issues such as, e.g., subsidies, food security and digital trade can only be properly addressed within a truly multilateral trading system. But at a time when the world seems to be on its way to a small number of (partially interconnected) geopolitical regions, the role of the WTO may increasingly resemble an interconnector between these regions: maybe thinking of the WTO will mean increasingly thinking of an interface and clearing house for the FTAs and CUs associated with these regions. It is worth remembering that Article XXIV (5) and (8) do not allow the creation of FTAs/CUs in order to sabotage MFN, i.e. with the sole or main purpose to discriminate. The requirement of "substantially all the trade", but also the rather restrictive interpretation of Article XXIV (5) GATT would seem to ensure that regional *integration* means more that trying to establish a protectionist *cordon sanitaire* against trading partners that are politically more distant than other. That later insight indeed may stay relevant in that new model.

References

Bhagwati J (1991) The world trading system at risk. Princeton, Princeton Legacy Library

Bhagwati J (1993) Regionalism and multilateralism: an overview. In: De Melo J, Panagariya A (eds) New dimensions in regional integration. Cambridge University Press, Cambridge, pp 22–51

Chase K (2006) Multilateralism compromised: the mysterious origins of GATT Article XXIV. World Trade Rev 5(1):1–30

Cottier T, Foltea M (2006) Constitutional functions of the WTO and Regional Trade Agreements. In: Bartels L, Ortino F (eds) Regional Trade Agreements and the WTO legal system. Oxford University Press, Oxford, pp 43–76
Curzon G (1965) Multilateral commercial diplomacy: the general agreement on tariffs and trade and its impact on national commercial policies and techniques. Michael Joseph, Ltd., London
Dam K (1970) The GATT, law and international economic organization. University of Chicago Press, Chicago
Dörr O, Schmalenbach K (eds) (2012) Vienna convention on the law of treaties – a commentary. Springer, Berlin
Gardner R (1956) Sterling–Dollar Diplomacy; The origins and the prospects of our international economic order. McGraw-Hill, New York
Hahn M (2021) Je t'aime … Moi non plus: Rechtsfragen des Verhältnisses Schweiz – EU. ZBJV 2(2021):77–125
Hahn M, Van der Loo G (eds) (2020) Law and Practice of the Common Commercial Policy. The first 10 years after the Treaty of Lisbon. Brill, Leiden
Haight F (1972) Customs Unions and Free-Trade Areas under GATT: a reappraisal. J World Trade Law 6(4):391–404
Hindelang S, Moberg A (2020) The art of casting political dissent in law: The EU'S framework for the screening of foreign direct investment. Common Market Law Rev 57(5):1427–1460
Irwin D, Mavroidis P, Sykes A (2008) The genesis of the GATT. Cambridge University Press, Cambridge
Lockhart N, Mitchell A (2005) Regional Trade Agreements under GATT 1994: an exception and its limits. In: Mitchell A (ed) Challenges and prospects for the WTO. Cameron May Ltd, London, pp 217–252
Matsushita M, Schoenbaum T, Mavroidis P, Hahn M (2015) The World Trade Organization — law, practice, and policy, 3rd edn. The Oxford International Law Library, Oxford
Odell J, Eichengreen B (1998) The United States, the ITO, and the WTO: exit options, agent slack, and presidential leadership. In: Krueger A (ed) The WTO as an international organization. University of Chicago Press, Chicago, pp 181–209
Odendahl K (2012) Commentary to Art. 41 VCLT. In: Dörr O, Schmalenbach K (eds) Vienna convention on the law of treaties. Springer, Berlin, pp 719–733
Tevini A (2011) Article XXIV GATT. In: Wolfrum R, Stoll PT, Hestermeyer H (eds) WTO: Trade in goods. Max Planck Commentaries on World Trade Law, Band: 5. Martinus Nijhoff Publishers, Leiden, pp 616–661
World Trade Organization, Secretariat (1995) Regionalism and the World Trading System. WTO, Geneva

Michael Hahn is Professor of Law at the University of Bern, Managing Director of its Institute of European and International Economic Law and a Director at its World Trade Institute; he is also an Honorary Professor at the University of Waikato School of Law in Hamilton, New Zealand. He holds degrees from the University of Heidelberg and the University of Michigan Law School. Michael is on the list of arbitrators for CETA, CPTPP and the SADC-EU Economic Partnership Agreement and teaches, researches and consults on international trade law, Swiss-EU bilateral relations and EU external relations law.

Services Trade Liberalisation in the Australia—EU FTA: Progress But No Quantum-Leap

Charlotte Sieber-Gasser

Contents

Abstract Australia declared services trade liberalisation in the Australia-European Union Free Trade Agreement (*AUEFTA*) negotiations a priority, while an impact assessment by the EU indicated no measurable impact on sectoral output for services in the *AEUFTA* in services. The two sides will not only have to agree on the relative importance of the services chapter, but also on the type of regulatory structure pursued. At this point, the outcome of negotiations remains unknown. While some elements of substantial liberalisation are expected in the liberalisation of trade in professional services along with temporary movement of persons, and in education services, the currently proposed regulatory structure of the *AEUFTA* service chapter suggests limited regulatory innovation. However, both parties have confirmed their intention to deepen liberalisation within the scope of their respective schedule of commitments beyond their Trade in Services Agreement (TiSA) offers in 2016.

C. Sieber-Gasser (✉)
University of Zurich, Zurich, Switzerland

M. Bungenberg, A. Mitchell (eds.), *The Australia-European Union Free Trade Agreement*, Special Issue, https://doi.org/10.1007/978-3-030-91448-6_4

Given that both parties have furthermore confirmed their commitment to modernisation and deepening of international rules in services trade liberalisation in the plurilateral forum of TiSA negotiations, the *AEUFTA* service chapter may therefore serve also as a stepping-stone to subsequent successful conclusion of plurilateral TiSA negotiations.

1 Introduction

Services are a key ingredient of successful global value-added chains; they enable high-quality production and are necessary for markets to converge. In an increasingly specialised and globalised economy, know-how is often transferred through services, and hence, today services lie at the heart of overall economic performance.[1] Rather untypically, services trade regulation has its roots in the multilateral and not in the preferential forum: the first comprehensive rules for the liberalisation of trade in services were established in the *General Agreement on Trade in Services* (GATS)[2] as part of the Uruguay-Round negotiations of the WTO in the late 1980s and early 1990s. At the time, regulation of and obligations in the liberalisation of trade in services were new and largely untested. Hence, the GATS was understood to be a stepping-stone to further, more refined services trade regulation and subsequent rounds of negotiations over increasing liberalisation. WTO members therefore remained cautious with regard to the level of liberalisation to which they committed under the multilateral GATS. Instead, they turned to negotiations of Preferential Trade Agreements (PTAs) in services, in which they committed to more extensive trade liberalisation in services with hand-picked partners, while negotiations at the multilateral level (i.e. "Doha-Round") regarding the initially envisaged gradual modernisation of the GATS rules remained blocked until today.[3]

More recently, the plurilateral negotiations of the *Trade in Services Agreement* (TiSA)[4] came close to modernising trade in services rules at least on the plurilateral level (limited to the signatories of the agreement): Since the entry into force of the GATS in 1995, the share of services trade has increased worldwide, and particularly in so-called industrialised economies, like the European Union (EU) or Australia. Technological advancements, cheaper and more accessible transportation and

[1] Sieber-Gasser (2016), p. 30.

[2] *General Agreement on Trade in Services* (GATS), 15 April 1994, available online: https://www.wto.org/english/docs_e/legal_e/26-gats.pdf.

[3] Sieber-Gasser (2016), pp. 110–115.

[4] *Trade in Services Agreement* (TiSA), 21 negotiation rounds until 17 November 2016, negotiations between 23 WTO members (incl. the EU and Australia) are on hold since. More information available online: https://ec.europa.eu/trade/policy/in-focus/tisa/ (last accessed 9 September 2021); Kerneis (2017), pp. 143–144.

internet rendered services substantially more "tradeable" and relevant than was the case when the initial GATS rules were negotiated. Hence, critical aspects of services trade liberalisation today are not addressed by the GATS, along with a number of new types of services which did not exist at the time of the negotiation of the GATS, but play a critical role in the global economy today. For instance, the supply of services through the internet—arguably the most common cross-border supply of services today—is not specifically addressed by the GATS, and neither are regulatory issues regarding services which form an integral, inseparable part of manufacturing.[5] TiSA would have modernised in particular the rules regarding e-commerce, the cross-border supply of telecommunication services, and aspects of temporary movement of service suppliers along with transparency and recognition of licenses and diplomas. As negotiations have not yet been concluded, PTAs remain the preferred forum for the advancement and modernisation of applicable rules in services trade liberalisation.

Since the EU and Australia are both members of the WTO and therewith of the GATS, the *Australia-EU PTA* has to comply with the PTA-requirements established in the GATS in order to qualify for the Most-favoured Nation (MFN) exception in GATS Article V: They are required to agree to substantial sectorial coverage (in terms of number of sectors, volume of services trade and no a priori exclusion of any of the modes of supply) and to the absence or elimination of substantially all discrimination within covered sectors.[6] It is generally agreed that in order to comply with the quantitative requirements of GATS Article V, WTO members may exclude 1-2 services sectors from their PTAs in services as long as these sectors are not substantial in the sense of covered volume of services trade. Furthermore, the qualitative requirement of GATS Article V of "absence or elimination of substantially all discrimination" is generally considered to be fulfilled if Market Access obligations and National Treatment obligations in the PTA go beyond the scope of the respective GATS commitments.

Other than that, however, Australia and the EU are quite free in defining the kind of rules and the levels of liberalisation they wish to apply to their bilateral services trade. Hence, theoretically a comprehensive *AEUFTA* regulating among others e-commerce, manufacturing services, preferential treatment of environment-related services, mutual recognition of licenses and diplomas along with substantial commitments in data protection and the temporary movement of labour would be fully in line with the GATS. An ambitious services chapter could even contribute to global standard setting in services trade liberalisation in the twenty-first century.

Obviously, trade in services is closely intertwined with manufacturing, e-commerce and digital trade, and with global value-added chains. Less immediately obvious is the fact that services trade liberalisation is also linked with labour migration (alas "temporary"; mode 4 supply of services "through the presence of natural persons in the territory of another country"), with investment (mode 3 supply

---

[5] Antimiani and Cernat (2015); Peng (2020).

[6] GATS Article V; Sieber-Gasser (2016), pp. 135–152. See also Jacobsson (2019).

of services "through commercial presence"), and with sustainability. Assessing the comprehensiveness of a PTA in services therefore requires to take into consideration not only the actual "services" chapter, but the overall role services trade liberalisation plays throughout the entire agreement. Ultimately, the level of ambition in the services chapter of a particular PTA is a relatively reliable indicator of the overall to be expected integration of the value-added chains between the PTA partners—and therewith of the overall to be expected economic benefit of the PTA as a whole.

2 General Scope and Structure of Preferential Services Trade in *AEUFTA*

2.1 Starting Point

Important to keep in mind when assessing the bilateral services trade liberalisation between Australia and the EU is the fact that while services are considered to be of particular relevance in the negotiations and attributed with a great potential of economic benefits for both sides—these assessments pre-date Brexit: the majority of EU Foreign Direct Investment (FDI) in Australia in 2016 originated in the United Kingdom (UK).[7] Brexit has a particularly strong impact on the services negotiations in the *AEUFTA*, given that the UK "takes almost half of Australia's services exports to the EU (four times more than Germany) and provides more than a third of Australia's services imports from the EU (twice as much as Germany). Of Australia's exports of financial services to the EU, the UK takes nearly 80 per cent"[8] The Australian services industry is therefore particularly keen on a PTA with the UK—perhaps even keener than on a PTA with the EU. Given that there is a potential that the UK might offer more favourable treatment compared to the EU, the current negotiations are in fact, from a point of view of the EU, a race against time. Negotiations between Australia and the UK started in early summer 2020 and the parties have confirmed that they aim at securing the agreement in "record time".[9]

On the other hand, Brexit might actually provide Australia with new opportunities to step-up for some of the potential gaps in services supply which the departure of the UK is to leave in the EU internal market: past market shares are therefore likely of limited informational value with regard to a post-Brexit future relationship between Australia and the EU. Drake-Brockman even notes: "it couldn't be clearer that services loom twice as large in the overall trading relationship with the EU than

[7]Drake-Brockman (2018), p. 14.

[8]Drake-Brockman (2018), p. 30.

[9]Smyth J and Payne S, 'Australia looks for UK trade deal 'by end of 2020'', *Financial Times*, 17 June 2020, https://www.ft.com/content/750b31e2-63ca-404f-be03-0753c294e8a9 (last accessed 9 September 2021).

on average with other trading partners. From an Australian perspective, this suggests that they deserve perhaps twice as much public policy attention."[10]

The European Commission, however, concludes in its impact assessment that "for the EU there is no measurable impact on sectoral output for services" in an *AEUFTA* in services.[11] The focus of the EU appears to be on the elimination of tariffs on goods in order to catch up with China, the US, Japan and South Korea, which all are accorded preferential treatment by Australia based on their respective PTAs. Furthermore, it is considered problematic by the European Commission that EU investors are accorded different treatment in Australia depending on their respective country of origin and that they are overall in a less favourable position compared to investors from countries with which Australia has some form of investment protection agreement.[12] High on the EU agenda ranks also addressing general issues such as digital trade and sustainability, which are however, not linked with services trade in general in the impact assessment.[13]

The apparent disinterest of the EU in bilateral services trade liberalization with Australia may come as a surprise given that to date, the two markets trade services on the basis only of the global minimum standard as established in the GATS and given that the EU is by far the biggest exporter and importer of services worldwide (with a significant trade surplus).[14] Economic benefits from an increase in services trade liberalisation are generally considerable, given that the general level of barriers to services trade is still quite high globally.[15] This is particularly true also because evidence and experience show that an increase in services trade leads to higher exports of both goods and services as a side-effect of services-fuelled integration in global value chains.[16] Because of the geographic distance between Australia and the EU, integration in global value-added chains has been limited to date, hence, the potential economic benefits of an increase in bilateral services trade liberalisation are likely to be considerable also for the EU thanks to a boost in bilateral value-added chains and an increase in legal security in mode 3 supply of services (through commercial presence/investment) from the EU to Australia.[17]

---

[10] Drake-Brockman (2018), p. 19.

[11] European Commission (2017) Impact Assessment. Recommendation for a Council Decision authorizing the opening of negotiations for a Free Trade Agreement with Australia. SWD(2017) 293 final, 13 September 2017, Brussels, p. 30.

[12] European Commission (2017) Impact Assessment. Recommendation for a Council Decision authorizing the opening of negotiations for a Free Trade Agreement with Australia. SWD(2017) 293 final, 13 September 2017, Brussels, p. 7.

[13] European Commission (2017) Impact Assessment. Recommendation for a Council Decision authorizing the opening of negotiations for a Free Trade Agreement with Australia. SWD(2017) 293 final, 13 September 2017, Brussels, p. 10.

[14] Kerneis (2017), p. 142.

[15] Drake-Brockman (2018), p. 17.

[16] See also Drake-Brockman (2018).

[17] Kerneis (2017), pp. 158–159.

The services sector is the largest and fastest growing employer in Australia and accounted in 2018 for 85% of Australian jobs.[18] Also in bilateral trade with the EU services are the dominant sector in Australia's export to the EU.[19] While the geographic distance constitutes a challenge to bilateral trade integration, it is also an advantage in particular in services trade: Australian and EU service providers are in the right time zone to cover each other's night shifts, e.g. in telemedicine and customer services.[20] Australia focuses its negotiating mandate for bilateral services trade liberalisation with the EU primarily on education, financial and professional services, the facilitation of temporary labour mobility and regulatory coherence. In addition, commitments on telecommunications rank high in the Australian negotiating mandate.[21] Tricky from an Australian perspective is the fact that services trade is not entirely within the competence of the EU, plus the various EU members still have varying degrees of liberalisation in place. Services trade negotiations with the EU are therefore much more complex than goods trade negotiations.[22]

The EU mandate, on the other hand, clarifies that other than audio-visual services, no sector should be a priori excluded from the scope of the agreement. The EU expects an outcome of the negotiations which goes beyond the Parties' WTO commitments and beyond the offers submitted in the context of TiSA negotiations. The EU mandate focuses on transparency, mutual recognition, horizontal provisions—which could all be covered by Australia's reference to "regulatory coherence"—along with telecommunication services, financial services, delivery services and international maritime transport services.[23]

2.2 *New Global Standard Setting in AEUFTA?*

Both parties obviously have a common—strong—interest in (1) regulatory coherence along with elimination of behind-the-border-barriers to services trade for instance through (2) mutual-recognition of certificates and diplomas, and commitments to liberalisation and/or facilitation in the sectors of (3) financial and (4) telecommunication services as well as in clarifying the applicable rules and scope of market access with regard to the (5) temporary movement of natural persons. Neither

[18] Drake-Brockman (2018), p. 17.

[19] Drake-Brockman (2018), p. 16.

[20] Obviously, this works more readily in English speaking countries; however, language barriers can be overcome.

[21] Australian Government, Department of Foreign Affairs and Trade, Australia—EU Free Trade Agreement: *Summary of Negotiating Aims and Approach*, https://www.dfat.gov.au/sites/default/files/a-eufta-summary-of-negotiating-aims-and-approach.pdf (last accessed 9 September 2021).

[22] Drake-Brockman (2018), p. 27.

[23] Council of the European Union (2018) Negotiating Directives for a Free Trade Agreement with Australia. 7663/18 ADD 1 DCL 1, 25 June 2018, Brussels. https://www.consilium.europa.eu/media/35794/st07663-ad01dc01-en18.pdf (last accessed 9 September 2021), p. 12.

mandate seems to explicitly link services trade liberalisation with other, related chapters in the negotiations. While in the EU draft proposal investment and services are part of the same Title ("Investment Liberalisation and Trade in Services"), they are divided into separate chapters, linked by a few general provisions (mainly definitions) in Chapter I. In the EU draft proposal cross-border trade in services is defined as follows:

(i) *From the territory of a Party into the territory of the other Party; or*
(ii) *In the territory of a Party to the service consumer of the other Party*

Hence, "cross-border trade in services" is basically limited to GATS modes 1 and 2 supply of services. Mode 3 supply of services (through commercial presence) is dealt with in Chapter II "Investment Liberalisation" of the same Title, while mode 4 supply of services (through presence of natural persons) falls within the scope of Chapter IV "Entry and Temporary Stay of Natural Persons for Business Purposes" of the same Title. With this structure, both temporary labour migration and investment regulation are effectively extended in scope beyond the limited realm of services trade alone. Even though the proposed structure does not explicitly cover all four modes of supply as defined and established in the GATS, it therefore nevertheless fulfils the obligation of GATS Article V to not a priori exclude one mode of supply.

While this structure more or less reflects the structure of services trade liberalisation in the *Comprehensive and Economic Trade Agreement* (CETA)[24] between the EU and Canada, it is new for Australia: for instance, the PTA between Australia and the US is based on the more common structure of services trade liberalisation which covers modes 1, 2 and 4 as part of "cross-border supply of services" and subsumes mode 3 under "covered investments",[25] while the more recent PTA between Australia and Japan along with the *Regional Comprehensive Economic Partnership* (RCEP) follow entirely the GATS structure and explicitly refer to all four modes of supply in the definition of "cross-border trade in services".[26] Hence, it will be interesting to see which of the regulatory structures ultimately succeeds in the negotiations. Regarding the actual scope of liberalisation embedded in a services chapter, the regulatory structure may matter—but does not need to. Ultimately, the general provisions along with the individual schedules of commitments are more decisive regarding the actual scope and extent of liberalisation and potential harmonisation.

Nevertheless, the variety in the regulatory structure of the definition of "cross-border trade in services" is a good example of the global race in standard setting

---

[24] Comprehensive Economic and Trade Agreement (CETA), 14 January 2017, https://eur-lex.europa.eu/legal-content/EN/TXT/?uri=CELEX:22017A0114(01) (last accessed 9 September 2021).

[25] Article 10.14, Chapter Ten (Cross-border Trade in Services), *Australia-US Free Trade Agreement*, February 2004.

[26] Article 9.2, Chapter 9 (Trade in Services), *Australia-Japan Economic Partnership*, July 2014; Article 8.1, Chapter 8 (Trade in Services), *Regional Comprehensive Economic Partnership*, November 2020.

currently taking place: clearly the rules of services trade require an update and need to be adjusted to twenty-first century economic and technological realities (e-commerce, digital trade, manufacturing services, aso.). PTAs are a way in this race to establish the respective preferred set of more modern rules, therewith perhaps creating a preference over time in the so-called "spaghetti-bowl effect" for the more widely established regulatory standard.[27]

Generally, however, the level of ambition on both sides appears to be limited with regard to the modernisation of services trade rules; perhaps the services chapter in the *AEUFTA* will aim at a compromise between the US- and the EU-approach and therewith contribute to a new emerging global consensus regarding regulatory structure and scope of modern services trade rules—however, it is at this moment unlikely that the parties will be experimenting with revolutionary new regulation of services trade liberalisation.

3 Services of Particular Interest in the Proposals

The following paragraphs discuss in more detail the negotiating mandates in services sectors identified by either Australia or the EU as a priority in the on-going *AEUFTA* services trade negotiations. Generally speaking, the identified priorities in services trade negotiations are mostly in line with priorities in other—current or previous—PTA negotiations of both Australia and the EU. Perhaps striking is the fact that transportation services are not considered a priority by either party. Given the geographical distance between Europe and Australia, trade liberalisation in transportation services would seem to be of potential interest, particularly with regard to an intended increase in bilateral goods trade. However, current publicly available negotiating mandates for the *AEUFTA* services chapter neither explain nor specifically refer to transportation services.

[27] Cottier et al. (2015).

3.1 Audio-Visual Services

According to the draft proposal by the EU, audio-visual services are explicitly excluded from the scope of application of the *AEUFTA*.[28] This is in line with the EU Negotiating Directives, which clearly state:[29]

> In line with Article V GATS, the Agreement should have substantial sectorial coverage and should cover all modes of supply. The Agreement should have no a priori exclusion from its scope other than the exclusion of audio-visual services.

If trade in audio-visual services between Australia and the EU does not in volume amount to a substantial share in overall bilateral services trade, excluding audio-visual services from the scope of application of the *AEUFTA* can indeed be in line with the requirements established in GATS Article V. Since the current levels of bilateral trade in audio-visual services are low, excluding audio-visual services from the scope of application of the *AEUFTA* is therefore compatible with GATS Article V per se. Whether it is a smart decision is an entirely different question.

Generally, the EU excludes audio-visual services from the scope of liberalisation or regulatory commitment in cross-border trade in services, investment and digital trade in its PTAs. This policy is arguably in line with Article 167 of the Treaty on the Functioning of the European Union, which emphasizes the specific nature of audio-visual services and the need to protect European cultural diversity. EU members are granted therefore the right to regulate domestically in the area of audio-visual services. Hence, the EU has only limited competence with regard to the negotiation of cross-border trade liberalisation in audio-visual services.[30]

However, as Parc and Messerlin rightly point out, both Australia and the EU have indeed already concluded some PTAs which do cover audio-visual services. Most prominently, both Australia and the EU each have a bilateral PTA with South Korea (Korea-EU *KOREU*; Australia-Korea *KAFTA*) which covers audio-visual services to some extent.[31] Those existing preferential commitments could serve as a minimum standard in new negotiations—at least as a benchmark of what the EU and Australia would theoretically be prepared to agree to. Hence, it is not immediately obvious—considering also the economic benefits from liberalisation in the film- and TV-industry for both sides—why audio-visual services are excluded entirely from

---

[28] See General Provisions, Article 1.1(5), European Commission (2018a) EU-Australia Trade Agreement Negotiations, initial text proposals, Services and Investment. 22 October 2018, Brussels. https://trade.ec.europa.eu/doclib/docs/2018/december/tradoc_157572.pdf (last accessed 9 September 2021), p. 2.

[29] Council of the European Union (2018) Negotiating Directives for a Free Trade Agreement with Australia. 7663/18 ADD 1 DCL 1, 25 June 2018, Brussels. https://www.consilium.europa.eu/media/35794/st07663-ad01dc01-en18.pdf (last accessed 9 September 2021), p. 12.

[30] See also Question for written answer E-002452/2019 to the Commission, Marie-Pierre Vedrenne (Renew) and Laurence Farreng (Renew); E-002452/2019, Answer given by Ms Malmström on behalf of the European Commission (6 September 2019).

[31] Parc and Messerlin (2018), p. 232.

the scope of application of the *AEUFTA*. Possibly, however, due to technological advancements and specifically the availability of Australian TV-channels in the EU and vice versa along with the possibility to access films and TV-productions through the internet, insisting on inclusion of audio-visual services in the mandate of *AEUFTA* may be politically costly and result merely in a reduction of already ineffective regulatory barriers—hence 'generate more costs than benefits'.[32]

3.2 Education Services

The internationalisation of higher education has rendered education services a lucrative market for both Australia and the EU. Through technology, internet and access to cheaper and faster transportation, education services have become easily tradeable in all four modes of services supply as established in the GATS. Trade in higher education services between the EU and Australia may, for example, take place in the following ways:

(a) *a student in the EU enrols for an online course taught by a professor in Australia (mode 1 supply of services—from the territory of one Party to the territory of the other Party);*
(b) *an Australian student enrols in an EU university for an EMBA (mode 2 supply of services—in the territory of a Party to the service consumer of the other Party);*
(c) *an Australian university establishes a satellite campus in the EU (mode 3 supply of services—through commercial presence)*
(d) *an EU expert travels to Australia for an intensive three week corporate training (mode 4 supply of services—through presence of natural persons),*

To date, the level of trade liberalisation in education services is generally low and liberalisation is limited substantially to private tertiary/higher education services and training services. Primary and secondary education along with any other public education are generally outside of the scope of the GATS and of PTAs.[33] It is important to note, that the exact scope of Market Access in trade in education services is generally established in the individual schedule of commitments, which are normally part of the services chapter of PTAs. At this moment, no information regarding the specific offers in the respective *AEUFTA* schedule of commitments is available to the public. Given that the EU draft proposal does not suggest a different regulatory structure (e.g. a separate Annex on trade in education services), it is assumed that the general provisions of the *AEUFTA* services chapter will apply to trade in education services and that the real extent to which Market Access for

[32] Parc and Messerlin (2018), p. 234.

[33] For a good overview see e.g. Sauvé P (2002) Trade, Education and the GATS: What's In, What's Out, What's All the Fuss About?. OECD/US Forum on Trade in Educational Services, Washington DC.

education services is indeed deepened will be established in the schedules of commitments alone.

Trade liberalisation in education services has been identified by Australia as one of the main objectives of the *AEUFTA* services chapter.[34] Given, that for instance Australia's export to China is dominated by education services, the focus on the Australian side on deepening Market Access in education services does not surprise. In 2018, Australian education services exports increased by 16.3% with approximately one third of the exports going to China. Of overall $35.8 billion Australian education services exports, $35.2 billion were mode 2 supply in higher education services (foreign students studying in Australia) in 2018.[35] Given the departure of the UK from the EU, Australian universities may indeed offer attractive alternatives to UK universities to EU students interested in studying abroad. European universities and research institutes are already the most significant partners of their Australian counterparts and bilateral cooperation in research and higher education is well established since more than two decades. According to Murray and Matera Europe is the most significant academic partner of Australia, "well ahead of Asia and the US in established knowledge-based relationships".[36]

Clearly, Australia has an interest in further extending trade in education services with the EU. Possibly, however, the scope for additional—even more substantial—Market Access in the *AEUFTA* remains limited, especially given the already well-established close partnership between Australian and European academic institutions. The EU indeed has only limited competence in negotiating substantial additional Market Access commitments because EU members have retained the right to regulate in various aspects of public and private education. This means that negotiating additional Market Access commitments with the EU requires bilateral negotiations with each EU member individually—and may result in the final treaty no longer qualifying as an EU-only agreement, but as a mixed agreement.[37]

Furthermore, and perhaps with the exception of corporate trainings, an increase in liberalisation in education services is politically disputed. Unions both in Australia

[34] Australian Government, Department of Foreign Affairs and Trade, *Australia-European Union Free Trade Agreement: Summary of Negotiating Aims and Approach*, https://www.dfat.gov.au/trade/agreements/negotiations/aeufta/Pages/summary-of-negotiating-aims-and-approach (last accessed 9 September 2021).

[35] Australian Government (2019) Trade in Services Australia 2018. Department of Foreign affairs and Trade, Statistics Section, Office of Economic Analysis. September 2019, p. 11.

[36] Murray P and Matera M (2019) Australia and the European Union: Trends and Current Synergies. Policy Report, University of Melbourne, May 2019, p. 14.

[37] If an EU trade agreement is "mixed", it (or the "mixed parts of it) has to be ratified by each EU member state individually and/or requires unanimity in the EU Council. For an overview of the EU ratification procedure regarding exclusive, shared and concurrent competences in foreign trade policy, see Puccio L (2016) A Guide to EU Procedures for the Conclusion of International Trade Agreements. EPRS Briefing October 2016, Brussels.

and in the EU are worried about the use of certain terms in the EU draft proposal:[38] Article 1.1(2)[39] says that Parties reaffirm the right to regulate within their territories to achieve legitimate policy objectives such as public education. Unions are worried that the terms "legitimate policy objectives", along with the term "public education" are not sufficiently clear and may endanger public funding and quality of education based on increasing competition through private education institutions. That the actual negotiation of substantial commitments in education services might be challenging can be observed also in the Brexit negotiations:[40]

> The inference often drawn is that public sector universities need not feel concerned. But what is patently obvious is that many 'public' universities, particularly in the UK, operate on a commercial basis.

Hence, the final outcome of negotiations in trade in education services will largely depend on the respective schedules of commitments. Substantial commitments might have implications for the EU ratification procedure, while the level bilateral cooperation and trade may in any case benefit from the UK's departure from the EU independent from additional liberalisation in *AEUFTA* (particularly from the perspective of Australia).

3.3 Professional Services and Temporary Movement of Persons

In particular high value-added knowledge-intensive business services (including professional and technical services) figure importantly in services exports from Australia to Europe. They account for roughly 30% and are growing.[41] On the other hand, linked with the substantial share of EU FDI in Australia, liberalisation of trade in professional services along with a deepening of commitments regarding the entry and temporary stay of natural persons for business purposes and the mutual recognition of professional qualifications is of critical interest to the EU as well.[42]

[38] See e.g. *EI-ETUCE-AEU-IEU-NTEU Joint Statement on the Ongoing Trade Negotiations Between EU and Australia*, 29 July 2019, available online: http://www.aeufederal.org.au/news-media/media-releases/2019/jul/290719 (last accessed 9 September 2021).

[39] Chapter 1, Article 1.1(2), European Commission (2018a) EU-Australia Trade Agreement Negotiations, initial text proposals, Services and Investment. 22 October 2018, Brussels. https://trade.ec.europa.eu/doclib/docs/2018/december/tradoc_157572.pdf (last accessed 9 September 2021), p. 2.

[40] Davies H, 'Trading in HE with the EU post-Brexit will not be easy', *University World News*, 16 November 2018, https://www.universityworldnews.com/post.php?story=20181115092307517 (last accessed 9 September 2021).

[41] Drake-Brockman (2018), p. 18.

[42] Council of the European Union (2018) Negotiating Directives for a Free Trade Agreement with Australia. 7663/18 ADD 1 DCL 1, 25 June 2018, Brussels. https://www.consilium.europa.eu/media/35794/st07663-ad01dc01-en18.pdf (last accessed 9 September 2021), p. 12.

Here, both Australia and the EU are likely to be prepared to agree to substantial commitments, both on the regulatory, as well as on the Market Access side.[43]

However, the current EU draft proposal suggests an offer from the EU side which—although ambitious—still lags behind what was achieved in the CETA both in terms of regulatory harmonisation and mutual recognition as well as in the duration of the temporary stay for business purposes. For example, as a baseline—still to be read in conjunction with the schedule of commitments and potential additional annexes—the EU agreed to the following general commitments regarding the length of stay, elimination of red tape and groups of persons covered in CETA, while the current EU AUEFTA draft proposal is less comprehensive in this regard:

CETA	EU AEUFTA draft proposal
Short-term business visitors: no requirement of work permit or other prior approval procedures, maximum length of 90 days in any **six**-month period (Article 10.9)	Short-term business visitors: no requirement of a work permit, economic needs test or other prior approval procedures, permissible length of 90 days in any **twelve**-month period (Article 4.3)
Contractual service suppliers and independent professionals: The length of stay is for a cumulative period of not more than **12** months, **with extensions possible at the discretion of the Party**, in any **24** month period or for the duration of the contract, whichever is less (Article 10.8)	Contractual service suppliers and independent professionals: The permissible length of stay shall be for a cumulative period of not more than **six** months in any **twelve**-month period, or for the duration of the contract, whichever is less (Article 4.4)
Key personnel: (a) specialists and senior personnel the lesser of three years or the length of the contract, with a possible extension of up to 18 months at the discretion of the Party; (b) graduate trainees the lesser of one year or the length of the contract; (c) investors one year, with possible extensions at the discretion of the Party; (d) business visitors for investment purposes 90 days within any six-month period (Article 10.7)	**N/A**

It is not immediately obvious to date, why this is the case, given that the EU experience with CETA appears so far positive and given that the general level of quality of education must normally be comparable between the EU, Canada and Australia. It is conceivable therefore that the length of stay, groups of eligible persons and scope of elimination of red tape with regard to the temporary movement of persons and professional services is still subject to negotiations. However, the current EU draft proposal in trade negotiations with New Zealand is practically

[43] See also Australian Government, Department of Foreign Affairs and Trade, Australia – EU Free Trade Agreement: *Summary of Negotiating Aims and Approach*, https://www.dfat.gov.au/sites/default/files/a-eufta-summary-of-negotiating-aims-and-approach.pdf (last accessed 9 September 2021).

identical with the EU *AEUFTA* draft proposal in this regard.[44] At least, both Australia and New Zealand ought to have good arguments on their side, should they insist on more substantial coverage than the one currently proposed in the EU draft.

3.4 Financial Services

Three years ago, two-thirds or more of trade in financial and insurance services between Australia and the EU were actually between Australia and the UK. This share is, hence, directly affected by Brexit. However, it is argued that the share is rather related to the fact that London is one of the global financial centres, and less to the fact that historic and cultural ties between the UK and Australia are particularly dense.[45] Since it is likely that with Brexit, new European financial centres are emerging (e.g. Dublin or Luxembourg), the share of trade in financial and insurance services between Australia and Europe will diversify between the UK and EU.

As equivalence negotiations in financial services between the UK and the EU are on-going, financial service providers in London have already opened their subsidiaries in the EU in vast numbers.[46] Given the size of the EU market compared with the size of the UK market, it is likely that liberalisation in financial services in *AEUFTA* remains attractive for Australia despite the departure of the UK from the EU common market. Ultimately, in recovering from the COVID-19 induced economic crisis, financial services will be of key relevance—not only with regard to their availability and competitiveness, but also with regard to their regulation and governance. Hence, general global circumstances point to the fact that trade liberalisation in financial services will be of interest to both parties of the *AEUFTA*.

3.5 Telecommunication Services

Telecommunication services along with internet access are key drivers of global value chains and economic integration in general. However, the telecommunications

[44]European Commission (2018b) EU-New Zealand Trade Agreement Negotiations, initial text proposals, Investment Liberalisation and Trade in Services. 25 September 2018, Brussels. https://trade.ec.europa.eu/doclib/docs/2018/december/tradoc_157580.pdf (last accessed 9 September 2021).

[45]Winters (2018), p. 69ff.

[46]Hall S (2021) Brexit: financial services face continued uncertainty – here's why. The Conversation, 19 January 2021, https://theconversation.com/brexit-financial-services-face-continued-uncertainty-heres-why-153486 (last accessed 9 September 2021).

sector remains highly fragmented and only partially privatised. In particular, the protection of universal services along with the allocation and use of scarce resources (such as frequencies and numbers, but also public infrastructure) require the continuance of an element of governmental control in an otherwise open market. Additionally, and more recently, the protection of user data and the governance of internet access and content have become a particular concern of regulators.

The recently concluded negotiations of RCEP[47] put a particular emphasis on the creation of trade opportunities in telecommunication services. In particular, Australia agreed in RCEP *inter alia* to grant flexibility in the choice of technology (e.g. the highly controversial 5G technology; Article 21), to enhance transparency and competition in international mobile roaming (Article 22), to non-discriminatory access to international submarine cable systems (Article 18), and to non-discriminatory access to and use of public telecommunications networks and services (Article 4).[48]

In comparison, the EU draft proposal provides for less detailed and comprehensive regulation in the mutual opening of telecommunication markets. Notably, the EU draft proposal makes no reference to "choice of technology" nor to "international mobile roaming", even though both aspects might be of relevance to the bilateral relationship between Australia and the EU as well.[49] Given that both the EU draft proposal in trade negotiations with New Zealand,[50] as well as the CETA Chapter on telecommunications[51] are almost identical with the EU *AEUFTA* draft proposal, it is possible that the EU is indeed not pushing for deeper integration in the telecommunications sector, even though RCEP might suggest that Australia could be prepared to open its market slightly more than is currently proposed.

4 Assessment of the Current Draft Chapter on Services

AEUFTA negotiations in services trade liberalisation are explicitly linked with previous cooperation and negotiation in the context of TiSA. Hence, starting point of negotiations of specific schedules of commitments certainly were the respective

[47] Regional Comprehensive Economic Partnership (RCEP), 20 November 2020, https://www.dfat.gov.au/trade/agreements/not-yet-in-force/rcep/rcep-text-and-associated-documents (last accessed 9 September 2021).

[48] Chapter 8, Annex 8B, "Telecommunications Services", RCEP.

[49] European Commission (2018a) EU-Australia Trade Agreement Negotiations, initial text proposals, Services and Investment. 22 October 2018, Brussels. https://trade.ec.europa.eu/doclib/docs/2018/december/tradoc_157572.pdf (last accessed 9 September 2021).

[50] European Commission (2018b) EU-New Zealand Trade Agreement Negotiations, initial text proposals, Investment Liberalisation and Trade in Services. 25 September 2018, Brussels. https://trade.ec.europa.eu/doclib/docs/2018/december/tradoc_157580.pdf (last accessed 9 September 2021).

[51] Chapter Fifteen, Telecommunications, CETA.

TiSA offers.[52] It is interesting to note that the EU explicitly refers to the offers made during TiSA negotiations and demands more substantial commitments.[53] It is unclear at this point, whether the EU itself is prepared to open its market beyond the scope of its TiSA offer—the draft chapter published by the EU in October 2018 does not appear to do so with respect to overall regulatory structure and innovation of services trade liberalisation.[54] However, possibly the EU along with Australia are able to deepen their schedules of commitments beyond the scope of their respective TiSA offers. If that were the case, the identified goal of the EU in *AEUFTA* services trade negotiations would be achieved while at the same time the chapter would not necessarily push regulatory boundaries of modern rules of services trade liberalisation beyond the scope of what is being applied already elsewhere.

4.1 Ambition

Typically, Australia would expect to add a ratchet-clause to the services chapter, along with a general MFN obligation.[55] The EU, on the other hand, is typically reluctant to commit to a ratchet-clause, specifically also since it wants to retain policy space for the imposition—if necessary—of trade restrictions to "new services". While at the time of TiSA negotiations, the EU resisted a general MFN obligation due to impending Brexit negotiations, possibly in the meantime the EU might be able to move on this position. This is particularly the case if Australia were to agree to a Brexit-type of exception to a general MFN obligation.

Ultimately, the proposed structure and scope of services trade liberalisation point to a rather cautious *AEUFTA* chapter. More recent statements at the WTO indicate that both parties are willing to re-engage in the modernisation of international rules governing services trade in the plurilateral forum of TiSA negotiations.[56] Bilateral negotiations in services trade liberalisation specifically may, therefore, be less of a priority for the time being. Hence, services trade-related regulatory innovation is to be expected in the *AEUFTA* chapters regarding investment and digital trade, while a

---

[52] Drake-Brockman (2018), pp. 28–29; see e.g. TiSA, EU Schedule of Specific Commitments, 2nd revised offer, 21 October 2016, https://trade.ec.europa.eu/doclib/docs/2016/november/tradoc_155091.docx.pdf (last accessed 9 September 2021).

[53] Council of the European Union (2018) Negotiating Directives for a Free Trade Agreement with Australia. 7663/18 ADD 1 DCL 1, 25 June 2018, Brussels. https://www.consilium.europa.eu/media/35794/st07663-ad01dc01-en18.pdf (last accessed 9 September 2021), p. 12.

[54] European Commission (2018a) EU-Australia Trade Agreement Negotiations, initial text proposals, Services and Investment. 22 October 2018, Brussels. https://trade.ec.europa.eu/doclib/docs/2018/december/tradoc_157572.pdf (last accessed 9 September 2021).

[55] Drake-Brockman (2018), p. 29.

[56] Australian Statement to the Trade Negotiations Committee, 25 February 2021, Geneva. Australian Permanent Mission and Consulate-General, Geneva, Switzerland, Liechtenstein.

deepening of existing obligations in individual schedules of commitments is to be expected within the scope of previous TiSA offers.

4.2 Potential for Greening the Economy Set Aside: Greener Trade in Services

Trade in services regulation typically does not distinguish between environment-related services and other services. However, particularly on a preferential basis,[57] such distinction could contribute considerably to successfully transition from conventional to more sustainable production in all economic sectors. For instance, services are critical for the construction of geothermal plants, the maintenance of solar panels, or the repair of a wastewater-treatment facility. Availability of high-quality and affordable environment-related services therewith has an immediate impact on longevity and effectiveness of environmental policies and investments.

While distinguishing between maintenance services for solar panels and maintenance services for a gas-fired power plant generally risks violating GATS obligations (since they might qualify as "like services and service suppliers"),[58] such distinction is possible with regard to preferential treatment in a trade agreement. Therewith, *AEUFTA* could fully liberalise environment-related services, while leaving their non-environment related counterparts at the level of TiSA offers. The therewith created integrated *AEUFTA* market for environment-related services would benefit not only availability and affordability of high-quality environment-related services in the *AEUFTA* market, but serve as a role-model for subsequent PTAs, and render the goal of achieving sustainable development through trade more comprehensive.[59] Credibility with regard to achieving mutual sustainable development through trade is becoming more and more relevant also for the successful ratification process: an increasing number of people and political parties in the EU, but also in Australia see international trade liberalisation critically. PTAs therewith require credible arguments to convince generally sceptical constituencies of their benefits—also, and importantly, with regard to the promotion of a more sustainable, environment-friendly economy through preferential trade liberalisation. Services are currently overlooked in this regard, leaving a substantial potential for greening the economy set aside.

---

[57] See Monteiro J-A (2016) Typology of environment-related provisions in regional trade agreements. WTO Staff Working Paper No. ERSD-2016-13, Geneva.

[58] The rules established under the GATT for likeness-analysis apply also to GATS, see *Argentina - Measures Relating to Trade in Goods and Services* – Report of the Appellate Body (9 May 2016) WT/DS453/AB/R.

[59] Sieber-Gasser (2021).

5 Concluding Remarks

While Australia declared services trade liberalisation a priority in *AEUFTA* negotiations, the EU puts its emphasis in negotiations rather on investment liberalisation and on the elimination of tariffs on goods. Hence, the starting point for bilateral services trade liberalisation between the EU and Australia is already disputed. Negotiations are further compounded by the fact that the EU and Australia follow a different regulatory logic in preferential services trade liberalisation in their previous PTAs. It will therefore not only be interesting to see which type of regulatory structure ultimately prevails in *AEUFTA*, but also to what kind of level of liberalisation the parties agree.

It is expected that audio-visual services will be excluded from the scope of application of the *AEUFTA* services chapter. Both parties have a genuine economic interest in deepening trade relations in professional services and the temporary movement of persons. Nevertheless, the current EU *AUEFTA* draft proposal is less ambitious in this regard than, for instance, the respective chapter in CETA. Australia in particular has a genuine interest in further liberalisation of education services. Whether and to what extend negotiations will result in more substantial liberalisation than offered previously in TiSA negotiations remains to be seen. While all of *AEUFTA* negotiations are critically impacted by Brexit, negotiations about trade liberalisation in financial services are particularly affected: three years ago, two-thirds of bilateral trade in financial and insurance services took place between Australia and the UK. Given global and regulatory circumstances at this time, regulation and liberalisation of financial services in *AEUFTA* will remain a priority for both parties, *alas* with uncertain outcome. Finally, the current EU *AEUFTA* draft proposal in telecommunications does not point to an ambitious outcome of negotiations. This is particularly notable given that Australia just agreed to more substantial and comprehensive liberalisation and governance of telecommunication services in RCEP.

While negotiations put an emphasis on sustainable development, the role of services trade in the transitioning from conventional to more sustainable production and value chains is set aside. Preferential treatment of environment-related services in *AEUFTA* would benefit longevity and effectiveness of environmental policies and investments both in Australia and in the EU. Furthermore, it would strengthen the comprehensiveness and credibility of the promise to achieve sustainable development through trade—an aspect of increasingly critical relevance for the ratification process and general support in constitutencies both in the EU and in Australia.

Ultimately, the services chapter itself is not expected to deliver substantial and particularly innovative and progressive rules with regard to services trade liberalisation. Such potential regulatory progression and innovation is more likely to be found in the services-related *AEUFTA* chapters on investment and digital trade. On the other hand, individual schedules of commitments in services trade liberalisation in *AEUFTA* are expected to be at least identical, if not more substantial than the offers submitted by both sides in TiSA negotiations in 2016. Therewith, the services chapter in AEUFTA is likely to have a role in re-enforcing the commitments of the EU and of Australia to engage on the plurilateral level of TiSA negotiations in the modernisation and deepening of international trade in services regulation.

References

Antimiani A, Cernat L (2015) Liberalizing global trade in mode 5 services: how much is it worth? J World Trade 52(1):65–83

Cottier T, Sieber-Gasser C, Wermelinger G (2015) The dialectical relationship of preferentialism and multilateralism. In: Elsig M, Dür A (eds) Trade cooperation: the purpose, design and effects of preferential trade agreements. Cambridge University Press, pp 465–495

Drake-Brockman J (2018) An Australian perspective on the Australia-EU Free Trade Agreement. In: Drake-Brockman J, Messerlin P (eds) Potential benefits on an Australia-EU Free Trade Agreement: key issues and options. University of Adelaide Press, pp 9–36

Jacobsson J (2019) Preferential services liberalization. Cambridge University Press, Cambridge

Kerneis P (2017) Gains for trade in services in an EU-Australia Free Trade Agreement: a European perspective. In: Elijah A, Kenyon D, Hussey K, van der Eng P (eds) Australia, the European Union and the New Trade Agenda. Australian National University Press, pp 139–162

Parc J, Messerlin P (2018) Audio-visual services. In: Drake-Brockman J, Messerlin P (eds) Potential benefits on an Australia-EU Free Trade Agreement: key issues and options. University of Adelaide Press, pp 225–244

Peng SY (2020) A new trade regime for the servitization of manufacturing: rethinking the goods-services dichotomy. J World Trade 54(5):669–726

Sieber-Gasser C (2016) Developing countries and preferential services trade. Cambridge University Press, Cambridge

Sieber-Gasser C (2021) Green(er) trade in services. In: Delimatsis P, Reins L (eds) Encyclopedia of environmental law. Edward Elgar Publishing, Cheltenham, p 48

Winters AL (2018) What difference does Brexit make. In: Drake-Brockman J, Messerlin P (eds) Potential benefits on an Australia-EU Free Trade Agreement: key issues and options. University of Adelaide Press, pp 61–73

Charlotte Sieber-Gasser is a Lecturer at Universities of Lucerne and Zurich, Switzerland, and Andrássy Budapest, Hungary. She specialised in International Economic Law, EU-Swiss Relations and in Swiss Constitutional Law. Charlotte currently teaches WTO-law, Swiss constitutional law and law of sustainable development and finishes her habilitation on the constitution of political rights in globalised Switzerland.

Digital Trade in the Australia—EU FTA: A Future-Forward Perspective

Neha Mishra

Contents

Abstract This paper assesses the significance of the Digital Trade Chapter of the Australia—EU FTA and focuses on the disciplines necessary to boost digital trade. In the ongoing negotiations, the EU and Australia are likely to agree upon conventional digital trade disciplines (e.g., e-signatures, e-authentication, paperless trading, customs duties on electronic transmissions) as well as provisions on online consumer trust and spam, and more contemporary disciplines on source code disclosure and data localisation. These disciplines can undoubtedly contribute to boosting digital trade between Australia and the EU. However, data flows and data protection will remain a sticky issue in the ongoing negotiations, given the differences in data protection laws of the EU and Australia, and the EU's exceptionally defensive approach in data protection. Instead of bypassing such issues, the FTA negotiators should view the negotiations as an opportunity to build mutual consensus and foster cooperation in formulating standards and mechanisms for data transfer. Further, the

N. Mishra (✉)
The Australian National University College of Law, Acton, ACT, Australia
e-mail: Neha.Mishra@anu.edu.au

M. Bungenberg, A. Mitchell (eds.), *The Australia-European Union Free Trade Agreement*, Special Issue, https://doi.org/10.1007/978-3-030-91448-6_5

negotiations provide an opportunity for adopting deeper disciplines on digital trade facilitation that can nurture start-ups as well as experimenting with novel models for regulatory cooperation in nascent policy areas including AI ethics and open government data.

1 Introduction

The European Union ("EU") and Australia started negotiating a Free Trade Agreement ("FTA") on 18 June 2018.[1] Since then, both parties have completed nine rounds of negotiations, the last round being from 30 November to 11 December in 2020.[2] In 2019, the two-way trade between Australia and the EU was estimated to be a total of AUD 85 billion.[3] The EU is Australia's second largest trading partner and the largest source of foreign investment in Australia,[4] while Australia was the EU's 21st largest trading partner in 2019 in merchandise trade.[5] Both the EU and Australia share a "long-standing and fruitful bilateral relationship",[6] with a "shared commitment to the rule of law, global norms and free and open markets".[7] Further, Australia and the EU converge on "many global economic issues and cooperate to promote international prosperity in the World Trade Organization and G20".[8]

[1]Department of Foreign Affairs and Trade ('DFAT'), Australia-European Union Free Trade Agreement, www.dfat.gov.au/trade/agreements/negotiations/aeufta/Pages/default#:~:text=Australia%20and%20the%20European%20Union,source%20of%20foreign%20investment1 (last accessed 9 September 2021).

[2]The reports of these negotiation rounds are posted by the DFAT and the European Commission ('EC'). See DFAT, A-EUFTA News, www.dfat.gov.au/trade/agreements/negotiations/aeufta/Pages/aeufta-news (last accessed 9 September 2021); EC, Commission Reports on Latest Negotiating Round with Australia, https://trade.ec.europa.eu/doclib/press/index.cfm?id=2151 (last accessed 9 September 2021).

[3]DFAT, Australia-European Union Free Trade Agreement, www.dfat.gov.au/trade/agreements/negotiations/aeufta/Pages/default#:~:text=Australia%20and%20the%20European%20Union,source%20of%20foreign%20investment1 (last accessed 9 September 2021).

[4]These statistics refer to EU27 and the United Kingdom. See DFAT, Australia-European Union Free Trade Agreement, www.dfat.gov.au/trade/agreements/negotiations/aeufta/Pages/default#:~:text=Australia%20and%20the%20European%20Union,source%20of%20foreign%20investment1 (last accessed 9 September 2021).

[5]EC, Client and Supplier Countries of the EU27 in Merchandise Trade (value %), https://trade.ec.europa.eu/doclib/docs/2006/september/tradoc_122530.pdf (last accessed 9 September 2021).

[6]See https://www.dfat.gov.au/geo/europe/european-union/Pages/european-union-brief (last accessed 9 September 2021).

[7]See https://www.dfat.gov.au/trade/agreements/negotiations/aeufta/Pages/default (last accessed 9 September 2021).

[8]DFAT, Australia-European Union Free Trade Agreement, www.dfat.gov.au/trade/agreements/negotiations/aeufta/Pages/default#:~:text=Australia%20and%20the%20European%20Union,source%20of%20foreign%20investment1 (last accessed 9 September 2021).

This paper focuses on the digital trade chapter in the *Australia—EU Free Trade Agreement* ("Australia – EU FTA"). Digital trade refers to all digitally enabled transactions facilitating the delivery of goods and services, irrespective of whether this occurs virtually or physically.[9] With the growing digitalisation of the economy, electronic commerce chapters (or digital trade chapters, as they have more recently been named) have become commonplace in Preferential Trade Agreements ("PTAs").[10] The first generation of electronic commerce chapters were developed at the turn of this century by the United States ("US") and then subsequently adopted by Singapore and Australia in several of their bilateral trade agreements.[11] Since then, the number of trade agreements containing provisions on electronic commerce have increased substantially.[12] Further, recent PTAs cover a much broader range of electronic commerce issues, and in greater depth, including rules in sensitive areas such as data flows and data localisation, source code disclosure/trade secret protection, and framework for personal information protection.[13] The discussion in Sect. 3 on the evolution of Electronic Commerce chapters in Australian and EU FTAs also reflects this trend, although Electronic Commerce Chapters in EU FTAs have generally been narrower in scope compared to Australian FTAs.

Services trade, including in digital services, is an important component of the Australia-EU trade relations.[14] Further, several opportunities remain untapped for expanding digital trade between Australia and the EU.[15] Thus, a high-quality digital trade agreement between the EU and Australia can create several positive outcomes including: (i) enhancing economic opportunities for digital businesses in both the EU and Australia; (ii) reducing business uncertainty for Australian and European businesses in the digital sector; and (iii) creating greater interconnectivity between the two markets and reducing digital trade protectionism, including blatant data localisation measures.

This paper discusses how the digital trade chapter in the Australia—EU FTA can enable secure and open digital trade, as well as provides insights on the possible areas of agreement and disagreement between the parties on possible digital trade provisions. Section 2 discusses the overlapping policy preferences on digital trade between the EU and Australia. Section 3 compares the evolution of Electronic

---

[9]This term encompasses B2B, B2C and C2C transaction, thus covering all forms of commercial transactions in the supply chain. The Organisation for Economic Cooperation and Development (OECD) has also developed a similar definition of "digital trade". See OECD, The Impact of Digitalisation on Trade, http://www.oecd.org/trade/topics/digital-trade/ (last accessed 9 September 2021).

[10]The term PTAs refers to all bilateral, regional, and megaregional trade agreements outside of the WTO. See generally Burri and Polanco (2020).

[11]Monteiro and Teh (2017), pp. 5–6.

[12]Burri and Polanco (2020), pp. 193–196.

[13]Burri and Polanco (2020), pp. 193–196.

[14]See https://www.dfat.gov.au/trade/agreements/negotiations/aeufta/Pages/summary-of-negotiating-aims-and-approach (last accessed 9 September 2021).

[15]Lee-Makiyama (2018), pp. 212, 214.

Commerce Chapters in Australian and EU PTAs. These two sections argue that although Australia and the EU share common ideas regarding the liberalisation of digital trade and reduction of digital protectionism, the Electronic Commerce Chapters in their PTA have historically diverged, particularly due to the EU's distinct regulatory approach in data privacy and digital regulation and tendency to focus on low hanging issues related to trade facilitation, consumer trust, and customs duties on electronic transmissions. However, with the growing importance of digital trade in the global economy, the EU appears to have embraced the need to address modern digital trade issues in its PTAs such as cross-border data flows, data localisation, and dealing with variable regulatory frameworks on data protection in different countries.[16] One such example is the recently concluded *EU—UK Trade Cooperation Agreement* ("EU-UK TCA") between the EU and the United Kingdom ("UK").

Against this background, Sect. 4 analyses the legal and policy implications of the text proposed by the EU on "digital trade"[17] in the Australia—EU FTA and suggests possible areas of improvement.[18] Based on past PTA practices of both countries, this section argues that the EU and Australia are likely to agree on several provisions pertaining to digital trade, especially in uncontroversial areas such as electronic signatures and authentication, paperless trading, customs duties on electronic transmissions, online consumer protection, spam, and frameworks for electronic transactions.[19] Further, agreement is also expected with regard to some modern-day digital trade provisions such as source code disclosure requirements and, potentially, prohibitions on protectionist data localisation requirements.

However, to significantly boost digital trade between the EU and Australia, the Australia—EU FTA must also address the potential obstacles to the transfer of data between the two regions. In that regard, the differences in data protection and privacy laws of the EU and Australia and the exceptionally defensive approach of the EU on privacy remains a compelling political and legal barrier. Rather than leaving this issue untouched, the paper suggests that the EU and Australia must use the FTA negotiations as a platform to jointly explore avenues for cooperation in data regulation, including facilitating data transfers for digital trade. Further, this paper suggests that the FTA negotiations provide an opportunity for both the parties to consider new disciplines that may facilitate digital start-ups including deeper digital

[16]See, e.g., European Parliament, Towards a Digital Trade Strategy, Doc no A8-0384/2017 (29 November 2017), https://www.europarl.europa.eu/doceo/document/A-8-2017-0384_EN.pdf (last accessed 9 September 2021).

[17]Unlike most of its previous PTAs, the EU uses the title "digital trade" for the relevant chapter, instead of electronic commerce. Some scholars believe digital trade signifies a broader scope of economic activities as compared to electronic commerce. See Burri (2016).

[18]EC, Draft Proposal for Australia – EU FTA (Digital Trade Chapter), http://trade.ec.europa.eu/doclib/docs/2018/december/tradoc_157570.pdf (last accessed 9 September 2021).

[19]See Report of the 7th round of negotiations for a Free Trade Agreement between the European Union and Australia, 4–15 May 2020, https://trade.ec.europa.eu/doclib/docs/2020/may/tradoc_158762.pdf (last accessed 9 September 2021).

trade facilitation mechanisms, as well as experiment with new models of regulatory cooperation on digital trade.

2 Significance of Digital Trade in Australia and the EU

Both Australia and the EU recognise the importance of digital trade in their economic growth.[20] This section identifies the common policy goals and priorities on digital trade of Australia and the EU and, thereafter, discusses the potential for growth of digital trade between the two parties.

Australia has, time and again, emphasised its ambition to maximise the economic benefits of digital trade and become a global leader in the digital economy.[21] Further, there is a greater acknowledgement within Australia that digitalisation of micro, small and medium sized enterprises ("MSMEs") will lead to greater economic welfare and improved digital inclusion.[22] In addition to the services industry,[23] Australia has also recognised the economic importance of digital technology in several traditional sectors such as agriculture, mining, and manufacturing.[24] The Australian government considers modern and comprehensive trade agreements an important tool to ensure international opportunities for Australian businesses in the digital sector, and a vital component of Australia's foreign cyber-policy.[25] Thus, in

[20] See generally https://www.dfat.gov.au/trade/services-and-digital-trade/Pages/e-commerce-and-digital-trade#:~:text=Digital%20trade%20is%20an%20increasingly,as%20further%20grow%20our%20economy (last accessed 9 September 2021); European Parliament, Towards a Digital Trade Strategy, Doc no A8-0384/2017 (29 November 2017), https://www.europarl.europa.eu/doceo/document/A-8-2017-0384_EN.pdf (last accessed 9 September 2021).

[21] See generally Depart of Industry, Science, Energy and Resources (Australian Government), *Australia's Tech Future* (2018), https://www.industry.gov.au/sites/default/files/2018-12/australias-tech-future.pdf (last accessed 9 September 2021), p. 7; Australian Trade and Investment Commission, Investment opportunities in digital technologies in Australia (2016) , https://www.austrade.gov.au/ArticleDocuments/5567/Investment-opportunities-in-Australian-Digital-technologies.pdf.aspx (last accessed 9 September 2021); Parliament of the Commonwealth of Australia, Trade and the digital economy. Joint Standing Committee on Trade and Investment Growth (2018); DFAT, Australia's Cyber Engagement Strategy (2017); Meltzer (2018).

[22] See generally Parliament of the Commonwealth of Australia, Trade and the digital economy. Joint Standing Committee on Trade and Investment Growth (2018).

[23] Depart of Industry, Science, Energy and Resources (Australian Government), *Australia's Tech Future* (2018), https://www.industry.gov.au/sites/default/files/2018-12/australias-tech-future.pdf (last accessed 9 September 2021) (2018), pp. 6–7.

[24] Depart of Industry, Science, Energy and Resources (Australian Government), *Australia's Tech Future* (2018), https://www.industry.gov.au/sites/default/files/2018-12/australias-tech-future.pdf (last accessed 9 September 2021), pp. 7–8; Meltzer (2018), p. iii.

[25] Along with cybersecurity, cybercrime, international security and cyberspace, internet governance and cooperation, human rights, and democracy online, technology for development, and cyber-affairs, digital trade is one of the pillars of Australian International Cyber Engagement Strategy. See DFAT, Australia's Cyber-Engagement Strategy (2017).

its “Summary of Negotiating Aims and Approach” for the Australia—EU FTA, the Australian government identified the following objective with regard to the Digital Trade Chapter:[26]

> We are seeking to establish ambitious digital trade commitments that strike a balance between facilitating modern trade and ensuring appropriate protections for consumers. High-quality rules on issues such as data flows and localisation will create a more certain and secure online environment and support increased growth of e-commerce between Australia and the EU.

This negotiating objective reflects Australia’s commitment to promoting free and open markets for digital trade including liberalising data flows and eliminating data localisation measures. At the same time, the government acknowledges the significance of the right to regulate in important policy areas of the digital economy such as digital privacy, cybersecurity, cybercrimes, and online consumer protection.[27]

Like Australia, the EU has recognised the importance of digital trade for economic growth and especially for creating opportunities for MSMEs.[28] Historically, the EU has opted to include a minimal framework on e-commerce in its PTAs.[29] However, in recent years, the EU has indicated its preference to adopt more ambitious provisions on digital trade so as to create a level-playing field for e-commerce companies and eliminate unjustified data localisation requirements and other discriminatory measures.[30] This policy approach is also reflected in the relatively ambitious proposals advanced by the EU in the Joint Statement Initiative (“JSI”) on Electronic Commerce of the World Trade Organization (“WTO”).[31] Similarly, as detailed in Sect. 4, the text proposed by the EU for the digital trade chapter in the ongoing Australia—EU FTA negotiations is much more comprehensive than its previous PTAs.

Australia and the EU appear to have several overlapping interests and motivations with respect to negotiating the digital trade chapter in their bilateral FTA, despite their distinct regulatory frameworks on privacy and data protection. The Framework Agreement signed in 2017 by Australia and the EU indicate that both parties are committed to creating “an environment conductive to greater bilateral trade and

[26] See https://www.dfat.gov.au/trade/agreements/negotiations/aeufta/Pages/summary-of-negotiating-aims-and-approach (last accessed 9 September 2021).

[27] DFAT, 2019 Progress Report, https://www.dfat.gov.au/publications/international-relations/international-cyber-engagement-strategy/aices/chapters/2019_progress_report.html (last accessed 9 September 2021).

[28] See generally European Parliament, Towards a Digital Trade Strategy, Doc no A8-0384/2017 (29 November 2017), https://www.europarl.europa.eu/doceo/document/A-8-2017-0384_EN.pdf (last accessed 9 September 2021).

[29] See Sect. 3.1.

[30] European Commission, Trade for All (2015), p. 12, 13. See also Towards a Digital Trade Strategy.

[31] WTO, Joint Statement on Electronic Commerce, WTO Doc WT/L/1056 (25 January 2019); WTO, Joint Statement on Electronic Commerce, WTO Doc WT/MIN(17)/60 (13 December 2017).

investment".[32] Although this agreement does not include specific provisions on digital trade, it contains a provision on the protection of personal data, acknowledging the OECD Privacy Framework as a "relevant international standard" and the possibility of "exchange of information and expertise" and "cooperation between regulatory counterparts" on data protection-related issues.[33]

Further, Article 42 of the Framework Agreement broadly recognises the growing importance of ICT sector in facilitating economic development, the need for greater digital interconnectivity between Australia and the EU, and building a robust regulatory environment for digital consumers, including through regulatory cooperation in areas such as security, trust, and privacy. The Framework Agreement also contains provisions on cybercrime and cybersecurity, particularly emphasising the importance of cooperation in these areas[34] and identifying that the Budapest Convention on Cybercrime is the "global standard against cybercrime".[35] Finally, more broadly, the EU and Australia both support an open, secure, and free internet for the digital economy as well as advocate for the protection of human rights in an online environment.[36]

Several opportunities exist to generate mutually advantageous business opportunities for digital trade between Australia and the EU. For instance, the growing awareness of privacy and digital trust in Australia can incentivise the development of domestic robust and privacy-compliant digital technologies, which could find a market in the EU. Likewise, Australian consumers may be interested to purchase high-quality digital technologies from the EU. Further, investors in both the regions can find new opportunities for profitable ventures in emerging technologies such as Artificial Intelligence ("AI") and Internet of Things ("IoT"). These opportunities in the digital realm are well complemented by the fact that Australia and the EU share many underlying norms and values regarding the ethical use of emerging data-driven technologies such as AI.[37] Finally, being a leader in the Asia-Pacific including in technological research and development, Australia is an attractive base for European businesses to foray into the e-commerce sector in this region.

To date, Australia's trade in ICT goods and services has grown much faster with China, Korea and Japan as compared to the EU.[38] A notable difference is that

---

[32] Framework Agreement, Preamble.

[33] Framework Agreement, art. 40.

[34] Framework Agreement, art. 11, art. 36.

[35] Framework Agreement, art. 36(3).

[36] European Parliament, Towards a Digital Trade Strategy, Doc no A8-0384/2017 (29 November 2017), https://www.europarl.europa.eu/doceo/document/A-8-2017-0384_EN.pdf (last accessed 9 September 2021), pp. 6, 8.; DFAT, Internet Governance and Cooperation, https://www.dfat.gov.au/publications/international-relations/international-cyber-engagement-strategy/aices/chapters/part_5_internet_governance_and_cooperation.html (last accessed 9 September 2021).

[37] EPIC consortium, Getting AI Right: Australian-Europe collaboration potential to maximise AI. EPIC Project policy brief #4 (2019).

[38] EPIC consortium, Getting AI Right: Australian-Europe collaboration potential to maximise AI. EPIC Project policy brief #4 (2019), p. 5.

Australia has already entered into bilateral trade and investment agreements with these countries (although, further research is necessary to establish the exact causal connection between these agreements and increasing trade flows). Therefore, several incentives exist for both Australia and the EU to negotiate a high-quality digital trade chapter in the Australia—EU FTA.

3 Digital Trade Chapters in EU and Australian FTAs: A Comparative Assessment

As of early 2020, the EU had signed 18 PTAs with electronic commerce provisions.[39] On 30 December 2020, the EU signed a trade agreement with the UK, containing a comprehensive chapter on digital trade. Australia has included electronic commerce chapters in 14 out of a total of 16 PTAs that are currently in force.[40] Electronic Commerce Chapters in Australian PTAs are usually more comprehensive, deeper and contain larger number of binding provisions than EU PTAs, which have generally been short and focused on consumer-related issues.[41] This section looks at the general structure, scope, and kinds of provisions in the Electronic Commerce Chapters in Australian and EU PTAs and draws broad comparisons. Annex 1 contains a tabular comparison of electronic commerce provisions in EU PTAs and Annex 2 contains a tabular comparison of electronic commerce provisions in Australian PTAs.

3.1 Digital Trade Provisions in EU PTAs

Electronic commerce provisions in EU PTAs are included either as a separate chapter[42] or as a part of the trade in services chapter.[43] The inclusion of these provisions in the trade in services chapter indicates the EU's underlying position that electronic commerce falls within the realm of trade in services. In majority of its PTAs, the EU has included a minimal framework on electronic commerce, with similarly worded provisions on: (i) ban on customs duties on electronic transmissions; (ii) online consumer trust and protection; (iii) regulatory cooperation on issues

[39] Willemyns (2020), p. 229.

[40] See https://www.dfat.gov.au/trade/services-and-digital-trade/Pages/e-commerce-and-digital-trade (last accessed 9 September 2021).

[41] Willemyns (2020), p. 228.

[42] See, e.g., EU-Canada Comprehensive Economic and Trade Agreement ("CETA"); EU-Mexico Globalised Agreement; EU-UK TCA.

[43] See, e.g., European Union–South Korea Free Trade Agreement ("EU-KR FTA"); EU-Singapore Free Trade Agreement ("EU-SG FTA").

related to digital trade; (iv) no prior authorisation requirement for online services; and (v) electronic contracts, authentication, and signatures. Some recent PTAs also contain a provision on requirements for disclosure of source code.

EU PTAs generally recognise the importance of electronic commerce for economic growth.[44] However, several variations can be found in the preambular clauses of EU PTAs. For instance, the *EU-Canada Comprehensive Economic and Trade Agreement* ("CETA"), while setting out a broad objective of promoting electronic commerce, acknowledges that countries are not obligated to allow any form of delivery by electronic means, unless it is in accordance with the obligations of the PTA.[45] The Digital Trade Chapter in the *EU-Mexico Globalised Agreement* and the EU-UK TCA both contain a preambular provision, explicitly recognising that parties have a right to regulate to achieve "legitimate public policy objectives" including for "protection of public health, social services, public education, safety, environment or public morals, social or consumer protection, privacy and data protection, or the promotion and protection of cultural diversity".[46] The EU-UK TCA also states that the parties are not prevented from "adopting or maintaining" measures for public interest reasons contained in the general and security exception and the prudential carve-out.[47] The *EU-Singapore Free Trade Agreement* ("EU-SG FTA") recognises the importance of "the free flow of information on the internet".[48] In the *EU-Japan Economic Partnership Agreement* ("EU-Japan EPA"), the parties recognise the importance of technology neutrality in electronic commerce.[49]

Some EU PTAs clearly set out the scope and applicability of the Electronic Commerce Chapter. For instance, certain services have been excluded from the scope of the electronic commerce chapter in EU's bilateral trade agreements with Japan and Mexico: gambling and betting services, broadcasting services, audiovisual services, services of notaries or equivalent professions, and legal representation services.[50] The recent EU-UK TCA leaves out audiovisual services from the scope of the digital trade chapter.[51] In addition to these sectors, the *Mexico-EU Globalised Agreement* excludes government procurement.[52]

Some EU PTAs contain a provision on "no prior authorisation", requiring that parties must endeavour to not impose "prior authorisation or any other requirement

---

[44] See, e.g., CETA, art. 16.2.1; EU-Vietnam Free Trade Agreement ("EU-VN FTA"), art. 8.50.

[45] See, e.g., CETA, art. 16.2.2.

[46] Mexico – EU Globalised Agreement, art. 1.2 (Chapter on Digital trade); EU-UK TCA, art. DIGIT.3. Similar provisions are also included in the EU-Singapore FTA, *EU-Japan Economic Partnership Agreement* ("EU-Japan EPA") and EU-Vietnam FTA.

[47] EU-UK TCA, art. DIGIT.4.

[48] EU-SG FTA, art. 8.57.3.

[49] EU-Japan EPA, art. 8.70.3.

[50] See, e.g., Japan – EU EPA, art. 8.70.5; *Mexico – EU Globalised Agreement*, art. 1.4 (Chapter on Digital Trade).

[51] EU-UK TCA, art. DIGIT.2.2.

[52] *Mexico – EU Globalised Agreement*, art. 1.4(f) (Chapter on Digital Trade).

having equivalent effect on the provision of services by electronic means".[53] This provision does not apply for authorisation schemes not specifically targeted at digital services and does not apply to telecommunication services.[54] This language was modified in the recent EU-UK TCA, where the relevant provision is framed in binding terms stating that a party "shall not require prior authorisation of the provision of a service by electronic means solely on the ground that the service is provided online".[55] This provision does not apply to telecommunications services, broadcasting services, gambling services, legal representation services or to the services of notaries or equivalent professions.[56]

Another common provision in many EU PTAs is on open internet access that requires parties to ensure that domestic laws do not restrict choices of services available to internet users, that they are able to connect to devices of their choice and have access to information on the network management practices of internet service providers.[57]

Another area commonly addressed in several EU PTAs is the recognition of the validity of electronic contracts and prohibition on parties from denying validity of electronic signatures or authentication methods on the sole basis that they are in an electronic form.[58] In order to facilitate electronic commerce, some provisions also encourage the use of interoperable standards for electronic signatures and authentication methods.[59] Under the EU-SG FTA, the parties further agree that they will "examine the feasibility of having a mutual recognition agreement on electronic signatures in the future".[60]

EU PTAs generally contain a provision on customs duties on electronic transmissions, although the language is not always identical. For instance, CETA restricts "customs duty, fee, or charge on a delivery transmitted by electronic means" but do not restrict any internal taxes or charges on electronic deliveries, provided it is otherwise consistent with the PTA.[61] The term language "delivery transmitted by electronic means" varies from Australian PTAs, which tend to follow US PTAs, in restricting "customs duties on electronic transmissions, including content transmitted electronically".[62] However, in some PTAs such as the EU-Japan EPA, the

---

[53] See, e.g., EU-Japan EPA, art. 8.75(1); *Mexico – EU Globalised Agreement*, art. 4.1 (Chapter on Digital Trade).

[54] See, e.g., EU-Japan EPA, art. 8.75(2); Mexico – EU Globalised Agreement, art. 4.2 (Chapter on Digital Trade).

[55] EU-UK TCA, art. DIGIT.9.1.

[56] EU-UK TCA, art. DIGIT.9.2.

[57] *Mexico – EU Globalised Agreement*, art. 10 (Chapter on Digital Trade). However, this provision is not binding as the language used is "shall endeavour to ensure".

[58] See, e.g., *Mexico – EU Globalised Agreement*, arts. 5, 6 (Chapter on Digital Trade); EU-Japan EPA, arts. 8.76, 8.77.

[59] See, e.g., *Mexico – EU Globalised Agreement*, art. 6.4 (Chapter on Digital Trade).

[60] EU-Singapore FTA, art. 8.60.1.

[61] See, e.g., CETA, art. 16.3.

[62] See, e.g., USMCA, art. 16.3.1; SADEA, art. 5.

EU-Vietnam Free Trade Agreement ("EU-VN FTA"), the EU-SG FTA, the EU-UK TCA and the *EU-Mexico Globalised Agreement*, the provision simply prohibits "customs duties on electronic transmissions".[63] In one of its submissions under the WTO JSI, the EU proposal suggested language similar to Australian PTAs: "members shall not impose customs duties on electronic transmissions, which include the transmitted content".[64] This trend suggests increasing convergence between the EU and other countries.

Several EU PTAs recognise the importance of data protection for ensuring consumer trust,[65] emphasising that "the development of electronic commerce must be fully compatible with international standards of data protection".[66] In fact, the EU-CARIFORUM FTA contains an entire chapter on personal data protection, setting out the common interest of the parties to protect privacy rights of individuals and maintaining effective data protective regimes consistent with international standards.[67] This chapter further sets out the baseline requirements of a data protection framework including specifying principles including purpose limitation, transparency in data collection and processing, security-by-design, and data access and rectification.[68] The chapter also sets out requirements pertaining to processing sensitive data with additional safeguards[69] and onward data transfers i.e. personal data can only be transferred to those countries with an adequate privacy framework.[70]

Other EU PTAs contain a more basic provision on personal information protection. For instance, Article 16.4 of the CETA states:

> Each Party should adopt or maintain laws, regulations or administrative measures for the protection of personal information of users engaged in electronic commerce and, when doing so, shall take into due consideration international standards of data protection of relevant international organisations of which both Parties are a member.

The EU-UK TCA contains a provision recognising the unqualified right of the parties to maintain measures for personal data protection and privacy, including

[63] See, e.g., EU-JAPAN EPA, art. 8.72; EU-SG FTA, art. 8.78; Mexico – EU Globalised Agreement, art. 3 (Chapter on Digital Trade); EU -VN FTA, art. 8.51; EU-UK TCA, art. DIGIT.8.

[64] Joint Statement on Electronic Commerce. EU Proposal for WTO Disciplines and Commitments Relating to Electronic Commerce, INF/ECOM/22, 26 April 2019, para. 2.5.

[65] See, e.g., CETA art. 16.4.

[66] EU-SG FTA, art. 8.57.4; EU-Korea FTA, art. 8.57.4; EU-CARIFORUM FTA, art. 119.2. See also EU-Japan EPA, art. 8.78.3.

[67] EU CARIFORUM FTA, art. 197.

[68] EU CARIFORUM FTA, art. 199(a).

[69] EU CARIFORUM FTA, art. 199(a).

[70] EU CARIFORUM FTA, art. 199(a).

pertaining to cross-border data transfers provided that these are measures of "general application".[71]

EU PTAs also usually contain a high-level provision on online consumer protection, whereby parties recognise the importance of consumer trust, agreeing to adopt a framework for online consumer protection to prohibit fraudulent and deceptive commercial practices, and acknowledging the importance of inter-state cooperation on consumer protection issues.[72] Another provision relevant to consumer trust common to many EU PTAs is the requirement for parties to adopt a regulatory framework for unsolicited commercial electronic messages or spam.[73]

Some recent EU PTAs include a provision prohibiting the "transfer of, or access to, source code of software owned by a juridical or natural person of the other Party".[74] This provision is inspired from the megaregional trade agreement, *Comprehensive and Progressive Trans-Pacific Partnership Agreement* ("CPTPP"), as discussed in the next section.[75] In order to balance commercial interests (i.e. protecting proprietary interests of companies) and public interests (e.g. protecting citizens against algorithmic discrimination), the restrictions on source code disclosure are qualified by different exceptions. For instance, the *Mexico-EU Globalised Agreement* provides a carve-out where disclosure of source code is necessary to achieve a legitimate public policy objective (e.g. in accordance with general, security exceptions or prudential carve-outs),[76] or if required by a judicial body to remedy a violation of competition law and enforcement of intellectual property law.[77] The obligations on the disclosure of source code also do not apply "in the context of a public procurement transaction or a freely negotiated contract".[78] Further, any restrictions on the disclosure of source code does not "affect the right of a Party to take any action or not disclose any information that it considers necessary for the protection of its essential security interests relating to the procurement of arms, ammunition or war materials, or to procurement indispensable for national security or for national defence purposes".[79] In the EU-Japan EPA, the prohibition on source code disclosure does not apply to "the transfer of or granting of access to source code in commercially negotiated contracts, or the

[71] EU-UK TCA, art. DIGIT.7. The term 'general application' refers to 'conditions formulated in objective terms that apply horizontally to an unidentified number of economic operators and thus cover a range of situations and cases'. See EU-UK TCA, art. DIGIT.7, n.34.

[72] See, e.g., *Mexico – EU Globalised Agreement*, art. 7 (Chapter on Digital Trade); EU-Japan EPA, art. 8.78.

[73] See, e.g., *Mexico – EU Globalised Agreement*, art. 8 (Chapter on Digital Trade); EU-Japan EPA, art. 8.79.

[74] See, e.g., EU-Japan EPA, art. 8.73; *Mexico – EU Globalised Agreement*, art. 9 (Chapter on Digital Trade).

[75] CPTPP, art. 14.17.

[76] *Mexico – EU Globalised Agreement*, art. 9.2 (a) (Chapter on Digital Trade).

[77] *Mexico – EU Globalised Agreement*, art. 9.3 (Chapter on Digital Trade).

[78] *Mexico – EU Globalised Agreement*, art. 9.2 (b) (Chapter on Digital Trade).

[79] *Mexico – EU Globalised Agreement*, art. 9.2 (c) (Chapter on Digital Trade).

voluntary transfer of or granting of access to source code, for instance in the context of government procurement"[80] and does not affect application of competition or intellectual property law.[81] Further, this agreement explicitly recognises that parties can adopt any measure consistent with the general and security exceptions.[82]

EU PTAs often contain a high-level provision to enhance cooperation and dialogues on electronic commerce between trade partners. Under the CETA, the EU-VN FTA, the EU-CARIFORUM FTA and the EU-SG FTA, the scope of such dialogues on electronic commerce extends to the recognition of electronic signatures, liability of intermediaries for transmission or storage of information, spam, online consumer protection, and personal information protection.[83] Under *the Mexico-EU Globalised Agreement*, the parties agree on cooperating on a broad range of areas such as electronic trust and authentication methods, treatment of direct marketing communications, addressing MSME concerns in e-commerce, cybersecurity issues, and online consumer protection.[84] In addition to several of the above issues, the EU-Korea FTA also includes cooperation between the parties on paperless trading.[85] The EU-Japan EPA contains a unique provision on stakeholder engagement, requiring parties to convene dialogues with their domestic civil society in a representative manner.[86]

The EU-UK TCA is the first EU PTA to contain a binding provision on cross-border data flows. This provision prohibits parties from restricting cross-border flows by: (i) requiring the use of local computing facilities or network elements, including those that are domestically approved or certified; (ii) imposing local storage or processing requirements for data; and (iii) subjecting cross-border transfer of data to local storage requirements or use of local computing facilities or network elements.[87] However, the PTA also requires the implementation of this provision will be reviewed within 3 years of the agreement coming into force. The EU-Japan EPA and the Mexico-EU Globalised Agreement contain a review clause on cross-border data flows that allow the parties to assess the need for inclusion of provisions on the free flow of data into this Agreement after 3 years after the PTA enters into force.[88]

[80] EU-Japan EPA, art. 8.73.1.

[81] EU-Japan EPA, art. 8.73.2.

[82] EU-Japan EPA, art. 8.73.3.

[83] CETA, art. 16.6; EU-CARIFORUM FTA, art. 120; EU-Singapore FTA, art. 8.61 EU -VN FTA, art. 8.52.

[84] *Mexico – EU Globalised Agreement*, art. 11 (Chapter on Digital Trade).

[85] EU-KOREA FTA, art. 7.49(e).

[86] EU-Japan EPA, art. 16.16.

[87] EU-UK TCA, art. DIGIT.6.

[88] EU-Japan EPA, art. 8.81; *Mexico – EU Globalised Agreement*, art. XX (Chapter on Digital Trade).

A unique requirement in EU PTAs is a provision setting out the scope of computer and related services. Computer and related services are defined quite broadly in several EU PTAs to include services providing:[89]

> …(a) consulting, strategy, analysis, planning, specification, design, development, installation, implementation, integration, testing, debugging, updating, support, technical assistance or management of or for computers or computer systems;
>
> (b) computer programs plus consulting, strategy, analysis, planning, specification, design, development, installation, implementation, integration, testing, debugging, updating, adaptation, maintenance, support, technical assistance, management or use of or for computer programs;
>
> (c) data processing, data storage, data hosting or database services;
>
> (d) maintenance and repair services for office machinery and equipment, including computers; or
>
> (e) training services for staff of clients, related to computer programs, computers or computer systems, and not elsewhere classified.

Further, these PTAs recognise the "important distinction between the enabling service such as web-hosting or application hosting and the content or core service that is being delivered electronically such as banking, and that in such cases the content or core service is not covered by CPC 84".[90]

With regard to inscribing committees in various service sectors in their schedules, the EU has generally preferred positive listing in its PTAs, whereby the EU explicitly lists the various sectors in which it undertakes commitments on market access and national treatment.[91] This approach has served the EU well in protecting emerging service sectors from unplanned liberalisation.[92] However, while negotiating CETA with Canada, the EU agreed to provide a more liberalising approach of providing negative list for services,[93] whereby the parties only list those sectors/sub-sectors where they wish to make reservations for market access and national treatment obligations. The negative list consisted of Annex I (reservations with regard to existing measures) and Annex II (reserving possible future measures). The EU also considered a hybrid approach for inscribing commitments in service sectors in the stalled Trade in Services Agreement, consisting of a positive list for market access and negative list for national treatment.[94]

---

[89] See, e.g., EU-KR FTA, art. 7.25.3; EU-SG FTA, art. 8.21.3; EU-VN FTA art. 8.22.3; EU-UK TCA, art. DIGIT.7; EU-CARIFORUM FTA, art. 188.

[90] EU-KR FTA, art. 7.25.4; EU-SG FTA, art. 8.21.4; EU-VN FTA art. 8.22.4.

[91] See generally EC, Services and investment in EU trade deals Using "positive" and "negative" lists, April 2017, http://trade.ec.europa.eu/doclib/docs/2016/april/tradoc_154427.pdf (last accessed 9 September 2021).

[92] Elms (2017), p. 47.

[93] Elijah (2017), p. 60.

[94] EC, Services and investment in EU trade deals Using "positive" and "negative" lists, April 2017, http://trade.ec.europa.eu/doclib/docs/2016/april/tradoc_154427.pdf (last accessed 9 September 2021).

3.2 Digital Trade Provisions in Australian PTAs

The extent and depth of provisions in most Australian FTAs is much more comprehensive and liberalising than Electronic Commerce Chapters in EU FTAs. Many of Australia's recent PTAs closely follows the language contained in the megaregional CPTPP. Significant deviations are observed in certain agreements such as the *China—Australia FTA* ("ChAFTA"), where the Electronic Commerce Chapter does not contain provisions on data localisation or cross-border data flows and is also not subject to dispute settlement. Further, certain PTAs pre-dating the CPTPP are not as comprehensive as the recent Australian PTAs such as those with Peru (*Peru—Australia Free Trade Agreement* or "PAFTA"), Hong Kong (*Hong Kong—Australia Free Trade Agreement* or "HK-AFTA"), Singapore (*Singapore—Australia Digital Economy Agreement* or "SADEA"), and Indonesia (*Indonesia—Australia Economic Partnership Agreement* or "IAEPA").

Preambular provisions in Australian PTAs usually recognise the economic opportunities provided by electronic commerce and the importance of consumer confidence in electronic commerce,[95] but do not typically recognise the right to regulate in the digital context which is common to many EU PTAs. The scope of application of Electronic Commerce Chapter in Australian PTAs applies to measures adopted or maintained by a party that affect trade by electronic means.[96] This language is usually not included in most EU PTAs. Some Australian PTAs exclude government procurement and government data (including data collected and processed on behalf of the government) from scope of the Electronic Commerce Chapter.[97] Further, financial service providers are typically excluded from the Electronic Commerce Chapter in Australia's PTAs.[98]

Unlike any of EU PTAs, some Australian PTAs contain a provision on non-discrimination of digital products prohibiting a party from providing less favourable treatment to digital products of the other party, subject to the non-conforming measures agreed to between the parties and consistent with the provisions on intellectual property.[99] Under the *Japan—Australia Economic Partnership Agreement* ("JAEPA"), this obligation also does not apply in the case of government procurement, state subsidies and services supplied by the

[95] See, e.g., HK-AFTA, art. 11.1.1; IAEPA, art. 13.2.1; PAFTA, art. 13.2.1; CPTPP, art. 14.2.1; ChAFTA, art. 12.1 (only recognising the economic growth and opportunities provided by e-commerce and the importance of avoiding barriers to e-commerce); JAEPA, art. 13.1 (also recognises the principle of technology neutrality in e-commerce, similar to the Japan-EU EPA).

[96] See, e.g., CPTPP, art. 14.2.2; HK-AFTA, art. 11.1.2; IAEPA, art. 13.2.2; PAFTA, art. 13.2.2; SADEA, art. 2.1.

[97] See, e.g., CPTPP, art. 14.2.3; HK-AFTA, art. 11.1.3; IAEPA, art. 13.2.3, art. 13.2.4; PAFTA, art. 13.2.3; KAFTA, art. 15.1; SADEA, art. 2.2.

[98] See, e.g., HK-AFTA, art. 11.2 (Definition of covered persons); CPTPP, art. 14.1 (Definition of covered persons).

[99] See, e.g., JAEPA, art. 13.4; PAFTA, art. 13.4; CPTPP, art. 14.4; SADEA, art. 6.

government.[100] Under the PAFTA, SADEA and CPTPP, this obligation also does not apply to broadcasting services.[101]

Like the EU PTAs, most Australian PTAs contain provisions on electronic signatures and electronic authentication, requiring parties to recognise the validity of electronic signatures and ensuring secure methods for electronic authentication, including encouraging the use of interoperable standards.[102] Some Australian PTAs also encourage parties to "work toward the mutual recognition of electronic signatures issued or recognised by either Party".[103]

Many Australian PTAs also provide that parties must adopt a domestic framework for electronic transactions consistent with international standards such as UNCITRAL Model Law on Electronic Commerce 1996 or the United Nations Convention on the Use of Electronic Communications in International Contracts.[104] The ChAFTA only references the UNCITRAL Model Law and adds other relevant international standards may be taken into account in devising domestic legal frameworks on electronic transactions.[105] The recently signed SADEA recognises international principles for transfer of electronic records such as the UNCITRAL Model Law on Electronic Transferable Records.[106] Further, certain Australian PTAs require that parties must endeavour to avoid "any unnecessary regulatory burdens on electronic transactions" and "facilitate input by interested persons in the development of its legal framework for electronic transactions".[107] Similar provisions are not found in EU PTAs.

EU PTAs do not typically contain a provision on paperless trading. In contrast, most Australian PTAs contain at least a hortatory provision on paperless trading requiring parties to endeavour to: (i) provide trade administration documents in electronic forum; (ii) accept electronic submission of trade administration of documents, to the extent legally and practically feasible.[108] Under the ChAFTA, the provision on accepting electronic version of trade administration documents is legally binding on the parties.[109] Under the recent SADEA, Australia has agreed to more onerous provisions on paperless trading such as making electronic versions

[100] See, e.g., JAEPA, art. 13.4.

[101] PAFTA, art. 13.4.4; CPTPP, art. 14.4.4; SADEA, art. 6.4.

[102] See, e.g., HK-AFTA, art. 11.3; IAEPA, art. 13.5; See also ChAFTA, art. 12.6; JAEPA, art. 13.6; PAFTA, art. 13.6; CPTPP, art. 14.6; SADEA, art. 9.

[103] JAEPA, art. 13.6.4.

[104] See, e.g., HK-AFTA, art. 11.4.1; IAEPA, art. 13.9.1; PAFTA, art. 13.5.1; CPTPP, art. 14.5.1; KAFTA, art. 15.4.1; SADEA, art. 8.2.

[105] ChAFTA, art. 12.5.1.

[106] SADEA, art. 8.4.

[107] See, e.g., HK-AFTA, art. 11.4.2; IAEPA, art. 13.9.2; PAFTA, art. 13.5.2; CPTPP, art. 14.5.2. See also ChAFTA, art. 12.5.2 (language is slightly different).

[108] See, e.g., HK-AFTA, art. 11.10; IAEPA, art. 13.4; JAEPA, art. 13.9; PAFTA, art. 13.9.

[109] ChAFTA, art. 12.9.1.

of all trade administration documents available and accepting electronic submissions of trade administration documents.[110]

Australian PTAs generally prohibit imposition of customs duties on electronic transmissions, although the language somewhat varies across PTAs. Some PTAs prohibit customs duties on "electronic transmissions, including content transmitted electronically" but do not prohibit parties from imposing internal taxes, fees or charges on content transmitted electronically.[111] Other PTAs simply state that parties will not impose customs duties on electronic transmissions.[112] Under the ChAFTA, Australia and China agree to not maintain its practice of imposing customs duties on electronic transmissions consistent with the WTO moratorium under the Work Programme on Electronic Commerce.[113] This means that if WTO parties do not renew the moratorium, then China will not be bound by the provision anymore.[114] The language on customs duties on electronic transmissions in Australian PTAs diverges from EU PTAs, although, as explained earlier in Sect. 3.1, some convergence can now be observed.

Similar to EU PTAs, Australian PTAs contain high-level provisions on online consumer protection and spam. The most common provision on online consumer protection requires parties to adopt legal framework to protect consumers from "fraudulent and deceptive commercial practices" in electronic commerce and recognises the importance of cooperation on online consumer protection.[115] However, some other provisions on online consumer protection are weaker in nature, where the PTA parties only recognise the importance of online consumer protection for electronic commerce (i.e. providing "protection that is at least equivalent to that provided for consumers using other forms of commerce"), without any binding obligations.[116] Similarly, for spam, the relevant provision in Australian PTAs requires parties to adopt or maintain measures for regulating spam such as facilitating the ability of recipients to prevent reception of spam and providing consent mechanisms for spam.[117]

Australian PTAs recognise the importance of personal information protection for electronic commerce but diverge from EU PTAs in significant ways: (i) they are usually not as detailed and comprehensive (e.g. EU-CARIFORUM FTA, discussed in the previous section); and (ii) they do not provide an unqualified right for parties

[110] SADEA, art. 12.1, art. 12.2. In addition, it has agreed on other provisions including single electronic window and developing data exchange systems for trade administration documents.

[111] See, e.g., CPTPP, art. 14.3; HK-AFTA, art. 11.6; PAFTA, art. 13.3; SADEA, art. 5.

[112] See, e.g., JAEPA, art. 13.3; KAFTA, art. 15.3.

[113] ChAFTA, art. 12.3.1.

[114] ChAFTA, art. 12.3.2.

[115] See, e.g., HK-AFTA, art. 11.5; IAEPA, art. 13.6; PAFTA, art. 13.7; CPTPP, art. 14.7. See also SADEA, art. 15.

[116] See, e.g., JAEPA, art. 13.7; ChAFTA, art. 12.7.

[117] See, e.g., HK-AFTA, art. 11.11; IAEPA, art. 13.8; PAFTA, art. 13.13; CPTPP, art. 14.14; KAFTA, art. 15.9; SADEA, art. 19.

to adopt data protection laws i.e., such provisions must be inconsistent with trade obligations contained in the agreement, including for cross-border data transfers. Following the CPTPP,[118] several of Australia's other recent PTAs contain a provision requiring all parties to "adopt or maintain a legal framework that provides for the protection of the personal information of the users of electronic commerce".[119] The provision does not prescribe any standards or benchmarks for the legal framework but imposes a general requirement that parties "take into account principles or guidelines of relevant international bodies".[120] The CPTPP provides a further clarification in a footnote as to what constitutes framework for personal information protection:

> For greater certainty, a Party may comply with the obligation in this paragraph by adopting or maintaining measures such as a comprehensive privacy, personal information or personal data protection laws, sector-specific laws covering privacy, or laws that provide for the enforcement of voluntary undertakings by enterprises relating to privacy.[121]

This provision paves the path for parties to adopt their own version of a privacy law without having to comply with any specific international standards. However, this footnote has been omitted in most Australian PTAs including the HK-AFTA, PAFTA and IAEPA. This footnote was however retained in the recent SADEA.[122] Following a similar provision in the *United States—Mexico—Canada Agreement* ("USMCA"),[123] the SADEA added APEC Cross-Border Privacy Rules System ("CBPR") and the OECD Privacy Guidelines as examples of relevant international guidelines on data protection.[124]

The provision on personal information protection in many Australian PTAs also encourages the development of mutual recognition mechanisms between parties[125] and adoption of non-discriminatory practices in protecting e-commerce users from privacy violations.[126] Parties are also legally bound to publish information regarding their personal information protection laws such as how individuals can pursue remedies and compliance requirements for businesses handling personal data.[127] In the recent SADEA, Australia and Singapore recognised that the APEC CBPR was

---

[118] CPTPP, art. 14.8.2.

[119] See, e.g., HK-AFTA, art. 11.9.2; IAEPA, art. 13.7.2; PAFTA, art. 13.8.1. See also JAEPA, art. 13.8; KAFTA, art. 15.8. The language in ChAFTA, art. 12.8.2 is slightly different ("In the development of data protection standards, each Party shall, to the extent possible, take into account international standards and the criteria of relevant international organisations.").

[120] See, e.g., HK-AFTA, art. 11.9.2; IAEPA, art. 13.7.2; PAFTA, art. 13.8.2.

[121] CPTPP, art. 14.8.2, n 6.

[122] SADEA, art. 17.2, n.11.

[123] USMCA, art. 19.8.2.

[124] SADEA, art. 17.2.

[125] See, e.g., HK-AFTA, art. 11.9.5; IAEPA, art. 13.7.4; PAFTA, art. 13.8.5; CPTPP, art. 14.8.5.

[126] See, e.g., HK-AFTA, art. 11.9.3; IAEPA, art. 13.7.3; PAFTA, art. 13.8.4; CPTPP, art. 14.8.4.

[127] See, e.g., HK-AFTA, art. 11.9.4; IAEPA, art. 13.10.2.

a "valid mechanism to facilitate cross-border information transfers while protecting personal information".[128]

Unlike the EU, Australia has consistently adopted an open position on cross-border data flows and data localisation. The language used in most Australian PTAs is similar to the CPTPP provisions,[129] where parties are required to allow cross-border transfer of information for electronic commerce, including personal information.[130] Similarly, as regards data localisation, the relevant provision prevents parties from requiring covered businesses[131] to use local computing facilities as a condition for conducting business within the country.[132] However, parties can only adopt or maintain measures which restrict cross-border data transfers or require local data localisation to achieve a "legitimate public policy objective". Further, such measures must not be "applied in a manner which would constitute a means of arbitrary or unjustifiable discrimination, or a disguised restriction on trade".[133] In the IAEPA, in addition to the above, parties have agreed that they are not prohibited from adopting or maintaining any measures "necessary for the protection of its essential security interests".[134]

Unlike most other Australian PTAs where data transfers for financial services is covered in the Financial Services Chapter, the HK-AFTA and the SADEA contain provisions for cross-border data transfers and data localisation for financial services in the Electronic Commerce Chapter. The relevant provision in these two agreements imposes a general prohibition on restricting cross-border data transfer necessary for financial services or requiring financial service providers to use local computing facilities.[135] However, the prohibition on data localisation is subject to the requirement that financial regulators must have "immediate, direct, complete and ongoing access to information processed or stored on computing facilities that the covered financial person uses or locates outside the Area of the Party".[136] Further, if a financial service provider is unable to provide data access to financial regulators, it must be given a "reasonable opportunity to remediate a lack of access to information", "to the extent practicable", before governments impose data localisation requirements.[137] Finally, parties can adopt or maintain any measures pertaining to financial services to achieve a "legitimate public policy objective", provided that it is

[128] SADEA, art. 17.8.

[129] CPTPP art. 14.11, art. 14.13.

[130] See, e.g., HK-AFTA, art. 11.7.2; IAEPA, art. 13.11.2; PAFTA, art. 13.11.2; SADEA, art. 23.

[131] The definition of covered persons in these PTAs excludes financial service providers.

[132] See, e.g., HK-AFTA, art. 11.8.2; IAEPA, art. 13.12.2; PAFTA, art. 13.12.2.

[133] See, e.g., HK-AFTA, art. 11.7.3, art. 11.8.3; IAEPA, art. 13.11.3(a), art. 13.12.3(a); PAFTA, art. 13.11.3, art. 13.12.3.

[134] See, e.g., IAEPA, art. 13.11.3(b), art. 13.12.3(b).

[135] HK-AFTA, art. 11.15.1; art. 11.15.2; SADEA, art. 25.2.

[136] HK-AFTA, art. 11.15.2.

[137] HK-AFTA, art. 11.15.3. See also HK-AFTA, art. 11.15.4; SADEA, art. 25.3.

not "applied in a manner which would constitute a means of arbitrary or unjustifiable discrimination" or is "a disguised restriction on trade".[138]

Similar to some recent EU PTAs as discussed above in Sect. 3.1, recent Australian PTAs also contain prohibitions on the forced disclosure of source code that broadly follow the language of the provision of the CPTPP.[139] The relevant provision prohibits parties from requiring that companies transfer or provide access to source code of software to regulators "as a condition for the import, distribution, sale or use of such software, or of products containing such software, in its territory".[140] This provision applies to "mass-market software or products containing such software" but excludes "software used for critical infrastructure".[141] This provision is not applicable to "commercially negotiated contracts" which require for the "provision of source code",[142] or in circumstances, where a party may "requir [e] the modification of source code of software necessary for that software to comply with laws or regulations which are not inconsistent with this Agreement".[143] Further, some PTAs specify that the prohibition on disclosure of source code does not prevent companies from licensing their software on a "free and open source basis".[144] The prohibition on involuntary disclosure of source code does not apply to provision of source code for "patent applications", "granted patents", including "in relation to patent disputes", provided that there are "safeguards against unauthorised disclosure under the law or practice of a Party".[145] Additionally, thc IAEPA does not prohibit the parties from adopting or maintaining any source code disclosure requirements if "it considers" the measure "necessary for the protection of its essential security interests".[146]

Following the CPTPP,[147] recent Australian PTAs such as the PAFTA and SADEA contain a high-level provision recognising the benefits for consumers of open access to the internet and digital services (subject to "reasonable network management" by the internet service provider) as well as the importance of consumers being able to use devices of their choices to connect to the internet and access information regarding the network management practice of their internet service supplier.[148]

Like the EU PTAs, most Australian PTAs contain a high-level provision encouraging cooperation between the parties on various issues pertaining to e-commerce

[138] HK-AFTA, art. 11.15.5.

[139] See CPTPP art. 14.17.

[140] See, e.g., HK-AFTA, art. 11.12.1; IAEPA, art. 13.13.1; PAFTA, art. 13.16.1.

[141] See, e.g., HK-AFTA, art. 11.12.2; IAEPA, art. 13.13.2; PAFTA, art. 13.16.2.

[142] See, e.g., HK-AFTA, art. 11.12.3(a); IAEPA, art. 13.13.3(a); PAFTA, art. 13.16.3(a).

[143] See, e.g., HK-AFTA, art. 11.12.3(b); IAEPA, art. 13.13.3(b); PAFTA, art. 13.16.3(b).

[144] See, e.g., HK-AFTA, art. 11.12.3(c); SADEA, art. 28.3.

[145] See, e.g., HK-AFTA, art. 11.12.4; IAEPA, art. 13.13.4; PAFTA, art. 13.16.4.

[146] IAEPA, art. 13.13.5.

[147] CPTPP, art. 14.10.

[148] PAFTA, art. 13.10; SADEA, art. 20.

including sharing of information, best practices and experiences in those relevant area including personal information protection, online consumer protection, spam, security, electronic authentication, international cooperation initiatives, and self-regulatory models in electronic commerce, and capacity building for computer security incident response.[149]

In addition to conventional digital trade issues, the SADEA, modelled on the lines of the *Digital Economy Partnership Agreement* ("DEPA") between Singapore, Chile, and New Zealand, covers several new areas which have conventionally been left out of Electronic Commerce Chapter in PTAs. Some of these new areas include electronic invoicing,[150] electronic payments,[151] express shipments,[152] online safety,[153] data innovation,[154] open government data,[155] and artificial intelligence.[156]

4 Digital Trade in Australia-EU FTA: Possibilities and Challenges

At the outset of the negotiations, the EU released a draft text proposal for the Digital Trade Chapter[157] in the Australia—EU FTA.[158] The draft proposal is far more comprehensive than most of EU PTAs, discussed in Sect. 3.1 above. This section analyses this draft EU proposal, taking into account the past PTA practices of Australia and the EU, including the reports from the ongoing negotiations, as well as the significance of digital trade provisions in strengthening the economic

---

[149] See, e.g., HK-AFTA, art. 11.13; IAEPA, art. 13.3; CPTPP, art. 14.15 and art. 14.16; ChAFTA, art. 12.10. See also JAEPA, art. 13.10; PAFTA, art. 13.14, art. 13.15 (cooperation on cybersecurity). See further SADEA, art. 16 (cooperation on competition policy), art. 33, art. 32(fintech and regtech cooperation).

[150] SADEA, art. 10.

[151] SADEA, art. 11.

[152] SADEA, art. 13.

[153] SADEA, art. 18.

[154] SADEA, art. 26.

[155] SADEA, art. 27.

[156] SADEA, art. 31.

[157] The proposal suggests the chapter title as 'Digital Trade' and not electronic commerce. Some experts believe that the use of 'digital trade' as a chapter title acknowledges the broader scope and applicability of these provisions to economic transactions in the digital economy. See Anupam Chander, The Coming North American Digital Trade Zone, 9 October 2018, https://www.cfr.org/blog/coming-north-american-digital-trade-zone (arguing the same in the context of the USMCA, which is the first PTA to adopt this chapter title).

[158] Identical text proposed for ongoing negotiations between New Zealand and the EU. See https://trade.ec.europa.eu/doclib/docs/2018/december/tradoc_157581.pdf (last accessed 9 September 2021).

relationship between Australia and the EU. It then suggests certain areas for improvement and dialogues to adopt a future-forward approach in negotiating the digital trade chapter in the Australia—EU FTA.

4.1 EU's Proposed Digital Chapter in the Australia: EU FTA

4.1.1 Scope and Applicability of the Digital Trade Chapter

The proposed chapter applies to any measure "affecting trade enabled by electronic means" and only excludes audiovisual services.[159] Trade enabled by electronic means would refer to any economic activity enabled by the internet, irrespective of whether it involves physical or virtual products and services; it would also include intermediate forms of digital trade, such as B2B transactions, instead of only B2C transactions, which has traditionally been associated with e-commerce. Most Electronic Commerce Chapters in Australian PTAs apply to trade "affected" by rather than "enabled" by electronic means; while the term "affected" theoretically appears to have a broader application, both the terms in practice are likely to have a very similar scope of application. The exclusion of "audiovisual services" from the ambit of digital trade chapter is unlikely to be highly contentious between Australia and the EU, given Australian sensitivity towards audiovisual services.[160] The EU proposal interestingly does not contain any exclusions for government procurement or financial services, which is common to many PTAs, especially to which Australia has been a party.

4.1.2 Right to Regulate and Applicable Exceptions

The proposed text sets out an independent provision on the right to regulate, encompassing a broad number of "legitimate public policy objectives":[161]

> The Parties reaffirm the right to regulate within their territories to achieve legitimate policy objectives, such as the protection of public health, social services, public education, safety, the environment including climate change, public morals, social or consumer protection, privacy and data protection, or the promotion and protection of cultural diversity.

---

[159]EU proposal, Digital Trade Chapter, Australia – EU FTA, art. 1. This exclusion is because the European Commission does not have the capacity to negotiate on audiovisual services but individual members. See Lee-Makiyama (2018), p. 219.

[160]For e.g., in CPTPP, Australia included a NCM for the audiovisual sector with respect to its applicable obligations on national treatment, MFN, market access, performance requirements and local presence contained in the investment and trade in services chapter. CPTPP, Annex of Australia, https://www.mfat.govt.nz/assets/Trade-agreements/TPP/Annexes-ENGLISH/Annex-II.-Australia.pdf, p. 9. Similarly, in the GATS, Australia included audio-visual services in its MFN list and also not undertaken any commitments in the GATS Schedule.

[161]EU proposal, Digital Trade Chapter, Australia – EU FTA, art. 2.

This provision will presumably inform how the exceptions may be read in the agreement, which is currently in a draft form in the proposed text, indicating that the EU desires to include the general exceptions, the security exception and the prudential carve-out (in the context of financial services) (which may later be moved to a separate chapter applicable to the entire FTA).[162] Read together, these two provisions highlight the importance accorded by the EU to protecting the right to regulate the digital sector. Further, in the Electronic Commerce Chapters of other recent EU FTAs, some elements of the general exceptions have been slightly modified, for instance, the sub-clause allowing measures "necessary to protect public security or public morals or to maintain public order".[163] Given that both Australia and the EU accord high importance to regulating the digital sector and share common values on internet and digital services regulation, such a provision is unlikely to be pose difficulties during negotiation, although Australian negotiators may aim to align this wording with their existing PTAs.

4.1.3 Data Flows and Privacy

The next section of the proposed EU text deals with data flows and personal data protection. As is already evident from the reports of the first eight round of negotiations between the EU and Australia, these provisions will be the most complicated to negotiate. Article 5(1) of the proposed text sets out a strict prohibition on unjustified data localisation measures, reflecting EU's digital trade policy and identical to the language contained in the EU-UK TCA (discussed above in Sect. 3.1):

> The Parties are committed to ensuring cross-border data flows to facilitate trade in the digital economy. To that end, cross-border data flows shall not be restricted between the Parties by:
>
> (a) requiring the use of computing facilities or network elements in the Party's territory for processing, including by imposing the use of computing facilities or network elements that are certified or approved in the territory of the Party;
> (b) requiring the localisation of data in the Party's territory for storage or processing;
> (c) prohibiting storage or processing in the territory of the other Party;
> (d) making the cross-border transfer of data contingent upon use of computing facilities or network elements in the Party's territory or upon localisation requirements in the Party's territory

This provision is a horizontal clause applicable to all sectors and covering both personal and non-personal data. Further, the scope of this provision appears broad as it prohibits different forms of data localisation such as forced local storage and processing requirements (arguably, including data mirroring requirements), forced use of local servers and other computing facilities including local technologies and overseas data storage and processing, and prohibits imposing conditions on

[162] EU proposal, Digital Trade Chapter, Australia – EU FTA, art. 3.
[163] See, e.g., EU-VN FTA, art. 8.53(a).

cross-border data flows to use local "computing facilities" or "network elements" (arguably, including different forms of local content or performance requirements). The terms computing facilities and network elements are undefined but appear to be broad. A useful reference is the definition of computing facilities in the CPTPP: "computer servers and storage devices for processing or storing information for commercial use".[164] Similarly, network elements can refer to any networking infrastructure related to the internet. Similar to the EU-UK TCA, the EU proposes to review and assess the functioning of this provision 3 years after the agreement comes into force.[165] This caution is not surprising given that this is one of the early attempts by the EU to adopt a binding prohibition on data localisation.[166]

Predictably, the proposed EU text provides a broad provision on privacy, acknowledging that right to privacy is a "fundamental right" and is a precondition to facilitate digital "trust". Further, the proposed provision provides an unlimited scope for each party to adopt a privacy framework as they deem fit, including safeguards for cross-border data transfers, irrespective of the obligations contained in the FTA:

1. Each Party recognises that the protection of personal data and privacy is a fundamental right and that high standards in this regard contribute to trust in the digital economy and to the development of trade.
2. Each Party may adopt and maintain the safeguards it deems appropriate to ensure the protection of personal data and privacy, including through the adoption and application of rules for the cross-border transfer of personal data. Nothing in this agreement shall affect the protection of personal data and privacy afforded by the Parties' respective safeguards.
3. Each Party shall inform the other Party about any safeguard it adopts or maintains according to paragraph 2.
4. For the purposes of this agreement, 'personal data' means any information relating to an identified or identifiable natural person.

The EU and Australia have adopted a different approach in data protection in their respective PTAs.[167] The EU has consistently refused to include any provisions that could subject its privacy laws to trade obligations.[168] This approach is also reflected in the above provision proposed by the EU, intended to provide a blanket exemption for existing regulatory barriers for cross-border data flows under the GDPR. In contrast, Australia has generally taken a more liberal approach with respect to provisions on data protection in their PTAs. As discussed in Sect. 3.2, majority of

---

164 CPTPP, art. 14.1.

165 EU proposal, Digital Trade Chapter, Australia – EU FTA, art. 5.2.

166 See Sect. 3.1 above.

167 See Sects. 3.1 and 3.2 above.

168 See, e.g., European Parliament, Towards a Digital Trade Strategy, Doc no A8-0384/2017 (29 November 2017), https://www.europarl.europa.eu/doceo/document/A-8-2017-0384_EN.pdf (last accessed 9 September 2021) , p. 8 (See also para. 7: "Recalls that nothing in trade agreements shall prevent the EU and its Member States from maintaining, improving and applying its data protection rules").

Australian PTAs include a provision requiring parties to adopt a basic framework for protection of personal information. However, Australian PTAs do not include a carve out for domestic privacy law, implying that any measures in domestic privacy laws must be consistent with the obligations contained in the PTA or otherwise be justifiable under the exceptions available under the PTA.

This provision will probably be the most difficult area for negotiation. The provision proposed by the EU does not alleviate the concerns of Australian businesses that use or monitor personal data of EU residents and depend on data transfers out of the EU. Therefore, the Australian negotiators are likely to push back against the adoption of the provision in the current form.

4.1.4 No-Prior Authorisation

Similar to the language adopted the EU-UK TCA (discussed in Sect. 3.1), the proposed text for the Australia—EU FTA also includes a provision on "no prior authorisation":

1. A Party shall not require prior authorisation solely on the ground that a service is provided online, or adopt or maintain any other requirement having an equivalent effect.
2. Paragraph 1 does not apply to telecommunications services, broadcasting services, gambling services, or legal representation services, nor to services of notaries or equivalent professions to the extent that they involve a direct and specific connection with the exercise of public authority.[169]

This provision effectively means that a party cannot subject online service providers to authorisation or equivalent requirements solely on the grounds that they offer online services. The aim of the provision appears to be discouragement of authorisation or equivalent procedures aimed specifically at online services.[170] However, as Streinz argues, the dichotomy between online and offline services is diluted in the current digital world and, hence, the relevance of this provision appears less clear today.[171]

4.1.5 Other Digital Trade Provisions

The remainder of the proposed Digital Trade Chapter includes provisions typical to many modern digital trade/electronic commerce chapters in PTAs: (i) prohibition on customs duties on electronic transmissions; (ii) electronic contracts, signatures, and authentication; (iii) prohibition on forced disclosure of source code; (iv) requirement

[169] EU proposal, Digital Trade Chapter, Australia – EU FTA, art. 8.

[170] No prior authorisation requirements was also a part of the E-commerce Directive in the EU.

[171] Thomas Streinz, Tweet (20 January 2021) https://twitter.com/t_streinz/status/1351848132729065473 (last accessed 9 September 2021).

to adopt a framework on online consumer protection; (v) protection against spam; (vi) regulatory cooperation on digital trade.

The EU proposes banning any customs duties on electronic transmissions.[172] Electronic transmissions relates to the "supply of services",[173] reflecting EU's approach of treating all trade in digitally encoded products as trade in services; therefore, this provision does not apply to customs duties applied on goods delivered via electronic commerce. The EU and the US have been involved in a long-standing divide at the WTO, whether digital products constitute goods or services or both.[174] It remains unclear from the wording of the proposed provision if electronic transmissions refer only to transmissions or also to the content transmitted,[175] although the EU has taken a liberal approach on this issue in recent PTAs, as previously discussed in Sect. 3.1.

The proposed text includes a headnote for reservations, listing the services included under "computer and related services",[176] which would also inform the interpretation of the scope of EU's commitments under the Australia—EU FTA. The EU has proposed the adoption of the same schema for listing non-conforming measures as the CETA, consisting of Annex I and Annex II,[177] as discussed previously in Sect. 3.1.

Following the trend in several recent PTAs,[178] the EU has also proposed a provision prohibiting the forced disclosure of source code:[179]

> 1. A Party shall not require the transfer of, or access to, the source code of software owned by a natural or juridical person of the other Party.

---

[172] EU proposal, Digital Trade Chapter, Australia – EU FTA, art. 7(2).

[173] EU proposal, Digital Trade Chapter, Australia – EU FTA, art. 7(1).

[174] This topic has also been subject to extensive debate in the WTO, where the EU and the US have taken opposite sides. For more discussion, see Willemyns (2020), p. 233.

[175] However, note EU's proposal to JSI discussed above.

[176] This headnote reads:

1. Any of the following services shall be considered as computer and related services, regardless of whether they are delivered via a network, including the Internet: (a) consulting, adaptation, strategy, analysis, planning, specification, design, development, installation, implementation, integration, testing, debugging, updating, support, technical assistance or management of or for computers or computer systems; (b) computer programmes defined as the sets of instructions required to make computers work and communicate (in and of themselves), as well as consulting, strategy, analysis, planning, specification, design, development, installation, implementation, integration, testing, debugging, updating, adaptation, maintenance, support, technical assistance, management or use of or for computer programmes; (c) data processing, data storage, data hosting or database services; (d) maintenance and repair services for office machinery and equipment, including computers; and (e) training services for staff of clients, related to computer programmes, computers or computer systems, and not elsewhere classified.
2. For greater certainty, services enabled by computer and related services, other than those listed in paragraph 1, shall not be regarded as computer and related services in themselves.

[177] EU proposal, Investment Liberalisation and Trade in Services, Australia – EU FTA, art. 2.7.1.

[178] For a general discussion, see Mishra (2021), pp. 41–46.

[179] EU proposal, Digital Trade Chapter, Australia – EU FTA, art. 11.

2. For greater certainty:

(a) the general exception, security exception and prudential carve-out can apply to measures of a Party adopted or maintained in the context of a certification procedure; (b) paragraph 1 does not apply to the voluntary transfer of or granting of access to source code on a commercial basis by a natural or juridical person of the other Party, for instance in the context of a public procurement transaction or a freely negotiated contract.

3. Nothing in this Article shall affect: (a) requirements by a court, administrative tribunal or competition authority to remedy a violation of competition law; (b) intellectual property rights and their protection and enforcement; and (c) the right of a Party to take measures in accordance with Article [security and general exceptions of the Public Procurement Title].

The proposed text does not contain a definition of source code, but source code ordinarily refers to the instructions written by the computer in programming language. Notably, this provision does not include algorithms (for instance, unlike the USMCA). As discussed in Sect. 3.2, several Australian PTAs include a provision on source code disclosure and the EU has recently also agreed upon similar provisions in its PTAs.

The EU has proposed various provisions to facilitate electronic commerce such as removing obstacles for parties to conclude a contract by electronic means;[180] recognising electronic authentication methods and ensuring that their underlying performance standards are "objective, transparent and non-discriminatory";[181] and ensuring that parties provide effective protection to consumers against spam.[182] In the draft text, the EU has also included a provision on online consumer trust, requiring parties to adopt measures to prohibit fraudulent and deceptive commercial practices, promote fair commercial practices, reduce information asymmetry between consumers and e-commerce businesses, and provide adequate rights and remedies to aggrieved consumers.[183] As discussed in Sect. 3, these kinds of provisions are common to both EU and Australian PTAs, although the exact wording varies across the PTAs. These issues appear to be low hanging fruit and likely to be agreed upon by both sides during the Australia—EU FTA negotiations, as also indicated by available reports.[184]

Like many of its previous FTAs, the EU has proposed a provision on regulatory cooperation in areas such as electronic trust and authentication methods, spam, online consumer protection and other matters relevant to digital trade.[185] This provision however does not include cybersecurity cooperation, which seems surprising given that cybersecurity cooperation was included in the Framework

[180] EU proposal, Digital Trade Chapter, Australia – EU FTA, art. 9(1).

[181] EU proposal, Digital Trade Chapter, Australia – EU FTA, art. 10.

[182] EU proposal, Digital Trade Chapter, Australia – EU FTA, art. 13.

[183] EU proposal, Digital Trade Chapter, Australia – EU FTA, art. 13(1).

[184] See, e.g., Report of the 6th round of negotiations for a Free Trade Agreement between the European Union and Australia, 10-14 February 2020, https://trade.ec.europa.eu/doclib/docs/2020/february/tradoc_158656.pdf (last accessed 9 September 2021).

[185] EU proposal, Digital Trade Chapter, Australia – EU FTA, art. 14(1); art. 13(2).

Agreement and is not atypical of EU FTAs.[186] Further, the EU appears to exclude mechanisms for regulatory cooperation on privacy and data protection issues:

> For greater certainty, this provision shall not apply to a Party's rules and safeguards for the protection of personal data and privacy, including on cross-border transfers of personal data.

The above provision appears undesirable because it reduces the possibility for Australia and the EU to seek mechanisms for achieving interoperability between their privacy frameworks to facilitate cross-border flows of personal data. Given the importance of data-driven trade for the both the parties, this provision seems over-cautious and defensive, especially since the proposed chapter already contains strong provisions on data protection (Article 6) and right to regulate (Article 2).

Reports also indicate that Australia and the EU have agreed on a provision on open government data.[187] While the proposed text is not available, both the SADEA[188] and the EU-UK TCA[189] contain a non-binding provision on open government data, which although not identical, is similarly worded. The key objective is recognising that "facilitating public access to and use of government information contributes to stimulating economic and social benefit, competitiveness, productivity improvements and innovation".[190] Further, parties are encouraged to provide public data in a user-friendly and accessible manner, consistent with principles of data protection.[191] Given that this is a high-level and non-binding provision, to which Australia and the EU have agreed with other trading partners, it is quite likely that the final provision will be similarly worded as the EU-UK TCA. Further, reports also suggest that parties have agreed on provisions on paperless trading and open internet access. These provisions are likely to be modelled very similar to the existing provision in some recent PTAs.

Over-all, several of the digital trade provisions currently being considered to be included in the Australia—EU FTA will create an open and robust environment for digital trade and enhance opportunities for digital trade between the two regions. Further, disciplines on electronic transactions, e-signatures, paperless trading, and online consumer protection will be important in creating security and predictability in digital trade as well as reduce transaction costs for businesses. The inclusion of modern-day digital trade provisions such as disciplines on source code disclosure requirements and prohibition on data localisation are also welcome changes. In that regard, the Australia—EU FTA is likely to achieve a stronger balance between provisions requiring the free flow of data and other regulatory pre-requisites for enabling data flows such as privacy protection and consumer trust as compared to the

---

[186] See, e.g., Japan -EU EPA, art. 8.80(2)(c).

[187] Report of the 8th round of negotiations for a trade agreement between the European Union and Australia, September 2020, https://trade.ec.europa.eu/doclib/docs/2020/october/tradoc_158976.pdf (last accessed 9 September 2021).

[188] SADEA, art. 27.

[189] EU-UK TCA, art. DIGI.15.

[190] SADEA, art. 27.2; EU-UK TCA, art. DIGI.15.1.

[191] SADEA art. 27.3; EU_UK TCA, art. DIGI.15.2.

CPTPP.[192] The EU has also demonstrated its willingness to consider including disciplines on broader digital economy issues such as open government data. While several of these developments are positive, the General Data Protection Regulation ("GDPR") disciplines on cross-border data transfers will be a major barrier for Australian businesses intending to conduct business in the EU. These challenges are addressed in the next section.

4.2 *Placing the Australia—EU PTA in the Digital Trade Realm: A Future-Forward Approach*

The previous section identifies various provisions likely to be included in the Australia—EU PTA and their potential impact on digital trade between the parties. While the EU and Australia appear to be moving forward on several areas of digital trade in their trade negotiations, this section identifies three areas critical to strengthen their digital trade links: (i) identifying and agreeing upon relevant cooperation mechanisms and standards for data transfers and arriving at a consensus regarding how their respective data protection frameworks could be made interoperable; (ii) adopting new trade disciplines that can enable innovation by MSMEs, especially taking advantage of digitalisation; and (iii) experimenting with new forms of institutional cooperation in digital trade, including participation in parallel mechanisms at the OECD, G20, WTO and internet multistakeholder institutions. Of these three areas, an agreement on cross-border data transfers and data protection appears to be the most challenging.

4.2.1 Data Protection and Privacy

The biggest impediment that Australian businesses are likely to face while conducting digital trade with the EU is the incompatibility of their respective regulatory frameworks on data protection.[193] While a detailed discussion is outside the scope of this paper, the GDPR and the Privacy Act in Australia have several notable differences. First, the GDPR is much broader in scope and applies to all businesses that offer services in the EU or even monitor the behaviour of EU residents.[194] In contrast, the Privacy Act generally applies to specified entities with a turnover of more than 3 million AUD with the exception of those trading in

[192] See generally Mishra (2017).

[193] Lee-Makiyama (2018), p. 214.

[194] GDPR, art. 3.

personal information or providing health services.[195] Thus, even a sole Australian entrepreneur intending to offer digital services in the EU must comply with the GDPR. Further, the GDPR classifies a broader range of information as personally identifiable information, including tracking cookies. In the ongoing negotiations, the EU and Australia are working toward a common definition of personal data.[196] This is likely to be a challenging task given the different definition of personal data in the EU and Australian law.

Second, the GDPR provides individuals with broader scope of rights compared to the Australian data protection law such as the right to data portability, right to be forgotten and right not be subjected to automated decision-making, thereby increasing compliance burden for any business handling personal data of Europeans.

Most importantly, while Australia has adopted an accountability-based mechanism for cross-border data transfers,[197] the EU has adopted a prescriptive mechanism, whereby, data can only be transferred to countries that have obtained a positive adequacy finding (Australia has not obtained a positive adequacy finding, to date) or if the business can offer appropriate safeguards (e.g. Standard Contractual Clauses).[198] As the latter option entail huge compliance costs, most MSMEs in Australia are unlikely to be able to exercise that option.[199]

Adequacy findings require long bilateral negotiations. The EC considers several factors in adequacy negotiations pertaining to the foreign country including their data privacy/protection framework, respect for rule of law, international commitments to data protection, and the strength of their economic and political relationship with the European Union.[200] Although New Zealand has obtained a positive adequacy finding, it remains unclear if Australia will be able to achieve this in the future. Experts have pointed out how this may cause business uncertainty in the future, given that New Zealand entities offering their services in the EU will be unable to operate through their Australian subsidiaries.[201]

Given the importance of digital interconnectivity for digital trade between the EU and Australia, the EU must use the ongoing FTA negotiations with Australia as a platform to explore new mechanisms to enable cross-border data transfers between

[195] Office of the Australian Information Commissioner, Australian Privacy Principles Guidelines, https://www.oaic.gov.au/assets/privacy/app-guidelines/app-guidelines-july-2019.pdf (last accessed 9 September 2021).

[196] Report of the 8th round of negotiations for a trade agreement between the European Union and Australia, September 2020,https://trade.ec.europa.eu/doclib/docs/2020/october/tradoc_158976.pdf (last accessed 9 September 2021).

[197] The only restriction in Australian law is the cross-border transfer of e-health records. See Personally Controlled Electronic Health Records Act 2012 (Cth), s. 77.

[198] See GDPR, Chapter 5.

[199] Submission of the Australian Business in Europe, 27 June 2019, pp. 4–5, https://www.dfat.gov.au/sites/default/files/australian-business-in-europe-eufta-submission.pdf (last accessed 9 September 2021).

[200] GDPR, art. 45(2).

[201] Lee-Makiyama (2018), p. 214.

the two regions. The CPTPP and several Australian PTAs already contain a provision that encourages parties to explore mutual recognition mechanisms for their privacy frameworks, as discussed previously in Sect. 3.2. A similar provision must be considered in the context of Australia—EU FTA. Several experts have also indicated the advantages of including language in PTAs to foster interoperability among privacy regimes.[202] For instance, as Australia already endorses the APEC CBPR, the EU can explore possible compatibility between the mechanisms available under the GDPR and the CBPR certification mechanism. Further, as was the case while negotiating the Japan-EU EPA, the EU and Australia must consider engaging in parallel dialogues regarding negotiation of adequacy arrangements with Australia in the near future.

4.2.2 Boosting the Growth of MSMEs

The proposed digital trade chapter in the Australia—EU FTA currently does not contain any provisions tailored towards facilitating the growth of MSMEs. In that regard, provisions on electronic payments and e-invoicing found in the SADEA and DEPA and the provision on logistics in the DEPA provide a good foundation for enabling MSMEs struggling to integrate in the global e-commerce markets due to the uncertainties in the global e-commerce framework. Such provisions are particularly instrumental for both the EU and Australia due to the high possibility of dynamic innovation by digital start-ups in these countries.

The provision on logistics in the DEPA states:

1. The Parties recognise the importance of efficient cross border logistics which would help lower the cost and improve the speed and reliability of supply chains.
2. The Parties shall endeavour to share best practices and general information regarding the logistics sector, including but not limited to the following:

   (a) Last mile deliveries, including on-demand and dynamic routing solutions;
   (b) The use of electric, remote controlled and autonomous vehicles;
   (c) Facilitating the availability of cross-border options for the delivery of goods, such as federated lockers;
   (d) New delivery and business models on logistics.

Although it is not legally binding, a similar provision could facilitate greater cooperation between the EU and Australia to share best practices and help small companies navigate the problems around small-value shipments and managing demands in real-time.[203] Another useful example is the provision on electronic invoicing in the SADEA, which facilitates cross-border interoperability of their electronic invoicing frameworks and collaboration on initiatives that facilitate the adoption of electronic invoicing by domestic companies.[204] As both Australia and

[202] Meltzer (2018), p. ix.
[203] See generally Mitchell and Mishra (2020).
[204] SADEA, art. 10.

the EU are digitally developed with high regulatory expertise, such a provision appears feasible for both the parties to implement meaningfully.

Another useful example that the negotiators of the Australia—EU FTA can consider is the provision on electronic payments in the SADEA.[205] Some of the key features of this provision are: (i) requiring parties to be transparent about their laws and regulations on electronic payment services; (ii) encouraging the adoption of international standards for data exchange and messaging in electronic payment systems; (iii) encouraging regulatory sandboxes in the fintech sector; (iv) possibility of greater interoperability and competition by facilitating open platforms and architectures in electronic payment systems; and (v) recognising the importance of a proportionate risk-based approach in regulating electronic payment systems. A provision containing such high-level principles on electronic payments, albeit largely soft in nature, can still be critical in the growth of fintech start-ups providing services in both Australia and the EU.

4.2.3 Experimenting with New Models of Cooperation

As explained previously in Sect. 2, the EU and Australia share several common economic interests pertaining to the digital economy. The Australia—EU FTA can be critical in fostering sustainable cooperation between the two parties on relevant areas in digital trade. While some issues such as data transfer mechanisms may appear intractable in the short run, continued dialogues on these issues can help both parties to reach a practical solution to manage their regulatory differences on data protection.

In that regard, similar to some EU FTAs,[206] setting up a committee on electronic commerce with representatives from both parties will be helpful to not only monitor the implementation of the existing digital trade rules in the FTA but also explore new avenues where high-level disciplines may be beneficial. While the relevant FTA committee cannot and should not prescribe substantive norms and standards on these issues, it can facilitate transparent, informal dialogues and a common understanding between the parties on some of these issues including a consensus on the relevant international standard for data protection, cybersecurity, and AI regulation.

The DEPA and SADEA provide various examples where parties have agreed to engage in regulatory dialogues such as AI frameworks, data innovation, fintech/regtech, and digital competition policy. Such disciplines will also be relevant for digitally advanced countries in the EU to develop greater regulatory cooperation with their Australian counterparts. In turn, such cooperation can translate into meaningful policy advocacy and action in other international fora such as the WTO (e.g., JSI negotiations), G20 (e.g., facilitating the data free flow with trust framework) and the OECD (e.g., reforms on digital taxes). Similarly, the EU and

[205] SADEA, art. 11.

[206] See, e.g., EU-KR FTA, art. 7.3.

Australia could develop a common position in the ICT standardisation debates in various internet multistakeholder and private standard-setting organisations.

Sectoral regulators in Australia and Singapore have currently signed several memoranda of understanding in areas such as electronic invoicing, data protection, fintech and regtech, and data innovation to exchange best practices, share information and potentially, develop a common position on specific issues.[207] Such an approach could also be replicated under the Australia—EU FTA. In the long run, novel cooperation mechanisms between like-minded partners will be critical in building greater transnational consensus and facilitating international regulatory cooperation in digital trade. The Australia—EU FTA provides an opportunity to explore and experiment with such mechanisms, which must not be lost.

5 Conclusion

The Australia—EU FTA lays an important foundation for strengthening the economic relationship between the EU and Australia. The Digital Trade Chapter in this FTA can contribute to this relationship, given the immense potential for increasing digital trade between the EU and Australia. This mutual economic interest is well complemented by the shared values of the EU and Australia regarding the development of data-driven technologies and internet governance.

Historically, Australia and the EU have adopted different approaches in their Electronic Commerce Chapters in PTAs. While Australia has adopted more comprehensive electronic commerce chapters with deeper commitments, the EU has stuck to a more bare-bones framework focusing largely on consumer trust and electronic transactions-related issues. However, in recent years, greater convergence can be observed in their PTA practices, with the EU agreeing upon provisions on source code disclosure requirements and data localisation in its recent FTAs. Based on these developments, it appears that the Australia—EU FTA will contain several digital trade disciplines including e-signatures, e-authentication, paperless trading, customs duties on electronic transmissions, online consumer trust and spam, trade disciplines on source code disclosure, and data localisation. Public reports also indicate that both parties are considering new areas such as open government data. However, the framing of the provisions on transborder data flows and data protection is likely to be a sticky issue for the parties. The EU's draft proposal indicates its preference to provide a blanket exemption for its GDPR disciplines on cross-border data flows. This approach is however not suited to Australian business interests and does not align with their past FTA practice.

---

[207] See DFAT, Australia-Singapore Digital Economy Agreement, https://www.dfat.gov.au/trade/services-and-digital-trade/Pages/australia-and-singapore-digital-economy-agreement (last accessed 9 September 2021).

Instead of bypassing such tricky issues, the negotiators of the Australia -EU FTA must see the negotiations as a meaningful opportunity to deliberate upon more ambitious digital trade disciplines that are mutually beneficial and essential to create new digital trade opportunities, especially for MSMEs in their respective economies. In that regard, the negotiators should remain mindful that the negotiations offer an opportunity to build mutual consensus and foster cooperation in data regulation, including data transfer mechanisms and standards. Further, the FTA negotiations provide an opportunity to consider deeper disciplines on digital trade facilitation that can nurture digital start-ups and experiment with novel models for regulatory cooperation to facilitate trade in emerging technologies such as AI and fintech.

Annex 1: Comparison of Electronic Commerce Chapters in EU PTAs

	CETA	EU-Mexico Globalised Agreement	EU-KR FTA	EU-SG FTA	EU-VN FTA	Japan-EU EPA	EU-CARIFORUM FTA	EU-UK TCA
Objective and purpose: Economic growth, boosting trade opportunities	✓	✓	✓	✓	✓	✓	✓	✓
Specific recognition of right to regulate	✗	✓	✗	✓	✓	✓	✗	✓
Specific scope or exclusions	✗	✓	✓	✓	✓	✓	✗	✓
Non-discrimination of digital products	✗	✗	✗	✗	✗	✗	✗	✗
Customs duties on electronic transmissions	✓	✓	✗	✓	✗	✓	✗	✓
Online consumer protection	✓	✓	✗	✗	✗	✓	✗	✓
Framework for protection of personal information	✓	✗	✗	✗	✗	✗	✓	✓
Cybersecurity-dedicated provision	✗	✗	✗	✗	✗	✗	✗	✗
Data Localisation	✗	✗	✗	✗	✗	✗	✗	✓

(continued)

	CETA	EU-Mexico Globalised Agreement	EU-KR FTA	EU-SG FTA	EU-VN FTA	Japan-EU EPA	EU-CARIFORUM FTA	EU-UK TCA
Cross-border transfer of information	✗	✗	✗	✗	✗	✗	✗	✓
Domestic regulation in e-commerce	✗	✗	✗	✗	✗	✓	✗	✗
No prior authorisation requirement	✗	✓	✗	✗	✗	✓	✗	✓
Open Internet Access	✗	✓	✗	✗	✗	✓	✗	✗
Electronic signatures and authentication	✓	✓	✗	✗	✗	✓	✗	✓
Spam	✓	✓	✗	✗	✗	✓	✗	✓
Involuntary disclosure of source code	✗	✓	✗	✗	✗	✓	✗	✓
Transparency in e-commerce	✓	✗	✗	✗	✗	✓	✗	✗
Definition of computer services	✗	✗	✓	✓	✓	✗	✓	✓
Dialogues/cooperation on e-commerce	✓	✓	✓	✓	✓	✓	✓	✓
Paperless trading	✗	✗	✓	✗	✗	✗	✗	✗
Open Government Data	✗	✗	✗	✗	✗	✗	✗	✓
Separate Chapter	✓	✓	✗	✗	✗	✗	✓	✓

Annex 2: Comparison of Electronic Commerce Chapters in Australian FTAs

	CPTPP	ChAFTA	HK-AFTA	IAEPA	KAFTA	PAFTA	JAEPA	SADEA
Objective and purpose—Economic growth, boosting	✓	✓	✓	✓	✓	✓	✓	✓

(continued)

	CPTPP	ChAFTA	HK-AFTA	IAEPA	KAFTA	PAFTA	JAEPA	SADEA
trade opportunities etc.								
Specific recognition of right to regulate in Section/Chapter on Electronic Commerce	✗	✗	✗	✗	✗	✗	✗	✗
Specific scope or exclusions from Electronic Commerce Chapter	✓	✗	✓	✗	✗	✓	✗	✓
Non-discrimination of digital products	✓	✗	✗	✗	✗	✓	✓	✓
Customs duties on electronic transmissions	✓	✓	✓	✗	✓	✓	✓	✓
Online consumer protection	✓	✓	✓	✓	✓	✓	✓	✓
Protection of personal information	✓	✓	✓	✓	✓	✓	✓	✓
Cybersecurity-dedicated provision	✓	✗	✗	✗	✗	✓	✗	✓
Data Localisation	✓	✗	✓	✓	✗	✓	✗	✓
Cross-border transfer of information	✓	✗	✓	✓	✗	✓	✗	✓
Domestic regulation in e-commerce	✗	✗	✗	✗	✓	✗	✓	✓
Open Internet Access	✓	✗	✗	✗	✗	✓	✗	✓
Electronic signatures and authentication	✓	✓	✓	✓	✓	✓	✓	✓
Spam	✓	✗	✓	✓	✓	✓	✗	✓
Involuntary disclosure of source code	✓	✗	✓	✓	✗	✓	✗	✓
Transparency in e-commerce	✗	✓	✗	✓	✗	✗	✗	✓
Definition of computer services	✗	✗	✗	✗	✗	✗	✗	✗
Dialogues/cooperation on e-commerce	✓	✓	✓	✓	✗	✓	✓	✓
Paperless trading	✓	✓	✓	✓	✓	✓	✓	✓
Domestic electronic transactions framework	✓	✓	✓	✓	✓	✗	✗	✓
Logistics, express shipments	✗	✗	✗	✗	✗	✗	✗	✓
Electronic invoicing	✗	✗	✗	✗	✗	✗	✗	✓
E-Payments	✗	✗	✗	✗	✗	✗	✗	✓
Digital Identities	✗	✗	✗	✗	✗	✗	✗	✓
Artificial Intelligence	✗	✗	✗	✗	✗	✗	✗	✓

(continued)

	CPTPP	ChAFTA	HK-AFTA	IAEPA	KAFTA	PAFTA	JAEPA	SADEA
Open Government Data	✗	✗	✗	✗	✗	✗	✗	✓
Data Innovation	✗	✗	✗	✗	✗	✗	✗	✓
Separate Chapter	✓	✓	✓	✓	✓	✓	✓	✓

References

Burri M (2016) Designing future-oriented multilateral rules for digital trade. In: Sauvé P, Roy M (eds) Research handbook on trade in services. Edward Elgar (online), pp 331–356

Burri M, Polanco R (2020) Digital trade in preferential trade agreements. J Int Econ Law 23(1): 187–220

Elijah A (2017) Is the CETA a Road Map for Australia and the EU? In: Elijah A et al (eds) Australia, the European Union and the new trade agenda. ANU Press, Canberra, pp 55–74

Elms D (2017) Understanding the EU–Singapore Free Trade Agreement. In: Elijah A et al (eds) Australia, the European Union and the new trade agenda. ANU Press, Canberra, pp 35–54

Lee-Makiyama H (2018) E-commerce and digital trade. In: Drake-Brockman J, Messerlin P (eds) Potential benefits of an Australia-EU Free Trade Agreement: key issues and options. University of Adelaide Press, Adelaide, pp 211–224

Meltzer JP (2018) Digital Australia: an economic and trade agenda. Global Economy and Development Working Paper 118, Brookings

Mishra N (2017) The role of the Trans-Pacific Partnership Agreement in the internet ecosystem: uneasy liaison or synergistic alliance? J Int Econ Law 20(1):*31–60*

Mishra N (2021) International trade law meets data ethics: a brave new world. N Y J Int Law Polit 53(2):305–374

Mitchell, AD, Mishra, N (2020) Digital trade integration in preferential trade agreements. ARTNeT Working Paper Series No. 191, Asia-Pacific Research and Training Network on Trade:1-54.

Monteiro JA, Teh R (2017) Provisions on electronic commerce in regional trade agreements. WTO Working Paper ERSD-2017-11, World Trade Organization

Willemyns I (2020) Agreement forthcoming? A comparison of EU, US, and Chinese RTAs in times of plurilateral e-commerce negotiations. J Int Econ Law 23(1):221–244

Neha Mishra is a lecturer at the ANU College of Law. She was previously postdoctoral fellow at the Centre for International Law, National University of Singapore. Neha holds a doctorate degree in law from the University of Melbourne (Australia)m and has also held visiting research positions at the Max Planck Institute Luxembourg and the World Trade Organization. She completed her undergraduate degree in law from National Law School Bangalore (India), LLM in Public International Law from London School of Economics (UK), and Master's in Public Policy from National University of Singapore (Singapore). Neha is a dual-qualified lawyer (UK and India) and has previously practised law with Herbert Smith Freehills LLP in London and Economic Laws Practice in Delhi. She also served as a lecturer at National Law School of India University (Bangalore). While studying in Singapore, Neha also interned with the Government Relations Teams at eBay Singapore and Microsoft Singapore, working on a wide variety of legal and policy issues related to internet and digital trade regulation. Neha currently researches on international economic law, digital trade and data governance.

Investment Screening and Market Access in the AEUFTA

Jarrod Hepburn

Contents

Abstract This chapter examines issues of investment screening and investment market access in the negotiations for the Australia-European Union Free Trade Agreement (AEUFTA). It provides an overview of the general purpose of the envisaged provisions on investment screening and investment market access in the AEUFTA, as well as an assessment of the particular value of these provisions in the Australia-EU relationship. The AEUFTA could potentially address both issues, by offering enhanced market access in particular sectors and/or by offering higher screening thresholds. Nevertheless, evidence remains unclear on whether higher screening thresholds play a significant role in encouraging more investment. As well, in light of current economic and political uncertainties, the treaty partners may also be tempted to include broad negative list reservations to their market access commitments, preserving maximum flexibility to meet future policy challenges.

Preparation of this article was supported by the Australia-Germany Joint Research Co-operation Scheme, operated jointly by Universities Australia and the Deutscher Akademischer Austauschdienst. I thank Fabian Blandfort and Tristram Feder for valuable assistance.

J. Hepburn (✉)
Melbourne Law School, Carlton, VIC, Australia
e-mail: j.hepburn@unimelb.edu.au

M. Bungenberg, A. Mitchell (eds.), *The Australia-European Union Free Trade Agreement*, Special Issue, https://doi.org/10.1007/978-3-030-91448-6_6

1 Introduction

This chapter examines issues of investment screening and investment market access in the negotiations for the Australia-European Union Free Trade Agreement (AEUFTA), commenced in 2018.

Australia and the European Union (EU) have a significant investment relationship. In 2018, the EU27 was the second-largest source of foreign investment in Australia, after the United States,[1] and the EU27 was the third-largest destination of outbound Australian investment, after the United States and United Kingdom.[2] The negotiations for the AEUFTA aim to "set a benchmark" for trade and investment agreements, demonstrating "what can be achieved between like-minded partners".[3] Amongst many other goals, Australia hopes to "[i]mprove market access for Australian investment and increase investment into Australia, supporting economic growth",[4] while the EU seeks the "progressive and mutual liberalisation of ... foreign direct investment with regard to establishment by eliminating restrictions to market access and national treatment".[5]

This chapter aims to provide an overview of the general purpose of the envisaged provisions on investment screening and investment market access in the AEUFTA (Sect. 2), as well as an assessment of the particular value of these provisions in the Australia-EU relationship (Sect. 3).

2 Barriers to Entry of Foreign Investment: Screening and Market Access

Inflows of foreign goods and services into a state's economy are often perceived negatively by domestic constituencies. Foreign goods compete with locally-produced goods, and potentially displace local production jobs. Similarly, foreign

[1] Australian Government, Department of Foreign Affairs and Trade (2020) Statistics on Who Invests in Australia. www.dfat.gov.au/trade/resources/investment-statistics/statistics-on-who-invests-in-australia (last accessed 9 September 2021).

[2] Australian Government, Department of Foreign Affairs and Trade (2020) Statistics on Where Australia Invests. www.dfat.gov.au/trade/resources/investment-statistics/statistics-on-where-australia-invests (last accessed 9 September 2021).

[3] Australian Government, Department of Foreign Affairs and Trade (2019) Australia-European Union Free Trade Agreement. www.dfat.gov.au/trade/agreements/negotiations/aeufta/Pages/default (last accessed 9 September 2021).

[4] Australian Government, Department of Foreign Affairs and Trade (2018) Australia-European Union Free Trade Agreement: Objectives. www.dfat.gov.au/trade/agreements/negotiations/aeufta/Pages/australia-european-union-fta-objectives (last accessed 9 September 2021).

[5] Council of the European Union (2018) Negotiating Directives for a Free Trade Agreement with Australia. www.consilium.europa.eu/media/35794/st07663-ad01dc01-en18.pdf (last accessed 9 September 2021).

service providers compete with and may displace local alternatives. States are therefore frequently tempted to place barriers to entry on foreign goods and services, in the well-known forms of tariffs, quotas, behind-the-border regulations, and others.[6]

Inflows of foreign capital, by contrast, are often perceived as beneficial to a host state's economy. Foreign investment may underpin new local businesses or permit existing local businesses to grow, creating new employment in the local economy. Both Australia and the EU, for instance, take a positive view of foreign investment. According to the Australian government, foreign investment "has helped build Australia's economy and will continue to enhance the wellbeing of Australians by supporting economic growth and innovation into the future".[7] Similarly, for the EU, "foreign investment tends to benefit host countries as well as home countries" by "contributing to economic growth, job creation and integration in global value chains".[8]

Because of this, states have historically found fewer reasons to impose barriers to the entry of foreign investment capital, compared to foreign goods and services. In the latter context, international instruments (such as the WTO Agreements) have focused on removing barriers to trade in goods and services. In the context of foreign investment, by contrast, formal barriers to entry are less likely to exist. Instead, the factor more likely to discourage or prevent foreign investment in a host state is the perception of a risk of harm or interference that investments may suffer *after* their entry to and establishment in the host state. Therefore, international instruments on foreign investment have traditionally targeted these post-establishment risks, rather than pre-establishment barriers to entry.[9]

Typical bilateral investment treaties (BITs) contain a range of substantive protections for foreign investors and investment applying post-establishment, such as the guarantees on fair and equitable treatment, expropriation and discrimination. These protections are usually backed by the enforcement mechanism of international arbitration. By contrast, BITs rarely contain pre-establishment commitments, instead leaving it to states' sovereign discretion under customary international law as to whether to admit the entry of any particular foreign investment. While many BITs do contain clauses on promotion of investments, these clauses are typically framed in weaker language, at most obliging the state to ensure that domestic laws are properly applied when making a decision on entry of foreign investments, and otherwise simply calling on the host state to create conditions favourable for foreign investment. Article 3(1) of the Australia-Lithuania BIT provides an example: "Each Party shall encourage and promote investments in its territory made by investors of the

---

[6] Alschner (2017), p. 379.

[7] Australian Government, Foreign Investment Review Board (2021) General guidance. firb.gov.au/general-guidance (last accessed 9 September 2021).

[8] European Commission (2020) Investment. ec.europa.eu/trade/policy/accessing-markets/investment/ (last accessed 9 September 2021).

[9] Alschner (2017), p. 379.

other Party and shall, in accordance with its laws, regulations and investment policies applicable from time to time, admit investments." Although such clauses may be justiciable under the investor-state arbitration mechanism in a typical BIT, they have rarely been the subject of disputes.[10]

States are thus usually not constrained by international law in deciding whether to permit the establishment of foreign investment in their territory. Furthermore, as noted above, states usually have less reason to deny entry of foreign investment, compared to entry of foreign goods and services. Nevertheless, in some situations, states do have reason to exercise their discretion to restrict entry of investment. For instance, the presence of foreign capital in a domestic sector may entail foreign control of that sector. In sectors of a state's economy that are critical for national security or are culturally or politically sensitive, this foreign control can be concerning, particularly if the capital is sourced from a foreign state-owned enterprise. Short-term portfolio investment in an economy by foreign entities can also affect monetary stability, leading to a need for capital controls. As well, large-scale foreign investment (for instance, in a mine) may create problems such as environmental pollution or disruption of local communities living near the site.[11]

As a result, despite the lesser desire for barriers to entry for foreign investment compared to barriers to trade, most countries do impose such investment barriers in practice, at least to some degree.[12] Most prominently, these barriers often include screening mechanisms, under which authorities review proposals for new (or expanded) foreign investment against specified criteria before deciding whether to admit the proposals. Barriers also include tools such as quotas (capping the number of entities within a given economic sector) or equity limits and joint venture requirements (capping the foreign partner's shareholding at a specified percentage).[13]

Investment treaties—or rather, in practice, investment chapters of preferential trade agreements (PTAs)—have begun including provisions designed to mitigate these investment barriers to entry, thereby encouraging investment liberalisation. These provisions take a variety of forms. The oldest form of such provisions—pioneered by early US treaties on "friendship, commerce and navigation", and appearing most prominently in the North American Free Trade Agreement (NAFTA) in 1992—guarantees national treatment in the pre-establishment phase for foreign investment, subject to a "negative list" of excluded sectors.[14] Some other treaties, by contrast, adopt a "positive list" form, guaranteeing both national treatment (a relative protection) and market access (an absolute protection) for foreign

[10] But see, e.g., *White Industries Australia Ltd v India* (UNCITRAL), Final Award, 30 November 2011, pp. 88–91.

[11] Alschner (2017), p. 379.

[12] Bonnitcha et al. (2017), p. 174.

[13] Drake-Brockman and Messerlin (2018), p. 194.

[14] North American Free Trade Agreement (1992) Articles 1102 and 1108, Annexes I–III. www.sice.oas.org/trade/nafta/naftatce.asp (last accessed 9 September 2021).

investors only in specified sectors. A more recent third form consists of a combination of the two approaches, offering pre-establishment national treatment and market access, but subject to a negative list.[15] Notably, recent EU agreements, including CETA and the EU-Japan agreement, adopt this third form,[16] and (as discussed below) it is likely to be adopted in the AEUFTA as well.

To combat screening requirements, PTA provisions typically take the form of reservations to screen only those investments the value of which falls above a specified monetary threshold. When the threshold specified in the reservation is higher than the previously applicable threshold, a larger number of investments will fall below the threshold, and will not require screening under the host state's regime. The monetary thresholds may vary depending on the economic sector, but investors from treaty partner states will typically receive better treatment (i.e., a higher threshold) in any given sector than investors from non-partner states.

Many economists argue that states should take such liberalising measures (such as reducing screening thresholds, offering pre-establishment national treatment, or guaranteeing market access for foreigners) unilaterally, rather than only in the context of a negotiated treaty with a partner state (or organisation such as the EU).[17] Indeed, an obligation on investment liberalisation in a treaty arguably offers no additional confidence to foreign investors beyond an equivalent obligation assumed unilaterally in national law, since there is nothing at risk for the investor if the state reneges on the obligation (given that no investment has yet been made). The more likely function of a treaty obligation on liberalisation is instead to serve as a broader signalling device, indicating more generally that the host state is a favourable investment destination. Whether this signal is effective, though, depends on whether investors are sophisticated enough to recognise the signal within the often complex provisions of such treaties.[18] Empirical evidence on this remains unclear.[19]

From the state's perspective, however, even if treaty obligations on liberalisation (such as an obligation to grant a higher screening threshold to the treaty partner's investors) do not serve a direct purpose of encouraging investment, they offer the opportunity to serve an indirect purpose in negotiations. Australia (and perhaps most other states too) appears to take the view that its screening thresholds constitute a useful bargaining chip, allowing it to extract concessions on market access and other issues from a negotiating partner in return for a higher investment screening

---

[15] UNCTAD (2002), pp. 16–17; Alschner (2017), p. 380.

[16] Canada-European Union Comprehensive Economic and Trade Agreement (2016) Articles 8.4, 8.6 and 8.15, Annexes I–III; Agreement between the European Union and Japan for an economic partnership (2017) Articles 8.7, 8.8 and 8.12, Annexes 8-B-I and 8-B-II.

[17] Drake-Brockman and Messerlin (2018), p. 15.

[18] Bonnitcha et al. (2017), p. 175.

[19] Bonnitcha et al. (2017), p. 175.

threshold.[20] The success of this approach presumably depends on a gamble that the concessions thereby obtained will be worth more than the cost of refusing to unilaterally grant a higher threshold in any event.

Provisions relevant to investment market access in PTAs also include certain rules relating to trade in services, and general exceptions and security exceptions clauses. On trade in services, PTAs may make commitments, for instance, that no limits will be imposed on the number of service suppliers in a particular sector, or that foreign service suppliers are not required to have a physical presence or to establish in the host state in order to provide services in the state. Given the connections between trade in services and investment, these commitments will benefit foreign investors as well as foreign service suppliers (who may well be indistinguishable).[21]

Exceptions clauses, meanwhile, typically apply to all the obligations in a PTA, including obligations on both trade and investment. Any commitments on investment market access or on investment screening, therefore, may be subject to a general exception for measures taken to protect (for instance) human health, or to protect essential security interests. In March 2020, Australia reduced all of its foreign investment screening thresholds to $0, essentially meaning that all foreign investment entering the country would be screened. This reduction *prima facie* might appear to be inconsistent with Australia's treaty commitments, under which the state guaranteed investors from partner states a certain monetary threshold below which investments would not be screened. However, although not clear from public statements, Australia may be relying on exceptions clauses to justify this *prima facie* inconsistency, maintaining that the enhanced screening measures are necessary to protect the Australian economy against the coronavirus pandemic.[22]

Leaving aside these provisions on services and exceptions, however, this chapter focuses more closely on the AEUFTA provisions on investment market access and on investment screening.[23]

[20] Drake-Brockman and Messerlin (2018), p. 15; Bath (2017), p. 159: "The failure to standardize the thresholds suggests that the government is holding the ability to grant higher screening thresholds in reserve for [future] combined trade and investment negotiations.".

[21] Bonnitcha (2019), p. 641.

[22] The original announcement of the changes does not refer to Australia's treaty obligations: The Hon Josh Frydenberg (2020) Changes to foreign investment framework. ministers.treasury.gov.au/ministers/josh-frydenberg-2018/media-releases/changes-foreign-investment-framework (last accessed 9 September 2021). See also Minter Ellison (2020) COVID 19: new blanket restrictions on foreign investment. www.minterellison.com/articles/covid-19-new-blanket-restrictions-on-foreign-investment (last accessed 9 September 2021): Australia's pandemic response "appears to have the effect of overriding Australia's free trade obligations".

[23] See Charlotte Sieber-Gasser's chapter in this volume for discussion of services in the AEUFTA.

3 The AEUFTA and Investment Barriers to Entry

This section considers the potential value of the AEUFTA on questions of investment market access and screening, before turning to discuss the treaty's likely content based on public information available to date.

3.1 *Potential Value of the AEUFTA*

The AEUFTA's provisions on investment market access and screening could potentially increase investment flows between the two treaty parties, arguably bringing the benefits outlined in Sect. 2. Indeed, observers of both Australia and the EU have highlighted a perceived need for foreign investment in many sectors.

In various reports including specific submissions to Australia's AEUFTA consultation process, responders have contended for the benefits of increased foreign investment in Australia in the agriculture, mining, film and television, research and development, video games and alcohol sectors.[24] In agriculture, for instance, responders emphasised that Australian capital was not likely to be sufficient to meet the sector's needs over the next few decades, if Australian agricultural producers wished to access lucrative markets particularly in Asia.[25] In mining, the Minerals Council of Australia pointed to the benefits of foreign investment for access to new technology and infrastructure development, and suggested that EU investment in Australia would assist the EU to meet its "critical minerals strategy" by securing supply.[26] Meanwhile, in video games, industry submissions suggested that "Australian game developers are attractive partners to European studios for investments, collaborative projects, joint ventures and "work for hire" arrangements, given

[24]The submissions are available at www.dfat.gov.au/trade/agreements/negotiations/aeufta/submissions/aeufta-submissions (last accessed 9 September 2021).

[25]ANZ (2012) Greener pastures: the global soft commodity opportunity for Australia and New Zealand. media.corporate-ir.net/media_files/IROL/24/248677/ANZ_insight_3_Greener_Pastures.pdf (last accessed 9 September 2021) pp. 1–4. See also Voice of Horticulture (2016) Submission. www.pc.gov.au/__data/assets/pdf_file/0008/195974/sub042-agriculture.pdf (last accessed 9 September 2021); Australian Food & Grocery Council (2016) AFGC Submission. www.dfat.gov.au/sites/default/files/australian-food-and-grocery-council-eufta-submission.PDF (last accessed 9 September 2021) pp. 6–7.

[26]Minerals Council of Australia (2019) Australia-EU FTA: implications for Australia's mining industry. www.dfat.gov.au/sites/default/files/minerals-council-of-australia-eufta-submission.pdf (last accessed 9 September 2021) pp. 3–4. See also the EU's view on securing access to raw materials: European Commission (2015) Trade for all: towards a more responsible trade and investment policy. trade.ec.europa.eu/doclib/docs/2015/october/tradoc_153846.pdf (last accessed 9 September 2021) p. 14.

our talent and creativity and also Australia's advantageous time zone".[27] Conversely, the EU has its own needs for foreign investment. In the infrastructure sector, for instance, the European Investment Bank (EIB) estimates that economic infrastructure investment needs for energy, transport, water and sanitation, and telecoms are as much as €688 billion per year.[28]

In addressing these investment needs, the value of any AEUFTA provisions on investment screening and market access must, of course, be assessed against the current situation for investment flows between the parties. Sections 3.1.1 and 3.1.2 review the existing (potential) barriers to entry for foreign investment in Australia and the EU.

3.1.1 The Australian Screening Regime

For several decades, Australia has operated a foreign investment screening regime through its Foreign Investment Review Board (FIRB). Evolving over time,[29] the regime is complex and detailed, with specific rules depending on the size of the investment, the target economic sector of the investment, the country of origin of the foreign investor, the nature of the foreign investor (government-owned or private), and the type of asset being acquired. The regime essentially constructs a series of monetary thresholds for foreign investment, with the thresholds differing according to the factors just listed. Any proposed investment above the threshold must undergo a screening process at FIRB, which assesses applications case-by-case according to a "national interest" test. FIRB itself has no formal decision-making power; ultimate decisions on admission of investment are made by the Australian Treasurer on the advice of FIRB. The Treasurer has the power to accept or reject investments applications after screening, or to impose conditions on admission. The Treasurer also has the power to impose penalties for failure to obtain approval prior to proceeding with an investment; these penalties can be monetary or can entail divestiture orders.[30]

As an example of the regime's operation, foreign investments in Australian businesses require prior approval where the foreign investor is acquiring (or following the acquisition will hold) a stake of 20% of more in a business valued

---

[27]Interactive Games & Entertainment Association (2019) Submission. www.dfat.gov.au/sites/default/files/interactive-games-and-entertainment-association-eufta-submission.pdf (last accessed 9 September 2021) p. 4.

[28]European Parliamentary Research Service (2018) Investment in infrastructure in the EU: gaps, challenges and opportunities. www.iberglobal.com/files/2018-2/infrastructure_eu.pdf (last accessed 9 September 2021) p. 1.

[29]See Kawharu and Nottage (2017), p. 481 for an outline of the history of Australia's screening regime.

[30]For an overview, see Australian Government, Foreign Investment Review Board (2020) Guidance 1. firb.gov.au/sites/firb.gov.au/files/guidance-notes/G01-Overview.pdf (last accessed 9 September 2021).

at higher than a certain monetary threshold. In general, as of 2021, the threshold is A $281 million.[31] For investors from certain countries with which Australia has free trade agreements (currently Chile, China, Hong Kong, Japan, Korea, New Zealand, Peru, Singapore, the United States, and CPTPP countries), the threshold is A$1216 million. However, the threshold for these investors is also A$281 million if the acquisition is in a "sensitive industry", such as telecommunications, transport, defence, encryption, and nuclear including uranium or plutonium mining.[32]

A threshold of A$0 applies to all foreign *government* investors (including corporations in which a foreign government holds at least a 20% stake) from any country.[33] Such investors must always apply for approval where they are acquiring a "direct interest" (in general, either a stake of more than 10% or a de facto controlling stake)[34] in an Australian business.

If the foreign investor is proposing to acquire agricultural land, however, different thresholds apply. FIRB approval will be required where the acquisition would bring the cumulative total of the foreign person's agricultural land holdings in Australia to more than A$15 million. Again, a different threshold applies for foreign investors from certain countries with which Australia has free trade agreements. For instance, the threshold for Thai investors is A$50 million, while for investors from Chile, New Zealand and the United States, the threshold is A$1216 million.[35] Again, a threshold of A$0 applies to all foreign *government* investors.

Other thresholds and rules apply for acquisitions of residential land, commercial land, mining land, agribusinesses and media businesses.

When prior approval is required in the circumstances outlined above, the basic criterion against which a decision will be made is whether the foreign acquisition is contrary to the *national interest*. This concept is not defined in legislation. Instead, the Treasurer assesses the national interest of each application on a case-by-case basis. A broad range of factors typically affect this decision. These include:[36]

(1) whether the investment affects national security issues, based on advice from Australia's national security agencies;

[31] Australian Government, Foreign Investment Review Board (2020) Guidance 7. firb.gov.au/sites/firb.gov.au/files/guidance-notes/G07-Business.pdf (last accessed 9 September 2021).

[32] Australian Government, Foreign Investment Review Board (2020) Guidance 7. firb.gov.au/sites/firb.gov.au/files/guidance-notes/G07-Business.pdf (last accessed 9 September 2021).

[33] Australian Government, Foreign Investment Review Board (2020) Guidance 7. firb.gov.au/sites/firb.gov.au/files/guidance-notes/G07-Business.pdf (last accessed 9 September 2021).

[34] Australian Government, Foreign Investment Review Board (2020) Guidance 2. firb.gov.au/sites/firb.gov.au/files/guidance-notes/G02-Key_concepts.pdf (last accessed 9 September 2021) p. 16.

[35] Australian Government, Foreign Investment Review Board (2020) Guidance 3. firb.gov.au/sites/firb.gov.au/files/guidance-notes/G03-Agriculture.pdf (last accessed 9 September 2021). These two thresholds are *not* cumulative.

[36] Australian Government, Treasurer (2019) Australia's Foreign Investment Policy. cdn.tspace.gov.au/uploads/sites/82/2018/12/1-January-2019-Policy_.pdf (last accessed 9 September 2021).

(2) competition issues, such as whether a proposed investment may result in an investor gaining control over market pricing and production of a good or service in Australia;
(3) the impact of a foreign investment proposal on Australian tax revenues;
(4) the impact of the investment on the general economy, including the level of Australian participation in the relevant business following the foreign investment;
(5) the extent to which the investor operates on a transparent commercial basis and is subject to adequate and transparent regulation and supervision in their home state; and
(6) the corporate governance practices of foreign investors.

Higher degrees of scrutiny will be imposed on foreign government investors, larger investments, investments in sensitive businesses, and investments in agricultural land.

On top of all of these rules, since 1 January 2021, Australia has applied a new national security test. Since national security is already one factor considered in the national interest test discussed above, the new national security test applies only where the proposed investment would not otherwise be screened under the normal process. The new test is triggered when a foreign investment is proposed in certain newly-defined categories of "national security land" or "national security businesses". If the proposed investment falls within these categories, it must be screened regardless of whether it passes the applicable threshold discussed above. A wide range of sectors could be captured under these national security tests, including healthcare, education, telecommunications and data centres, transport, utilities, and even commercial real estate.[37]

Since 2015, applicants to FIRB must pay fees to have their investment application screened. The fees are calculated on a sliding scale depending on the value of the investment, rising to a maximum of A$500,000 (for an acquisition of an Australian business worth more than A$2 billion).[38]

As briefly described here, Australia's foreign investment screening regime thus appears to be quite onerous, comprising complex rules, application fees, broad discretionary review powers, and penalties including divestment orders. Commentators have criticised Australia's national interest test on the grounds that it is too vague and uncertain, and that it should be restricted solely to matters of defence and national security rather than other economic or governance factors.[39] Others have expressed concern that treating state-owned enterprises as foreign government investors, which are subject to greater scrutiny under Australia's regime, effectively discriminates against Chinese enterprises. As well, in 2016–17 for example,

---

[37] Australian Government, Foreign Investment Review Board (2020) Guidance 8. firb.gov.au/sites/firb.gov.au/files/guidance-notes/G08-National_Security.pdf (last accessed 9 September 2021).

[38] Australian Government, Foreign Investment Review Board (2020) Guidance 10. firb.gov.au/sites/firb.gov.au/files/guidance-notes/G10-Fees.pdf (last accessed 9 September 2021).

[39] A review of these criticisms and responses is contained in Bath (2012), pp. 16–19.

conditions were imposed on foreign investments in 40% of applications subject to screening.[40]

Nevertheless, supporters of the scheme observe that outright rejections are extremely rare in practice. Of 14,360 decided applications in 2016–17, only three applications were rejected; two of those applications related to the same project (a proposed 99-year lease of 50.4% of the electricity distribution network covering eastern Sydney).[41] In 2014–15, all of the 37,953 applications decided by the Treasurer were accepted.[42] (However, it is possible that some applications are never submitted because, after informal discussions with the government, the applicant feels that the application is unlikely to succeed.[43] Thus, the "rejection" rate in practice may be higher.) Supporters also argue that the case-by-case review approach provides flexibility, and that the regime has not deterred foreign investment into Australia. Other supporters contend that it is legitimate to consider competition concerns as part of the national interest test, since these concerns are potentially tied to strategic interests and national security.[44]

3.1.2 The EU Screening Regime(s)

EU states generally do not impose requirements such as foreign equity limitations or joint venture obligations for foreign investors.[45] Instead, the major formal impediment to foreign investment in EU member states consists of the screening mechanisms implemented by many EU states. As of January 2021, 16 EU member states,

---

[40] Australian Government, Foreign Investment Review Board (2018) Annual Report 2016–17. firb.gov.au/sites/firb.gov.au/files/2018/05/FIRB-16-17-Annual-Report.pdf (last accessed 9 September 2021) p. 22.

[41] These two rejected applications were filed by the final two bidders in the tender process, a Chinese state-owned enterprise and a publicly-listed Hong Kong company. The lease was later granted to two Australian companies. See Australian Government, Foreign Investment Review Board (2018) Annual Report 2016–17. firb.gov.au/sites/firb.gov.au/files/2018/05/FIRB-16-17-Annual-Report.pdf (last accessed 9 September 2021) p. 23.

[42] Australian Government, Foreign Investment Review Board (2018) Annual Report 2016–17. firb.gov.au/sites/firb.gov.au/files/2018/05/FIRB-16-17-Annual-Report.pdf (last accessed 9 September 2021) p. 23.

[43] See Kawharu and Nottage (2017), p. 487 for one possible example, in which a Chinese firm withdrew an application in 2016 after being asked to revise the application on very short deadlines.

[44] Bath (2012), p. 17.

[45] However, EU member states do maintain many specific restrictions affecting foreign investment. For instance, foreign (non-EU) purchasers of real estate in Austria require authorization from provincial authorities, which can be refused if the purchase is not in the public interest. See, e.g., Agreement between the European Union and Japan for an economic partnership (2017) Annex 8-B-I. trade.ec.europa.eu/doclib/docs/2018/august/tradoc_157232.pdf#page=11 (last accessed 9 September 2021) p. 20.

including the major economies of Germany, France, Italy and Spain, operate some form of investment screening.[46]

At present, member state screening regimes differ considerably, with some state regimes imposing quite minimal controls on the entry of foreign investment. As well, the remaining 11 EU member states, including Sweden, Czechia, Estonia and others, currently do not operate screening regimes at all. However, in 2019, the European Union introduced a new Screening Regulation (EU) 2019/452,[47] which took effect from 11 October 2020. The Regulation does not explicitly require harmonisation of member state screening regimes. Instead, it "establishes a framework for the screening by Member States of foreign direct investments into the Union on the grounds of security or public order and for a mechanism for cooperation between Member States, and between Member States and the Commission, with regard to foreign direct investments likely to affect security or public order". Thus, the intention is to set minimum standards for screening mechanisms in states that choose to adopt such mechanisms. Article 3 of the Regulation states that the "Member States may maintain, amend or adopt mechanisms to screen foreign direct investments in their territory on the grounds of security or public order". As a result, the general competence and responsibility for investment screening remains with EU member states, which may decide whether or not to establish or maintain a national system for scrutinising foreign investments. Indeed, it is arguable that the wording of the provision also implies an option to abolish existing national screening mechanisms.

In Article 4, the Regulation suggests factors that member states may consider when determining whether a foreign investment is likely to affect security or public order. These factors include the investment's effects on "critical infrastructure, whether physical or virtual, including energy, transport, water, health, communications, media, data processing or storage, aerospace, defence, electoral or financial infrastructure, and sensitive facilities, as well as land and real estate crucial for the use of such infrastructure", "critical technologies and dual use items" and "access to sensitive information, including personal data, or the ability to control such information". Furthermore, Article 4(2) states that the screening authorities may also take into account "whether the foreign investor is directly or indirectly controlled by the government, including state bodies or armed forces, of a third country, including through ownership structure or significant funding". The Regulation also establishes systems for cooperation and information sharing between member states and the European Commission, for instance permitting the Commission to submit an

[46] European Commission (2021) List of screening mechanisms notified by member states. trade.ec.europa.eu/doclib/docs/2019/june/tradoc_157946.pdf (last accessed 9 September 2021).

[47] Regulation (EU) 2019/452 of the European Parliament and of the Council of 19 March 2019 establishing a framework for the screening of foreign direct investments into the Union, OJ L 79I of 21.3.2019, p. 1.

opinion to member state authorities on whether a particular investment should be admitted or not.[48]

Despite the lack of any binding obligation on member states to harmonise their screening regimes with the Regulation (or even to maintain a screening regime at all), the Regulation seems likely to have a harmonising effect.[49] Indeed, following the Regulation's entry into force, EU members without screening mechanisms are beginning to implement them, in reliance on the Regulation's minimum standards.

Czechia, for instance, plans to introduce a mechanism to screen non-EU investments that could compromise national security or public order.[50] Screening would be subject to a threshold of an effective level of control of the target, such as acquiring at least 10% of the voting rights. While an investment in any sector could be subject to screening, investments in certain sectors (including defence, military, critical infrastructure, cybersecurity and others) would be automatically deemed to implicate security and public order concerns. The envisaged outcomes of screening could include rejection of the investment or imposition of conditions, with monetary penalties and divestment orders available for breaches. Similarly, Estonia is also reportedly developing a new screening regime on the basis of the EU Regulation.[51]

Furthermore, other EU states such as Austria and France have amended their existing regimes in order to bring them closer to the EU Regulation.[52] Austria's new regime, in force since July 2020, applies to foreign investment in specified sectors, and is triggered by an acquisition either of control of an Austrian company or of a specified shareholding percentage of the company, or by an acquisition of the

[48] Regulation (EU) 2019/452, Article 6.

[49] This is not least due to the principle of sincere cooperation in EU law under Article 4(3) TEU, which requires EU member states to, "in full mutual respect, assist each other in carrying out tasks which flow from the Treaties". Arguably, a decision to abolish an existing screening regime, or even a decision to maintain a significantly different screening regime compared to other member states, could amount to a deliberate undermining of the EU framework, in potential violation of this principle.

[50] Van Bael & Bellis (2020) Czech Republic. www.vbb.com/insights/FDI/Czech-Republic (last accessed 9 September 2021); Lexology (2020) Czech authorities to screen future foreign investments. www.lexology.com/library/detail.aspx?g=f85a19ab-e38f-4485-bf54-97e069e9f406 (last accessed 9 September 2021).

[51] United States Department of State (2020) 2020 Investment climate statements: Estonia. www.state.gov/reports/2020-investment-climate-statements/estonia/#report-toc__section-1 (last accessed 9 September 2021); Estonian Wind Power Association (2020) State to start screening impact of foreign investments on Estonia's economic security. www.tuuleenergia.ee/en/2020/06/state-to-start-screening-impact-of-foreign-investments-on-estonias-economic-security/ (last accessed 9 September 2021).

[52] On France, see French Treasury, Monetary and Financial Code. trade.ec.europa.eu/doclib/docs/2020/march/tradoc_158692.pdf (last accessed 9 September 2021); Jones Day (2020) French foreign direct investment rules set for overhaul. www.jonesday.com/en/insights/2020/01/french-fdi-rules-set-for-overhaul (last accessed 9 September 2021).

essential assets of the company.[53] For certain highly sensitive sectors specified in the new Austrian law, which include defence equipment, critical infrastructure, water, pharmaceuticals, vaccines and others, the specified shareholding percentage is 10%, meaning that an acquisition of more than 10% of the voting rights of a company in these sectors will be subject to screening.[54] Higher thresholds apply for investments in other sensitive sectors, including media, food supply, telecommunications, and traffic and transport.[55] Exceptions exist for foreign investments in businesses with fewer than 10 employees and an annual turnover of less than €2 million.[56] Nevertheless, the list of specified sectors is quite broad, and some observers worry that "the new approval regime (potentially) introduces a lot of red tape to FDI transactions in Austria".[57] The degree to which the new regime actually discourages Australian (or other foreign) investment in Austria may depend on the degree of scrutiny applied by Austrian authorities in applying the central test of a "threat to security or public order".[58]

3.1.3 Potential Benefits of the AEUFTA: Investment Screening

The AEUFTA offers the potential for reduction in the barrier to entry arguably posed by investment screening regimes. Potential mitigating measures for screening regimes would most obviously include raised screening thresholds and limited negative lists of sectors for which the possibility of screening is preserved. To the extent that the treaty might remove or reduce screening requirements for investment between Australia and the EU, it could contribute to investment liberalisation and increase investment flows, bringing the potential benefits outlined in Sect. 2.

Indeed, there is a degree of support amongst AEUFTA observers for a reduction in screening burdens, particularly on the Australian side (given the relatively newer and historically less burdensome EU screening regimes). Most notably, business groups have urged Australia to raise its screening thresholds for EU investors.[59] The

[53] Republic of Austria (2020) Investment Control Act. trade.ec.europa.eu/doclib/docs/2020/september/tradoc_158955.pdf (last accessed 9 September 2021).

[54] Republic of Austria (2020) Investment Control Act. trade.ec.europa.eu/doclib/docs/2020/september/tradoc_158955.pdf (last accessed 9 September 2021) Annex, Part 1.

[55] Republic of Austria (2020) Investment Control Act. trade.ec.europa.eu/doclib/docs/2020/september/tradoc_158955.pdf (last accessed 9 September 2021) Annex, Part 2.

[56] Republic of Austria (2020) Investment Control Act. trade.ec.europa.eu/doclib/docs/2020/september/tradoc_158955.pdf (last accessed 9 September 2021) Section 2(2).

[57] Lexology (2020) The new Austrian Investment Control Act – increased supervision of foreign direct investments in Austria. www.lexology.com/library/detail.aspx?g=5bd38104-1dfb-437c-9525-20f1a2611730 (last accessed 9 September 2021).

[58] Republic of Austria (2020) Investment Control Act. trade.ec.europa.eu/doclib/docs/2020/september/tradoc_158955.pdf (last accessed 9 September 2021) Section 3.

[59] Business Council of Australia (2018) Submission. www.dfat.gov.au/sites/default/files/business-council-of-australia-eufta-submission.pdf (last accessed 9 September 2021) p. 3;

Business Council of Australia, for instance, contends that higher thresholds for EU investors would encourage greater diversity of investment sources in Australia, thereby reducing the risks of reliance on a small number of source countries for foreign investment.[60] Others have noted that EU companies face higher screening thresholds in Australia compared to companies from Australia's other PTA partners, pointing to the relative disadvantage that this entails for EU companies.[61]

Nevertheless, these views depend on whether screening regimes do in fact discourage foreign investment. If investors are not significantly deterred by screening requirements, any efforts of the AEUFTA to reduce these requirements may provide little benefit.

In public consultations, both Australian and European business interests have asserted that Australia's screening regime, or at least the reduction of screening thresholds, deters foreign investment.[62] The Australian Productivity Commission has suggested that lower screening thresholds increases the "cost and complexity" of investing in Australia, which "ultimately risks deterring foreign investment".[63] Similarly, the Australian Lot Feeders' Association asserts that "[d]ecreasing the threshold . . . has potentially deterred a significant proportion of [foreign] buyers".[64] Outside the specific AEUFTA context, the World Bank has also maintained that, "[f]rom the investor's perspective, screening adds to their investment costs in the form of time delays, onerous compliance requirements, and what are generally described as 'hassle costs'. When an investment agency is also a screener/decisionmaker, the hassle cost can include the costs of rent-seeking behavior by corrupt agency officials."[65]

German-Australian Chamber of Industry and Commerce (2018) Updated submission regarding negotiations on an Australia-European Union free trade agreement. www.dfat.gov.au/sites/default/files/german-australian-chamber-of-industry-and-commerce-eufta-submission.PDF (last accessed 9 September 2021) pp. 3–4; ANZ (2016) Australia-European Union free trade agreement. www.dfat.gov.au/sites/default/files/anz-eufta-submission.PDF (last accessed 9 September 2021) p. 3.

[60] Business Council of Australia (2018) Submission. www.dfat.gov.au/sites/default/files/business-council-of-australia-eufta-submission.pdf (last accessed 9 September 2021) p. 11.

[61] European Commission (2017) Impact assessment. eur-lex.europa.eu/legal-content/EN/ALL/?uri=CELEX:52017SC0289 (last accessed 9 September 2021) p. 10.

[62] European Commission (2017) Impact assessment. eur-lex.europa.eu/legal-content/EN/ALL/?uri=CELEX:52017SC0289 (last accessed 9 September 2021) p. 61; Australian Government, Productivity Commission (2016) Regulation of Australian agriculture. www.pc.gov.au/inquiries/completed/agriculture/report/agriculture.pdf (last accessed 9 September 2021) pp. 527, 545, 546.

[63] Australian Government, Productivity Commission (2016) Regulation of Australian agriculture. www.pc.gov.au/inquiries/completed/agriculture/report/agriculture.pdf (last accessed 9 September 2021) p. 33.

[64] Australian Government, Productivity Commission (2016) Regulation of Australian agriculture. www.pc.gov.au/inquiries/completed/agriculture/report/agriculture.pdf (last accessed 9 September 2021) p. 546.

[65] World Bank (2010) Investment law reform: a handbook for development practitioners. openknowledge.worldbank.org/bitstream/handle/10986/25206/911740WP0Box3800Law0Reform0Handbook.pdf?sequence=1&isAllowed=y (last accessed 9 September 2021) pp. 32–33.

Such views do not purport to rely on concrete evidence of, for instance, a specific foreign investor deciding not to invest due to screening requirements, or a more general quantifiable drop in investment clearly attributable to the imposition or increase of screening requirements. However, in a 2019 OECD study of 60 countries, screening regimes were found to constitute the second most "effective" means of discouraging foreign investment, after direct restrictions on foreign equity participation.[66] The study authors suggest that this is because "conditions imposed [in screening regimes] can be arbitrary, inconsistent and lack in transparency", and that screening "can have a potentially dissuasive impact on FDI through the signal it sends, the projects rejected or reconfigured and the administrative burden and uncertainty it imposes on potential investors".[67]

Despite this, the OECD study acknowledges the variation in national screening regimes, making it "difficult to effectively grasp their importance in an indicator objectively".[68] Commenting on the study, Australia's Productivity Commission also warns that it "measures statutory restrictions and not how the measures are enforced", and "generally does not distinguish between positive and negative tests, nor the criteria used to assess whether investments can proceed".[69]

By contrast, the Australian government itself has suggested that there is "no evidence suggesting that the lower thresholds have deterred investment".[70] As noted above, the overwhelming majority of applications to Australia's FIRB have been approved to date, and investment flows into Australia have increased in recent decades.[71] Similarly, a report by the European Parliamentary Research Service found no correlation between investment flows into EU member states and whether the member state operated a screening regime. According to the report, "the presence or absence of an FDI screening mechanism does not seem to be a decisive factor [in foreign investment decision-making], notably if it operates under predictable

[66] Mistura F and Roulet C (2019) The determinants of foreign direct investment: do statutory restrictions matter?. OECD Working Papers on International Investment 2019/01, www-oecd%2D%2Dilibrary-org.eu1.proxy.openathens.net/finance-and-investment/the-determinants-of-foreign-direct-investment_641507ce-en (last accessed 9 September 2021) p. 38.

[67] Mistura F and Roulet C (2019) The determinants of foreign direct investment: do statutory restrictions matter?. OECD Working Papers on International Investment 2019/01, www-oecd%2D%2Dilibrary-org.eu1.proxy.openathens.net/finance-and-investment/the-determinants-of-foreign-direct-investment_641507ce-en (last accessed 9 September 2021) p. 15.

[68] Mistura F and Roulet C (2019) The determinants of foreign direct investment: do statutory restrictions matter?. OECD Working Papers on International Investment 2019/01, www-oecd%2D%2Dilibrary-org.eu1.proxy.openathens.net/finance-and-investment/the-determinants-of-foreign-direct-investment_641507ce-en (last accessed 9 September 2021) p. 15.

[69] Australian Government, Productivity Commission (2020) Foreign investment in Australia. www.pc.gov.au/research/completed/foreign-investment/foreign-investment.pdf p. 96.

[70] Australian Government (2019) Productivity Commission inquiry into the regulation of Australian agriculture: Australian government response. www.awe.gov.au/sites/default/files/2020-01/aus-govt-response-regulation-agriculture.pdf (last accessed 9 September 2021) p. 19.

[71] Australian Government, Productivity Commission (2020) Foreign investment in Australia. www.pc.gov.au/research/completed/foreign-investment/foreign-investment.pdf pp. 5–6.

conditions and the rule of law and is not extensively time-consuming".[72] A 2002 World Trade Organisation report noted a similar view, commenting that "a properly administered screening mechanism which provides for an expeditious assessment of an investment proposal on the basis of transparent criteria is not a hindrance to investment flows. On the contrary, it can provide an element of predictability in a host country's administration of the entry of foreign investment".[73]

The evidence on whether screening deters investment thus appears to remain somewhat mixed, with no "one-size-fits-all" answer. As a result, it is unclear whether the AEUFTA can offer any benefit in relation to investment screening. To the extent that clarity and transparency of screening regimes is central to avoiding deterrence of foreign investment, these factors are unlikely to be addressed in AEUFTA itself. Instead, it will fall to domestic law in Australia and EU member states to determine the kind of screening regime that operates, and the degree of transparency (for instance, on timelines, reason-giving and appeals) that it displays.

3.1.4 Potential Benefits of the AEUFTA: Other Barriers to Entry

The AEUFTA might also offer benefits by minimising other barriers to entry for foreign investment, apart from screening regimes.

Some respondents to the EU's 2016 public consultations on impact assessment of the AEUFTA complained about specific barriers to investment imposed by Australia. In particular, respondents highlighted the equity cap in the telecommunications and airlines sectors, and sectoral restrictions in postal delivery, distribution services, professional services (such as legal and accounting) financial services, gambling, aviation and maritime transport.[74] Indeed, Australia has had long-standing restrictions on foreign investment in specific industries. For instance, aggregate foreign ownership of the former state monopoly telecommunications provider, Telstra, is limited to 35%, while individual foreign shareholdings are limited to 5%.[75] Similarly, aggregate foreign ownership in an Australian airline (including the national airline Qantas) is limited to 49%, with any one foreign shareholding capped at 35%.[76] However, the EU's impact assessment modelling

[72] European Parliamentary Research Service (2018) EU framework for FDI screening. www.europarl.europa.eu/EPRS/EPRS-Briefing-614667-EU-framework-FDI-screening-FINAL.pdf (last accessed 9 September 2021) p. 3.

[73] World Trade Organization (2002) Modalities for pre-establishment commitments based on a GATS-type, positive list approach. docs.wto.org/dol2fe/Pages/FE_Search/FE_S_S009-DP.aspx?language=E&CatalogueIdList=103291,68566,66075,57538,47692&CurrentCatalogueIdIndex=4 (last accessed 9 September 2021) para. 10.

[74] European Commission (2017) Impact assessment. eur-lex.europa.eu/legal-content/EN/ALL/?uri=CELEX:52017SC0289 (last accessed 9 September 2021) p. 61.

[75] Telstra Corporation Act 1991 (Cth).

[76] Qantas Sale Act 1992 (Cth).

did not assess the economic impacts of investment liberalisation in these areas, because of the "difficulty in quantifying these impacts".[77]

Conversely, Australian scholars have contended that removal of EU barriers to private investment in research and development—including "complex and expensive" systems for protection of intellectual property compared to Australia, rules on movement of researchers, and commitments against forced technology transfer—would enhance Australian foreign investment in the EU.[78]

In theory, the AEUFTA could address these barriers by (for example) offering commitments to raise the Australian equity cap on airlines for EU investors, or by simplifying EU intellectual property rules. Nevertheless, whether any particular such barrier (such as the prohibition on majority foreign ownership of Qantas) should be removed for EU investors would require a detailed, multi-faceted assessment beyond the scope of this contribution, drawing widely on economic, strategic, social and cultural factors amongst others.

3.2 Likely Content of the AEUFTA

Section 3.1 above offered an assessment of the potential for the AEUFTA to contribute to investment liberalisation and greater investment flows, compared to the current situation. This Sect. 3.2 proceeds to consider whether the AEUFTA is likely to implement any of the possible commitments or measures identified in the previous section.

In relation to market access, one indication of the likely outlines of the final AEUFTA text is provided by a proposal tabled by the EU in October 2018 for discussion with Australia.[79] Chapter II of the proposal, entitled "Investment Liberalisation", contains several guarantees relevant to market access for foreign investors. Most notably, Article 2.3 offers a commitment to national treatment on establishment and operation of investment, thus adopting the liberalisation model pioneered for investment treaties by NAFTA. On its face, this provision would require Australia to admit EU investments (and vice versa) on the same terms as domestic investors—i.e., without screening. Article 2.4 offers a commitment to most-favoured-nation treatment for operation of investment, but states only that the EU "reserves the right to propose a text on most favoured nation treatment for establishment". Article 2.2, meanwhile, offers a commitment not to impose investment barriers including limitations on the number of enterprises in a sector,

---

[77] European Commission (2017) Impact assessment. eur-lex.europa.eu/legal-content/EN/ALL/?uri=CELEX:52017SC0289 (last accessed 9 September 2021) p. 20.

[78] Drake-Brockman and Messerlin (2018), pp. 201–202.

[79] European Union (2018) Investment liberalization and trade in services. trade.ec.europa.eu/doclib/docs/2018/december/tradoc_157572.pdf (last accessed 9 September 2021).

restrictions on the type of entity that foreign investors may employ for economic activity, and equity limits on foreign shareholdings.

However, all of these proposed commitments (as well as proposed commitments in Articles 2.5 and 2.6 on the nationality of senior management[80] and the non-imposition of performance requirements as a condition of establishment) are subject to Article 2.7. That clause provides exemptions for existing non-conforming measures to be listed in an Annex I, and for reservations to be listed in an Annex II. In the parties' other recent trade and investment agreements, similar Annexes are designed such that various sectors are reserved entirely from the pre-establishment commitments. In the 2014 Japan-Australia agreement, for example, Australia's Schedule to Annex 7 reserves the right to adopt or maintain any measure with respect to primary school education that does not conform to commitments on market access or national treatment.[81]

In relation to screening specifically, such Annexes (in the parties' other trade agreements) have also been designed to preserve the legality of pre-establishment screening regimes, but to implement higher screening thresholds for treaty partners compared to other states. Thus, when listing non-conforming measures to permit measures on pre-establishment screening, the Japan-Australia agreement reserves Australia's right to screen Japanese proposals to invest in Australian businesses worth more than A$1074 million.[82] By contrast, the Indonesia-Australia agreement reserves Australia's right to screen Indonesian proposals to invest in Australian businesses worth more than A$266 million.[83] While the EU's proposal offers a commitment on rights of review of screening decisions on investment establishment (in Article 5.2.3), this is subject to a carve-out in Article 5.1.2 for measures exempted under the Annexes.

Thus, it might be expected that similar exemptions and reservations will be included in negotiated Annexes to the EU proposals on investment liberalisation. Indeed, public reports on the negotiating rounds indicate that market access has been a central focus of some rounds. In September 2020, Australia reported that "[n]egotiators sought to improve on the already ambitious respective initial services and investment market access offers of each Party", and that "Australia

[80] This proposal matches an objective sought by Australia, suggesting that agreement will be reached relatively easily on this point. See Australian Government, Department of Foreign Affairs and Trade. Summary of negotiating aims and approach. www.dfat.gov.au/trade/agreements/negotiations/aeufta/Pages/summary-of-negotiating-aims-and-approach (last accessed 9 September 2021): "We will also seek an undertaking from the EU not to impose residency and/or citizenship requirements on senior representatives of Australian companies established in the EU".

[81] Japan-Australia Economic Partnership Agreement (2014) Annex 6. www.dfat.gov.au/sites/default/files/jaepa-annex-6.pdf (last accessed 9 September 2021) Part 1, section 2, paragraph 13.

[82] Japan-Australia Economic Partnership Agreement (2014) Annex 6. www.dfat.gov.au/sites/default/files/jaepa-annex-6.pdf (last accessed 9 September 2021) Part 1, section 2, paragraph 1(c). This figure is subject to indexing each year, meaning that it is now higher than A$1074 million.

[83] Indonesia-Australia Comprehensive Economic Partnership Agreement (2019) Annex I. www.dfat.gov.au/sites/default/files/iacepa-annex-i-schedule-of-australia.pdf (last accessed 9 September 2021) Schedule of Australia, section 1, paragraph A(a). This figure is also subject to indexing.

focused on our core commercial interests in pursuit of ambitious services and investment market access outcomes for Australian service suppliers and investors".[84] In October 2020, the EU reported that "[t]he main focus of this round was on market access, where both sides continued to respond to queries regarding each other's offers that were exchanged in an earlier round and to indicate additional market access priorities" and that "[t]here was steady progress in agreeing the services and investment liberalisation texts".[85] Although not specified, it might be assumed that these discussions focused on the detail of the exemptions and reservations in the negative list Annexes.

As discussed above, Australia maintains long-standing restrictions on foreign investment in specific industries, including airlines, airports and telecommunications. Australia's recent PTAs have included provisions to take account of this,[86] framed as reservations for existing measures that do not conform to the obligation of national treatment. It is likely that the AEUFTA will replicate these provisions. Nevertheless, in less sensitive areas (perhaps on foreign provision of legal services), there is likely to be scope for negotiated preferential access for EU investors. EU member states similarly maintain a range of existing non-conforming measures (such as Austria's requirement for provincial approval of foreign purchases of real estate) which they have reserved in other recent EU agreements.[87] Some of these measures might be subject to relaxation for Australian investors, in return for Australian concessions. Agriculture, however, is likely to be one point of disagreement, given long-standing restrictions and sensitivities in that sector in the EU.[88] The precise extent of the exemptions and reservations eventually included in the AEUFTA will indicate whether the treaty has achieved its objectives on investment market access.

One risk inherent in the negative list approach is naturally that any exemptions or reservations not included in the negative list will reduce the treaty parties' capacity to introduce new restrictions later.[89] In the context of North-South agreements, scholars have observed that the developed state often produces a longer negative list in their

---

[84] Australian Government, Department of Foreign Affairs and Trade (2020) Report on negotiating round eight. www.dfat.gov.au/trade/agreements/negotiations/aeufta/news/australia-eu-fta-report-negotiating-round-eight-14-25-september-2020 (last accessed 9 September 2021).

[85] European Commission (2020) Report of the 8th round of negotiations. trade.ec.europa.eu/doclib/docs/2020/october/tradoc_158976.pdf (last accessed 9 September 2021) p. 2.

[86] See, e.g., Japan-Australia Economic Partnership Agreement (2014) Annex 6. www.dfat.gov.au/sites/default/files/jaepa-annex-6.pdf (last accessed 9 September 2021).

[87] See, e.g., Agreement between the European Union and Japan for an economic partnership (2017) Annex 8-B-I. trade.ec.europa.eu/doclib/docs/2018/august/tradoc_157232.pdf#page=11 (last accessed 9 September 2021).

[88] Australian Government, Department of Foreign Affairs and Trade (2020) Market insights. www.dfat.gov.au/sites/default/files/european-union-market-insights-2021.pdf (last accessed 9 September 2021); European Commission (2018) EU-Australia trade agreement: launching trade negotiations with Australia. trade.ec.europa.eu/doclib/docs/2018/june/tradoc_156941.pdf (last accessed 9 September 2021).

[89] Kawharu and Nottage (2017), p. 479.

schedule compared to the developing state, illustrating the developed state's greater capacity to ensure flexibility for future policy changes.[90] Nevertheless, Bath has labelled Australia's treaties "arguably too prescriptive", pointing to difficulties experienced by Australia in introducing new screening requirements (in relation to sales of critical infrastructure assets to private investors) following changes in perceived risks.[91] This suggests that even developed states like the AEUFTA parties have sometimes overlooked certain risks and may be tempted to take a cautious approach in future, framing negative list schedules as broadly as possible (and thus liberalising as narrowly as possible) in order to preserve future flexibilities.[92]

In relation to screening, EU investors in Australia are at present subject to the general screening thresholds, not benefiting from any higher preferential thresholds.[93] In line with offers to its other treaty partners, it might be expected that Australia will offer higher screening thresholds to EU investors in the AEUFTA. However, Australia essentially maintains three informal tiers of screening thresholds, constructed in its various PTAs. The most favourable tier is generally enjoyed by investors from the USA, New Zealand and Chile, while the second tier generally applies to investors from Japan, South Korea, China, Singapore, Peru, Hong Kong and CPTPP countries. The third tier, offering the lowest thresholds, applies to investors from all other states, currently including EU states. It remains to be seen whether Australia would offer EU investors treatment under the first or second tier, or perhaps even a new tier.

Conversely, it also remains unclear whether the EU would offer higher screening thresholds for Australian investors in EU states. As described above, the various screening regimes of EU member states do not operate on monetary thresholds based on the value of the investment, in the same way as Australia's regime. Instead, the triggers for screening are typically based on acquisition of more than a specified percentage of voting rights in companies in particular sectors (often 10% for highly sensitive sectors and 25% otherwise). It seems unlikely that the AEUFTA will raise these thresholds for Australian investors, particularly since several of the screening regimes in EU states have only been implemented very recently.

---

[90] Bonnitcha et al. (2017), p. 177; Alschner (2017), p. 380.

[91] Bath (2017), p. 172.

[92] Cf Bonnitcha J (2020) The return of investment screening as a policy tool. www.iisd.org/itn/en/2020/12/19/the-return-of-investment-screening-as-a-policy-tool-jonathan-bonnitcha/ (last accessed 9 September 2021).

[93] See Sect. 3.1.3 above.

4 Conclusion

Screening regimes and restrictions on market access are some of the major formal barriers to entry encountered by foreign investors. The AEUFTA could potentially address both of these barriers, by offering enhanced market access in particular sectors and/or by offering higher screening thresholds. Australia may well offer EU investors screening thresholds similar to those granted to its other key "like-minded" trading partners, such as the United States and New Zealand. Nevertheless, evidence remains unclear on whether these higher thresholds play a significant role in encouraging more investment. Market access offers are clearly a key feature of the ongoing negotiations, and seem likely to produce at least some concessions useful to investors in each partner. However, in light of current economic and political uncertainties, the partners may also be tempted to include broad negative lists, preserving maximum flexibility to meet future policy challenges.

References

Alschner W (2017) Investment barriers-to-entry. In: Cottier T, Nadakavukaren Schefer K (eds) Elgar encyclopedia of international economic law. Edward Elgar, Cheltenham, pp 379–381

Bath V (2012) Foreign investment, the national interest and national security – foreign direct investment in Australia and China. Sydney Law Rev 34:5–34

Bath V (2017) Australia and the Asia-Pacific: the regulation of investment flows into Australia and the role of free trade agreements. In: Morosini F, Ratton Sanchez Badin M (eds) Reconceptualizing international investment law from the global South. Cambridge University Press, Cambridge, pp 146–187

Bonnitcha J (2019) Investment wars: contestation and confusion in debate about investment liberalization. J Int Econ Law 22:629–654

Bonnitcha et al (2017) The political economy of the investment treaty regime. Oxford University Press, Oxford

Drake-Brockman J, Messerlin P (eds) (2018) Potential benefits of an Australia-EU free trade agreement: key issues and options. Adelaide University Press, Adelaide

Kawharu A, Nottage L (2017) Models for investment treaties in the Asia-Pacific region: an underview. Ariz J Int Comp Law 34:461–528

UNCTAD (2002) Admission and establishment. United Nations, New York

Jarrod Hepburn is an Associate Professor at Melbourne Law School, University of Melbourne, Australia. His research interests lie largely in international economic law and general international law. His work has been published in journals including the American Journal of International Law, the International and Comparative Law Quarterly, the Journal of International Dispute Settlement, the Journal of World Investment and Trade, and the Melbourne Journal of International Law. Jarrod is the author of Domestic Law in International Investment Arbitration (Oxford University Press 2017). Jarrod holds the degrees of DPhil, MPhil and BCL from Balliol College, University of Oxford, as well as first-class honours undergraduate degrees in both law and software engineering from the University of Melbourne. Jarrod is admitted to practice law in Australian federal and state jurisdictions, and has experience in the Competition Group of a major Australian commercial law firm. He is also a long-time contributor to a specialised news service, Investment Arbitration Reporter, providing coverage and analysis of foreign investment disputes.

Panel Procedures Under the Proposed EU-Australia FTA

Angshuman Hazarika

Contents

Abstract State-to-state dispute settlement is a common feature in most modern trade agreements and EU Free Trade Agreements (FTAs) have been no exception with its trade agreements since the 2000s containing the possibility for state-to-state dispute settlement through panelists or arbitrators (Cornelia, Ensuring that state to state dispute settlement procedures under the EU FTAs do not end when they have just begun, 2020, p. 2.). While these provisions were largely unused for a long time, since 2018, the EU has been a part of four disputes based on dispute resolution proceedings in FTAs (Disputes against Ukraine, Southern African Customs Union, South Korea and Algeria. Progress on the proceedings can be monitored at https://ec.europa.eu/trade/policy/accessing-markets/dispute-settlement/bilateral-disputes/ (last accessed 9 September 2021).), The EU has recently received a favourable decision in the first concluded proceeding against Ukraine (Final Report of the Arbitration Panel, Restrictions applied by Ukraine on exports of certain wood products to the

A. Hazarika (✉)
Indian Institute of Management Ranchi, Ranchi, India

M. Bungenberg, A. Mitchell (eds.), *The Australia-European Union Free Trade Agreement*, Special Issue, https://doi.org/10.1007/978-3-030-91448-6_7

European Union, 11 December 2020, p. 125.), and mixed results in the second concluded proceeding against South Korea (Report of The Panel of Experts, Panel of Experts Proceeding Constituted Under Article 13.15 of the EU-Korea Free Trade Agreement, January 20, 2021, p. 77.). This line of recent disputes indicates that state-to-state dispute settlement procedures may have a significant role in the future and relevant clauses in the FTAs need to be carefully negotiated with a view to prevent procedural hurdles in future proceedings.

1 Introduction to Third Party State-to-State Dispute Settlement in FTAs

The EU has indicated that it will include state-to-state dispute settlement in its FTAs to ensure compliance with the rights and obligations under those agreements.[1] The binding methods of third-party state-to-state dispute settlement in FTAs can be divided into two broad groups:

(a) Treaties calling for the formation of a panel ("Panel procedure")
(b) Treaties which call for the framing of an arbitration panel ("Arbitration procedure")

The term third-party here refers to the fact that an external party here has been entrusted to resolve the dispute between the two disputing parties.[2] Establishment of a panel or an arbitration panel are common methods of third party based mechanisms for inter-state disputes.[3] For the purposes of this chapter, the two aforementioned methods have been found in a range of EU and Australian FTAs. Among the recent agreements, the possibility for formation of a Panel has been found in the yet to be signed EU-Mexico Global Agreement (Article X.4, Chapter- XX, Dispute Settlement), and the Proposed EU Text for the EU-Australia FTA as released in 2018 ('Proposed EU Text'). The possibility for formation of an arbitration panel has been found in the Comprehensive Economic and Trade Agreement ('CETA') (Article 29.6), the EU-Mercosur Association Agreement (Article 6, Chapter III- Dispute Settlement Procedures) and EU-Japan EPA (Article 21.7).

While traditionally arbitration and panel procedures were considered as alternatives,[4] a few differences can be seen on how these procedures have been utilized in the recent FTAs which have been concluded or are under negotiation by the EU. In terms of the text, differences begin with the classification of a panel decision as a "Panel Report" and the classification of a decision from an arbitral tribunal as an

[1]European Union, Dispute Settlement, https://ec.europa.eu/trade/policy/accessing-markets/dispute-settlement/ (last accessed 9 September 2021).

[2]Bilder (1989), p. 474 et seqq.

[3]UNCTAD (2003), pp. 30 et seqq.

[4]Holbein and Carpentier (1993), p. 537.

"award."[5] This situation has however changed in recent years with decision from an arbitral tribunal being referred to as a "report",[6] or even through a change of terminology so as to consider the decision as a "report" at the time of initial circulation among the parties and later on as an "award."[7]

Beyond the cosmetic changes, a review of the text of recent FTAs concluded by the EU which contained a provision for Arbitration procedure when compared to the Proposed EU Text which has a Panel procedure reveals a few noticeable differences primarily in the 'terms of reference' for Panels under the FTA which may indicate a slight difference in the role they are expected to perform.

First, the scope of 'the terms of reference' for an Arbitration procedure calls for the arbitration tribunal to issue 'a *ruling* (or, to rule) on the compatibility of the measures in question'.[8] On the other hand, in draft text of recent EU FTAs where a Panel procedure has been included, the Panel has been asked to '*make findings* on the conformity of the measure at issue'.[9] This may be a result of the fact that the text of dispute resolution provisions which relate to Panel proceedings are generally inspired from the text of the WTO DSU.[10] There, under Article 7 (1) DSU, WTO Panels are by default required to make 'findings' which when adopted by the DSU (automatically by reverse consensus, unless appealed) become binding.[11] For arbitral tribunals on the other hand, in the FTAs where they are found, they have been given the right to go ahead and make the ruling based on their own findings or examination.[12]

---

[5] See Articles X.11 and X.12, Chapter on Dispute Settlement of the EU-Mexico Agreement in principle announced on 21 April 2018 ('EU-Mexico Global Agreement') and Art 12.4, Chapter on Dispute Settlement, EU-Mercosur Association Agreement in principle announced on 28 June 2019 ('EU-Mercosur Association Agreement').

[6] Article 21.19, Agreement between the European Union and Japan for an Economic Partnership ('EU-Japan EPA'), OJ 2018 L 330/3; Article 15.12, Free Trade Agreement between the Government of Australia and the Government of the People's Republic of China, 2015 ('Australia-China FTA').

[7] Article 12, EU-Mercosur Association Agreement.

[8] Clause 9 (a), Annex 29-A, Comprehensive Economic and Trade Agreement ('CETA'), OJ 2017 L 11/23; Clause 11 (a), Annex 14-A, Free trade Agreement between the EU and Singapore ('EU-Singapore FTA'), OJ 2019 L 294/3; Clause 14 (a), Annex I, EU-Mercosur Association Agreement.

[9] Article X.9, Chapter on Dispute Settlement, Proposed Text for the EU-New Zealand FTA; Article X.9, Chapter on Dispute Settlement, Proposed EU Text.

[10] Chase (2013), p. 6.

[11] See, Article 7(1) and Article 11, Understanding on rules and procedures governing the settlement of disputes ('WTO DSU' or 'DSU'), 1869 U.N.T.S. 401; See also, Van den Bossche and Prevost (2021), p. 43.

[12] For example, See, the terms of reference under Clause 11 (a), Annex 14-A, EU-Singapore FTA: 'to examine, in the light of the relevant provisions of the Agreement, the matter referred to in the request for establishment of the arbitration panel made pursuant to Article 14.4; *to rule* on the compatibility of the measure in question with the provisions referred to in Article 14.2 *by making findings of law and/or fact*, together with the reasons thereof; and to issue a ruling in accordance with Articles 14.7 and 14.8.' See also, Article 14.7 (1), EU-Singapore FTA (same agreement) which

A second linked difference which can be linked to the difference of whether a panel/tribunal makes a 'ruling' or a 'finding' is seen in the 'binding' nature attributed to the decisions of an arbitral tribunal under the text of the FTAs. The EU FTAs which contains the provisions for an Arbitration procedure generally also contain a clause which specifically states that the 'ruling' shall be 'binding on the Parties.'[13] On the other hand, for proposed EU FTAs where the panel has been entrusted to make findings, the provision stating a 'binding' nature of the decision for the Panel is missing.[14] Instead, they contain a provision which states that the Parties shall accept decisions and reports of a Panel 'unconditionally'.[15] Like the previous issue, this provision may also be inspired from the WTO DSU wherein there is no clause stating the binding nature for a WTO Panel or Appellate Body (AB) report, but under Article 17 (14) DSU, there is a similar requirement for disputing parties to only accept an AB Report 'unconditionally'.

A third key difference between Panel procedure and Arbitration procedure is the difference in the treatment of the 'interim report' which is issued by an Arbitral panel from those by a Panel in a Panel procedure. It has been revealed from the text of the EU FTAs with an Arbitration procedure that, the arbitral tribunal has a power to 'modify' its interim report,[16] 'reconsider its report',[17] or even 'make any further examination',[18] based on comments by the parties to the interim report. Compared to this, the panels formed as a part of the Panel procedure only have a limited power to 'include a discussion of any written request by the Parties on the interim report and clearly address the comments of the Parties.'[19]

This difference may be linked to the fact that an arbitral tribunal is generally making a 'ruling' or 'award' which may be a final determination on the subject and

---

shows that the interim panel report on whose basis the arbitration panel ruling will be made sets out the findings of fact.

[13] Article 29.10 (1), CETA; Article 14.19 (2), EU-Singapore FTA; Article 12.8, EU-Mercosur Association Agreement; Article X. 12 (3), Chapter on Dispute Settlement, EU-Mexico Global Agreement. For an outlier FTA which does not contain the term 'binding' even with Arbitration procedure, see, Free Trade Agreement between the European Union and the Socialist Republic of Viet Nam, OJ 2020 L 186/3 ('EU-Vietnam FTA').

[14] See, EU Proposed Texts for Australia and New Zealand FTAs which do not contain a provision stating a binding nature of the decision of the Panel.

[15] Article X.23 (2), Chapter on Dispute Settlement, Proposed Text for the EU-New Zealand FTA; Article X.23 (2), Chapter on Dispute Settlement, Proposed EU Text.

[16] Article 14.7 (4), EU-Singapore FTA; Article X.12 (2), Chapter on Dispute Settlement, EU-Mexico Global Agreement; Article 12 (3), Chapter on Dispute Settlement, EU-Mercosur Association Agreement.

[17] Article 29.9 (2), CETA.

[18] Article 29.9 (2), CETA; Article 14.7 (4), EU-Singapore FTA; Article X.12 (2), Chapter on Dispute Settlement, EU-Mexico Global Agreement; Article 12.3, Chapter on Dispute Settlement, EU-Mercosur Association Agreement.

[19] Article X.12 (2), Chapter on Dispute Settlement, EU's proposed Text for Discussion for the EU-New Zealand FTA as released in 2018 ('Proposed Text for the EU-New Zealand FTA'); Article X.12 (2), Chapter on Dispute Settlement, Proposed EU Text.

hence the tribunal may need to reevaluate its conclusions on introduction of new information by the parties, so that it does not make an incorrect decision by ignoring information introduced later merely because it had moved ahead to the interim report phase. In EU FTAs where an Arbitration procedure is present, based on the exact requirements as prescribed under the terms of reference, the arbitral tribunal may issue a binding 'ruling', 'award', or even a 'report' to convey its adjudication.[20] Once the award or ruling is issued in an inter-state arbitration, it would become binding and is without appeal.[21]

On the other hand, a 'panel' under the Panel procedure, based on its terms of reference, is in most cases only making 'findings' and then 'delivering a report' which may contain 'conclusions' based on its findings, but it is generally not making any rulings or decisions.[22] Such a Panel limited by its terms of reference to findings may also be making 'decisions' also but for other purposes mentioned in the FTA itself, but not in the final report that it issues about the dispute.[23] This difference between 'decisions' and the 'report' for Panels is highlighted by the Proposed EU Text itself where they are always referred separately.[24]

The above assessment however does not mean that a panel is unable to make an adjudication or determination by going beyond the findings when the terms of reference explicitly ask it to. In fact, in a few recent Australian FTAs, panels have been explicitly asked to make determinations or recommendations in their terms of reference going beyond merely making findings.[25]

The actual implications for a decision of the panel as an arbitral award or as a panel report may be linked to certain other principles such as the requirement to comply with an arbitral award in good faith. This particularly emerges from the fact that in at least a few treaties which require the formation of an arbitration tribunal, there is an obligation 'to comply promptly and in good faith' with the decision of the

[20] See, 'Ruling' in Article 29.10, CETA; Article 14.8, EU-Singapore FTA; 'Award' in Article 12, EU-Mercosur Association Agreement; 'Report' in Article 21.19, EU-Japan EPA.

[21] Office of Legal Affairs (1992), p. 55. The fact that there is no appeal is explicitly mentioned in Article 12 (8) Chapter on Dispute Settlement, EU-Mercosur Association Agreement.

[22] See, Article 18.9, Australia- Hong Kong Free Trade Agreement, 2019 (A-HKFTA).

[23] For situations when the Panel makes decisions, See Article X.10- Decision on Urgency, Article X.14 (2)- Decision on reasonable period of time, Article X.15 (2)- Decisions in compliance review, Article X.16 (5)- Decision on temporary remedies, All in Chapter on Dispute Settlement, Proposed EU Text.

[24] For instance, See, Article X.23- Report and decisions of the Panel, Article X.8 (b)- Functions of the panel, Article X.18 (2)- Replacement of panelists, Proposed EU Text.

[25] See, For Determinations: Article 19.12 (2) Regional Comprehensive Economic Partnership Agreement ('RCEP'), 2020; For Recommendations, see: Article 12 (6), Australia-PACER Plus FTA, 2017; For both Determinations and Recommendations, See, Article 28.8 (1), Comprehensive and Progressive Agreement for Trans-Pacific Partnership, 2018 ('CPTPP'); Article 27.8, Peru-Australia Free Trade Agreement, 2018. ('PAFTA').

arbitral tribunal whether it be in the form of a report or an award.[26] Such a requirement can be traced back to the initial days of modern interstate arbitration as the requirement for compliance with arbitration awards in good faith was included in the Hague Convention of 1907.[27]

This can be distinguished from the requirement to merely "comply promptly" with the decision of a panel as seen in the Proposed EU Text and the Proposed Text for the EU-New Zealand FTA under negotiation, with no direct mention of good faith obligations for the same.[28] It can however be argued that owing to the presence of a requirement to 'comply promptly' with decision of a panel, there can be an implied good faith requirement in international law on the treaty parties to comply with any obligations imposed by a treaty (including the requirement to comply with panel decisions under the FTA).[29]

Lastly, in addition to the issue of compliance, panel proceedings in the form that they were seen even in the very recent Australian trade agreements with Peru, Chile, Hong Kong, Indonesia and the Pacific Islands (PACER+) did not contain reference to the possibility of submission of *amicus curiae* briefs which have traditionally also been excluded from panel proceedings in the WTO.[30] The Proposed EU Text however changes this situation and provides for *amicus curiae* submissions from natural and legal persons belonging to the Parties.[31]

2 Current Status of Panel and Arbitration Procedures in Recent EU and Australian FTAs

The EU and Australia have included panel procedures or state-to-state arbitration in all their recent known trade agreements. The preferred procedures among both of them in recent trade agreements entered into by these two Parties can be known from the following tables:

[26] See Article 15, Title XXX, Dispute Settlement, EU-Mercosur Association Agreement; Article 21.20, EU-Japan EPA; Article 14.9 EU-Singapore FTA: Article 14.8, Free Trade Agreement between the European Union and its Member States, and the Republic of Korea, OJ 2011 L 127/1 ('EU-South Korea FTA'); Article 15.12 EU-Vietnam FTA.

[27] Article 37, Convention for the Pacific Settlement of International Disputes, 1907, 2 AJIL Supp. 43 (1908).

[28] See Article X.13 (1), Chapter- Dispute Settlement, Proposed Text for the EU-New Zealand FTA and Article X.13, Chapter- Dispute Settlement, Proposed EU Text.

[29] Reinhold (2015), pp. 60 et seqq.; Uçaryılmaz (2020), pp. 53 et seqq.

[30] WTO, Participation in dispute settlement proceedings, https://www.wto.org/english/tratop_e/dispu_e/disp_settlement_cbt_e/c9s3p1_e.htm (last accessed 9 September 2021).

[31] Clause 39, Annex X, Rules of Procedure, Proposed EU Text.

For the European Union—Type of binding Third-party Dispute Resolution Procedures in EU Trade Agreements since 2015

Trade agreements since 2015	8[a]
Agreements with Panel procedure	0
Agreements with Arbitration procedure	8[b]

[a] The trade agreements since 2015 for the EU are: Kazakhstan (2015), Southern African Development Community Economic Partnership Agreement States (SADC EPA States) (2016), Canada (2016), Armenia (2017), Japan (2018), Singapore (2018), Vietnam (2019) and UK (2020). Data collected from UNCTAD Database, https://investmentpolicy.unctad.org/international-investment-agreements/groupings/28/eu-european-union- (last accessed 9 September 2021)
[b] European Union trade agreements with UK, Vietnam, Singapore, Japan, Armenia, Canada, SADC EPA States, Kazakhstan

For Australia—Type of binding Third-party Dispute Resolution Procedures in Australian Trade Agreements since 2015

Trade agreements since 2015	7[c]
Agreements with Panel procedure	6[d]
Agreements with Arbitration procedure	1[e]

[c] The trade agreements since 2015 for Australia are: China (2015), Pacific Agreement on Closer Economic Relations (PACER) Plus, Peru, Comprehensive and Progressive Agreement for Trans-Pacific Partnership (CPTPP), Indonesia, Hong Kong, Regional Comprehensive Economic Partnership (RCEP)
[d] Australian trade agreements: RCEP, Hong Kong, Indonesia, CPTPP, Peru, PACER Plus
[e] Australian trade agreement with China

For the purposes of the aforementioned review, we have considered the procedures as arbitration when the treaty itself has considered the procedure as "arbitration procedure" or "arbitration." While there may be variations among the trade agreements, the numbers reveal that the EU included arbitration procedures in all its trade agreements since 2015 while Australia had Panel procedures in all but one agreement (i.e. with China). This prima-facie indicates a preference of EU for Arbitration procedure and of Australia for Panel procedure respectively.

3 Current Status of Negotiations

The European Union has released a "Proposal for the EU-Australia FTA" for the negotiations. The status of negotiations as revealed from the latest round EU-Australia Trade Agreement and the initial text proposals reveals that dispute settlement through panel procedures will be the only mode of binding third-party dispute resolution under the treaty.[32] The report of negotiations at the end of the 11th round of negotiations reveals that the parties have:

[32] Articles X.4 and X.5, Panel Procedures, Proposed EU Text.

> reached agreement on the objectives for the Chapter, which include transparent, efficient and effective dispute settlement procedures. Negotiators also agreed in principle on many areas relating to the concrete operation of the dispute settlement mechanism but certain areas remain outstanding.[33]

The updates indicate that certain issues remain to be resolved between the parties, however they do not reveal if there have been any changes in the text proposed in the original draft proposed by the European Union which is discussed below.

3.1 EU Proposed Draft

The EU has proposed for "Panel Procedures" as a binding mode for dispute resolution under the treaty.[34] The inclusion of a dispute resolution procedure which includes consultation followed by the Panel procedures is referred to as the "Quasi-adjudicative" dispute settlement model,[35] which was seen for the first time for the EU in its FTA with Mexico which entered into force in 2000.[36]

The "Panel Procedures" prescribed by the EU through its proposed text are meant to come into play if the Parties,[37] are unable to resolve a dispute regarding the "interpretation and application of the provisions" of the Agreement through Consultations.[38] It has been clarified here that in case a request for consultations is not replied within a definite time period or if the consultations are not held, or if the Parties cannot reach a mutually agreed solution, then they may move to the next step of Panel procedures.

The scope of dispute resolution through the Panel procedures as prescribed under the Proposed EU Text *prima facie* indicates that declaratory claims which have been foreseen for certain treaties as a potential step for state parties to evaluate compatibility of a measure with the FTA before implementation may not be possible for the proposed EU-Australia FTA.[39] This is because of the inclusion of a specific provision in the Proposed EU Text which requires the complaining party to "identify the

[33] Report of the 11th round of negotiations for a trade agreement between the European Union and Australia 1–11 June 2021, p. 3.

[34] See Section C, Panel Procedures, Chapter on Dispute Settlement, Proposed EU Text.

[35] Robles (2006), p. 26.

[36] Economic Partnership, Political Co-ordination and Co-operation Agreement between the European Community and its Member States, of the one part, and the United Mexican States, of the other part, OJ 2000 L 276/45.

[37] It is unclear from the Proposed EU Text if a "Party" for the EU may mean only a member state or it means European Union.

[38] Clause 1, Article X.4, Chapter- Dispute Settlement.

[39] For the potential for declaratory claims under the state-to-state dispute settlement mechanism in an FTA, see, Lubambo (2020), p. 107.

measure at issue in its request, and explain how that measure constitutes a breach of the covered provisions".[40] With the requirement to identify the "measure" and the requirement to explain the "breach of the covered provisions", a declaratory claim to identify compatibility may no longer be possible.

In the proposed EU-Australia FTA, the provisions on the Panel procedures in the draft proposed by the European Union is a significant departure from the EU's practice in recent FTAs wherein it had chosen Arbitration procedure.[41] Panel procedure was the preferred dispute resolution mode for Australia in its recent FTAs and inclusion of this procedure may indicate EU's intention to come up with customized draft agreement proposals based on the counterparty. This customization may be possible based on prior observation that EU trade agreements do not have any standard dispute settlement procedure,[42] and EU does not have any "model FTA".[43] EU has however ensured that it includes

3.1.1 Scope of the Dispute Resolution Procedure

The scope of the Panel procedures in the Proposed EU Text extends to all disputes where the Parties have failed to resolve the dispute through Consultations.[44] However, certain specific subjects, sections or Chapters have however been explicitly excluded from the ambit of the dispute settlement provisions including the chapter on trade remedies,[45] the chapter on Anticompetitive Conduct, Merger control and Subsidies,[46] the chapter on Trade and Sustainable Development,[47] the Chapter on Good Regulatory Practices,[48] and the subject of readmission of natural persons.[49] There may also be additional requirements imposed before commencement of dispute resolution procedures such as the requirement for technical consultations.[50]

Among the chapters which have been excluded, the chapters on Trade remedies, the chapter on Anticompetitive Conduct, Merger control and Subsidies, and the chapter on Trade and Sustainable Development have specific dispute resolution

---

[40] Article X. 4 (2), Section C, Chapter on Dispute Settlement, Proposed EU Text.

[41] An analysis can be found in Table 1 above. The proposed EU-Mexico Global Agreement has a provision for formation of a panel.

[42] Szepesi (2004), p. 2.

[43] Woolock (2007), p. 2.

[44] Article X. 4, Section C, Chapter on Dispute Settlement, Proposed EU Text.

[45] See the following Articles of Proposed EU Text: Article X.5, Section B, Chapter on Trade Remedies; Article X.9, Section B, Chapter on Trade Remedies.

[46] See Article X.7, Section A, Chapter on Anticompetitive Conduct, Merger control and Subsidies, Proposed EU Text.

[47] See Article X.13, Chapter on Trade and Sustainable Development, Proposed EU Text.

[48] See Article X.12, Chapter on Chapter on Good Regulatory Practices, Proposed EU Text.

[49] See the following Articles of Proposed EU Text: Article 3, Annex on Movement of Natural Persons for Business Purposes, Chapter on Investment Liberalisation and Trade in Services.

[50] Article X. 15(2), Chapter on Sanitary and Phytosanitary Measures, Proposed EU Text.

procedures which are included in the chapter itself, a practice which is also seen in other recent EU and Australian FTAs.

3.1.2 Composition of the Panel

The Proposed EU Text calls for the formation of a panel with three panelists based on consultations between the parties and in case of a failure to agree, based on lists provided by the parties.[51] The qualification of the panelists, their code of conduct, replacement of panelists, and guidelines on suspension and termination of the panels are also provided in the Proposed EU Text.[52] The members of the panel are referred to as a "panelist".[53]

3.1.3 Procedure to Be Followed by the Panel

A separate Annex on "Rules of Procedure" for the Panel Procedure has been included in the Proposed EU Text which covers Appointment of Panelists, replacement of the Panelists, conduct of Hearings, Confidentiality, *Amicus curiae* submissions and Urgent cases. The Chapter through two separate articles supplement this Annex by providing for the procedure for "Decision on urgency", and guidelines and timelines for Interim and Final Report of the Panel.[54] The procedural framework has also been made flexible through inclusion of provisions for remote proceedings through telephone and computer links and by allowing the Panel to make decisions on procedural questions not covered by the FTA or its annexes, based on consultation with the Parties.[55]

The Rules of Procedure and Code of Conduct included in the Proposed EU Text indicate inspiration from both EU FTAs and Australian FTAs of that time. The EU has taken an effort to include specific provisions which were present in Australian FTAs but missing in EU FTAs signed or negotiated at the time of release of the Proposed EU Text. Conversely, provisions absent in Australian FTAs but present in EU-FTAs being negotiated at that time also find a place in the Proposed EU Text.

An example of the EU including provisions from its other contemporary FTAs can be seen in the form of provisions linked to *Amicus curiae* submissions, and *Ex*

[51] Article X. 5, Section C, Chapter on Dispute Settlement, Proposed EU Text.

[52] Articles X. 7, X.18 and X.20 Section C, Chapter on Dispute Settlement, Proposed EU Text; Annex XX, Code of Conduct for Panelists and Mediators, Proposed EU Text.

[53] Clause 1(e), I. Definitions, Annex XX. The members of a "panel" have been referred to as "arbitrators" under Articles X.23(1) and X.34(2), Section C, Chapter on Dispute Settlement, Proposed EU Text, which can be an indication that they are performing functions similar to an arbitrator.

[54] Articles X. 10, 11 and 12, Section C, Chapter on Dispute Settlement, Proposed EU Text; Annex XX, Code of Conduct for Panelists and Mediators, Proposed EU Text.

[55] Clause 13 and 16, Hearings, Annex X- Rules of Procedure, Proposed EU Text.

parte contacts being included in the Proposed EU Text. These provisions are not present even in the recent Australia-Indonesia CEPA,[56] or the Australia-Hong Kong FTA,[57] which were signed after the release of the Proposed EU Text,[58] neither were they present in the Australian FTAs in 2018. However, they are present in the EU-Singapore FTA and the EU-Vietnam FTA,[59] which were being negotiated around the same time as the release of the Proposed EU Text.[60] Consequently, provisions which provide for *Amicus curiae* submissions and *Ex parte contacts* found a place in the Proposed EU Text.[61]

On the other hand, an example of the EU attempting to include provisions from the Australian FTAs can be seen in the Code of Conduct part of the Proposed EU Text. The Code of Conduct includes a provision wherein an arbitrator is also responsible to disclose "any matters concerning actual or potential violations of this Code of Conduct at the earliest time he or she becomes aware of them."[62] This seems to be derived from a narrower provision in the China-Australia FTA which enables a panelist to disclose actual or potential violations by another panelist under certain situations.[63] Such a requirement to inform about violations by other parties is absent in both the EU-Singapore and EU-Vietnam FTAs of the same time discussed above.

3.2 Australian Objectives

The Australian objectives for the trade agreement reveal that it also intends to establish "a state-to-state dispute settlement mechanism that provides transparent and efficient procedures for settling disputes regarding the FTA."[64] In line with the Proposed EU Text, Australia also intends to exclude certain areas from dispute

[56] Indonesia-Australia Comprehensive Economic Partnership Agreement (IA-CEPA), entered into force on 5 July 2020.

[57] Australia-Hong Kong Free Trade Agreement (A-HKFTA) and associated Investment Agreement (IA) entered into force on 17 January 2020.

[58] The IA-CEPA was signed on March 4, 2019 and the A-HKFTA was signed on March 26, 2019. The Proposed EU Text is dated June 13, 2018.

[59] Clause 38-42, Annex 15-A, EU-Vietnam FTA. 2019; Clause 40-44, Annex 14-A, EU-Singapore FTA. 2018.

[60] The Final Text of the EU-Vietnam FTA was updated on 24 September 2018; The Final Text of EU-Singapore FTA was signed on 19 October 2018, https://trade.ec.europa.eu/doclib/docs/2018/april/tradoc_156716.pdf (last accessed 9 September 2021).

[61] Part XI and XII, Annex X- Rules of Procedure, Proposed EU Text.

[62] Clause 10, Annex XX, Proposed EU Text.

[63] Clause 11, Annex 15-A, Australia-China FTA.

[64] Australia-European Union Free Trade Agreement, Summary of negotiating aim and approach, https://www.dfat.gov.au/trade/agreements/negotiations/aeufta/Pages/summary-of-negotiating-aims-and-approach (last accessed 9 September 2021).

resolution without any explicit clarity on the subjects sought to be kept outside the ambit of dispute resolution proceedings.[65] It has however stated that exceptions for legitimate public policy has been planned.[66]

The likely exclusion of investor-state arbitration from the proposed EU-Australia FTA as indicated by the Proposed EU Text which does not contain such a provision is a major development which means that the panel procedures can be expected to deal with both trade and investment law disputes.[67] This is in line with the Australian objectives as well as the EU Negotiating Directives which only mention state-to-state dispute settlement.[68] Unless there is a major deviation from this position by the parties, this clears the air on the confusion on whether the EU would agree to sign an FTA which does not include provisions for the new investment court system proposed by the EU, and indicates that exceptions may be possible.[69]

3.3 Updates Provided by the Parties

The parties have recently indicated that negotiations for the Dispute Settlement chapter are ongoing and they "have resolved most outstanding issues."[70]

A timeline regarding the *progress in negotiations for the Dispute Settlement Chapter* can be seen from the official Reports of the Parties[71] on the negotiating rounds as shown in Table 1.

A review of the table indicates that broad agreement on most parts of the dispute settlement chapter in the agreement was reached in the second round itself and by round five only few issues remained outstanding. The reports from Australia indicate that Mediation may have been an important issues for the party and it has continued

[65] Article X. 2, Section A, Chapter on Dispute Settlement, Proposed EU Text.

[66] Objectives, https://www.dfat.gov.au/sites/default/files/australia-european-union-fta-objectives.pdf (last accessed 9 September 2021).

[67] See also, Report 183, Joint Standing Committee on Treaties, Australian Parliament, https://www.aph.gov.au/Parliamentary_Business/Committees/Joint/Treaties/AspectsPAFTArevisited/Report_183/section?id=committees%2Freportjnt%2F024238%2F26778#footnote12target (last accessed 9 September 2021).

[68] Objectives, Council of the European Union, Negotiating directives for a Free Trade Agreement with Australia, 7663/18, 25 June 2018, https://www.dfat.gov.au/sites/default/files/australia-european-union-fta-objectives.pdf (last accessed 9 September 2021).

[69] Chaisse and Renouf (2018), p. 285.

[70] Australia-EU FTA – Report on Negotiating Round Ten, 9–19 March 2021, https://www.dfat.gov.au/trade/agreements/negotiations/aeufta/news/australia-eu-fta-report-negotiating-round-ten-9-19-march-2021 (last accessed 9 September 2021).

[71] The Report of the Negotiating Rounds for Australia can be found at https://www.dfat.gov.au/trade/agreements/negotiations/aeufta/aeufta-news. The Report of the Negotiating Rounds for EU can be found at https://trade.ec.europa.eu/doclib/press/index.cfm?id=1865 (last accessed 9 September 2021).

Table 1 Reports on the 11 rounds of negotiation released by the Parties

Negotiating round	Dates	Updates from Australia	Updates from the EU
First	2–6 July 2018	Detailed and productive discussions reaching broad agreement on the objectives and expectations for the chapter	Discussed proposals and two annexes in detail. Exchanged information about FTA practice in the area. Detailed discussion on practice and positions of both parties. "Broad agreement on objectives and expectations for the Chapter, which include transparent, efficient and effective dispute settlement procedures."
Two	19–23 November 2018	Detailed discussion on Australia's responses to the EU's proposed Dispute Settlement Chapter. Broad agreement on dispute settlement process and further discussions on certain rules and procedures (such as timeframes, panelist expertise requirements and non-violation claims) and the EU's proposed mediation mechanism	Discussed proposals and two annexes in detail. Discussion took place on the basis of draft text consolidated after the first round. Reached agreement on the objectives for the Chapter, which include transparent, efficient and effective dispute settlement procedures. Agreement in principle on may areas relating to concrete operation of dispute settlement mechanism but with certain areas outstanding
Three	25–29 March 2019	Broad agreement on the Chapter and Annexes including EU's proposed mediation mechanism, subject to further discussions on certain rules and procedures (such as non-violation claims and timeframes)	Almost identical as Round two
Four	1–5 July 2019	Agreement on a number of procedural timelines	Almost identical as Round two
Five	14–18 October 2019	Further discussions on the chapter and annexes and progress on EU's proposed mediation mechanism	Detailed discussions on the Dispute settlement chapter and large parts provisionally agreed. Only few areas remain outstanding
Six	10–14 February 2020	No updates	No updates

(continued)

Table 1 (continued)

Negotiating round	Dates	Updates from Australia	Updates from the EU
Seven	4–20 May 2020	Further discussions on the chapter and annexes and EU's proposed mediation mechanism. Constructive discussion on cross-cutting issues including in exceptions chapter	Almost identical as Round two
Eight	14–25 September 2020	Progress on Mediation mechanism and rules of procedure	Almost identical as Round two
Nine	30 November–11 December 2020	Resolved most outstanding issues in the Dispute Settlement chapter	Almost identical as Round two
Ten	9–19 March 2021	Made progress and resolved most outstanding issues in the Dispute Settlement chapter	Almost identical as Round two
Eleven	1–11 June 2021	Discussion on EU's new procedural proposals. Resolved most outstanding issues	Almost identical as Round two

discussions on the issue. As of the final round, it appears from the statement of both the parties that most of the issues in the Chapter have been resolved with no major disagreements on the panel procedures. It however emerges from the Australian report that EU may have introduced new procedural proposals in this round. The exact nature of such proposals is however unknown.

4 Resolving the Final Kinks in the Dispute Settlement Procedure

The current status of the text is unknown which makes it difficult, if not impossible to predict what would be the current status of the text of the agreement relating to the panel procedures. In such a situation, an attempt has been made to suggest amendments to the text of the Proposed EU Text to make it more in line with the negotiating objectives and also prevent problems which arose in past dispute settlement proceedings. Considering that disputes under the third-party dispute settlement procedures of EU FTAs is now a reality, the parties would do well to iron out any kinks in the treaty text before the next inter-state dispute arises based on a FTA.

4.1 *Providing a Clear Understanding of the Term "Dispute"*

While the term "dispute" may prima facie appear to be self-explanatory, it may come as a surprise that international courts and tribunals have at multiple times been required to determine that there is indeed a dispute between the parties which require a resolution.[72] In the absence of a dispute between the parties, the panel (or the tribunal) is not able to accept a jurisdiction over the matter. Parties may create such a situation by refusing to take a position on a particular issue which may prevent the other party from moving towards the dispute resolution provisions.[73]

To prevent a situation where parties are not able to prevent proceedings from progressing based on the non-existence of a dispute by refusing to respond to an issue, it is recommended that a provision be included in the treaty which states that the refusal to take a position in a matter may indicate the existence of a dispute.[74]

4.2 *Inclusion of a Provision for Clarification on Panel Reports*

In view of the situation that certain panel reports may contain issues on which the parties to the dispute may not have a common understanding, a provision for a "Request for Clarification" on a panel report may be included in the treaty. A similar provision was seen in the EU-Mercosur Association Agreement which provides for a possibility for seeking a clarification on "determination or recommendation in the arbitral award that the requesting party considers ambiguous."[75]

Clear guidelines may be provided on the exact procedure to be followed for such requests for clarification and timelines may be set so that the provision is not used as a means to review a panel decision or to delay its implementation. As of now, only a possibility for translation of documents and interpretation of oral submissions of the Parties exists.[76]

---

[72] ICJ, Obligations concerning Negotiations relating to Cessation of the Nuclear Arms Race and to Nuclear Disarmament (Marshall Islands v. United Kingdom), Preliminary Objections, Judgment, I.C.J. Reports 2016, p. 833 at 849; PCA Case No. 2012-5, Republic of Ecuador v. United States of America, Award, 29 September, 2012; ICJ, Application of the International Convention on the Elimination of All Forms of Racial Discrimination (Georgia v. Russian Federation), Preliminary Objections, Judgment, I.C.J. Reports 2011, p. 70.

[73] Such a situation was seen in PCA Case No. 2012-5, Republic of Ecuador v. United States of America arising out of the USA-Ecuador BIT, wherein USA refused to take a position on an issue and denied that there was a dispute between the parties.

[74] Bernasconi-Osterwalder (2016), p. 259.

[75] Article 14, EU-Mercosur Association Agreement.

[76] Article XIV, Annex, Rules of Procedure, Proposed EU Text.

4.3 Dealing with Multiple Proceedings

The Parties may include appropriate provisions in the FTA to ensure that multiple disputes arising at the same time or linked disputes can be merged together to be dealt with by the same panel (consolidation of proceedings) instead of the need of the formation of a new panel and potential parallel proceedings. For instance, if there is a measure by an EU member state which affects the imports of a particular product from Australia, it may choose to commence consultation and panel proceedings under the issue.

Now, if at the same time, there are multiple similar measures by different EU member states which affect the interests of Australia, it may choose to commence multiple proceedings. This may make the dispute resolution proceedings cumbersome and may also lead to conflicting reports by the panels. To deal with such a situation, a possibility must be present for merging of multiple proceedings on similar issues arising at the same time and *res judicata* against raising a dispute which has been dealt with by a panel in the past based on ideal factual scenario.

4.4 Requirement for Repeat of Hearings Due to Replacement of a Panelist

While the Proposed EU Text provides the possibility for replacement of panelists,[77] a clause in rules of procedure requiring presence of all panelists during the entirety of the hearing,[78] lowers its usefulness. The presence of this requirement means that death or inability of a panelist leading to his/her replacement may be argued by the disputing parties as a ground for restarting the hearings.

A requirement to restart proceedings due to the replacement of a panelist may lead to extreme delay in the proceedings and may potentially lead to overshooting of the time periods fixed for release of interim and interim reports. The inclusion of a clause for freezing of the calculation of time period during the process of appointment of a new panelist is unlikely to help in this situation, since the extension of time is provided only for "the time necessary for the appointment of the new panelist",[79] and not for a restart of hearings.

In order to deal with this situation, the parties may include a provision which limits the requirement of restart of hearings only to exceptional scenarios such as the replacement of the chairperson.[80] For other situations such as replacement of another panelist, the tribunal may decide to use the transcripts which already have to be

[77] Article X.18, Section C, Chapter on Dispute Settlement, Proposed EU Text.

[78] Clause 25, Hearings, Annex X- Rules of Procedure, Proposed EU Text.

[79] Article X.18, Section C, Chapter on Dispute Settlement, Proposed EU Text.

[80] Such a provision is seen in Article 14, PCA Optional Rules for Arbitrating Disputes Between Two States.

prepared during the hearings,[81] or in exceptional situations require a part of the hearings to be repeated. Additionally, with the advances in available technology, parties may also require video recording of the proceedings along with preparation of transcripts which may further reduce delays.

5 Conclusion

The Proposed EU Text and the report on the negotiations released by EU and Australia indicate that the negotiations about the dispute settlement clauses may have reached the final stages with possibly only minor issues to be resolved. The Proposed EU Text which was based on negotiations between the parties and the prior experience of the EU in negotiating FTAs over several decades indicates that the EU has taken the best practices and clauses from the treaties and has been successful in including them in its proposed text to come up with a flexible and future dispute settlement framework which includes the latest advances in technology. It is however recommended that the parties consider the additional suggestions made in this chapter for streamlining the treaty to deal with some yet untouched potential procedural hurdles.

References

Bernasconi-Osterwalder N (2016) State-state dispute settlement in investment treaties. In: Singh K, Ilge B (eds) Rethinking bilateral investment treaties. Both Ends, Amsterdam, pp 256–262

Bilder RB (1989) International third party dispute settlement. Denver J Int Law Policy 17(3): 471–503

Chaisse J, Renouf Y (2018) Investor-state dispute settlement. In: Drake-Brockman J, Patrick M (eds) Potential benefits of an Australia-EU Free Trade Agreement- key issues and options. University of Adelaide Press, Adelaide, pp 281–313

Chase C, Yanovich A, Crawford JA, Ugaz P (2013) Mapping of dispute settlement mechanisms in regional trade agreements – innovative or variations on a theme?. WTO Staff Working Paper. WTO, Geneva

Cornelia F (2020) Ensuring that state to state dispute settlement procedures under the EU FTAs do not end when they have just begun. Eutip Policy Brief 1

Holbein JR, Carpentier G (1993) Trade agreements and dispute settlement mechanisms in the Western Hemisphere. Case West Reserve J Int Law 25(2):531–570

Lubambo M (2020) Entry rights and investments in services: adjudicatory convergence between regimes? In: Gáspár-Szilágyi S, Behn D, Langford M (eds) Adjudicating trade and investment disputes convergence or divergence? Cambridge University Press, Cambridge, pp 92–118

Office of Legal Affairs (1992) Handbook on the peaceful settlement of disputes between states. United Nations, New York

[81] Requirement to prepare transcripts under Clause 30, Hearings, Annex X- Rules of Procedure, Proposed EU Text.

Reinhold S (2015) Good faith in international law. UCL J Law Jurisprud 2(0):40–63
Robles ER (2006) Political and quasi-adjudicative dispute settlement models in the European Union Free Trade Agreements- Is the quasi-adjudicative model a trend or is it just another model?. WTO Staff Working Paper ERSD-2006-09
Szepesi S (2004) Comparing EU free trade agreements- Dispute Settlement. Inbrief, No. 6G
Uçaryılmaz T (2020) The principle of good faith in public international law. Estudios de Deusto 68(1):43–59
UNCTAD (2003) Dispute settlement: state-state. United Nations, New York and Geneva
Van den Bossche P, Prevost D (2021) Essentials of WTO law, 2nd edn. Cambridge University Press, Cambridge
Woolock S (2007) European Union policy towards Free Trade Agreements. ECIPE Working Paper, No. 03/2007

Angshuman Hazarika is an Assistant Professor for Ethics and Business Law at IIM Ranchi, India. He also teaches at IIIT Ranchi and IICM Ranchi. Prior to this, Angshuman worked as a Research Associate at Saarland University, Germany and has also worked in a leading law firm in India. He was awarded the Angela Merkel Scholarship by DAAD for his Master's Degree at the Europa-Institut, Saarbrucken, Germany. The special focus of his work is on investment arbitration with focus on state-to-state arbitration and the impact of investment arbitration on developing countries. He is also involved in work relating to the interface of foreign policy, trade and investment and he has worked on issues of investment screening and dispute resolution mechanisms for trade and investment issues.

Investment Protection in the AEUFTA: Missed Opportunities or Strategic Exclusions?

Esmé Shirlow

Contents

Abstract Negotiations between Australia and the European Union (EU) for a free trade agreement (the AEUFTA) appear to be nearing completion. Based on the EU's negotiating mandate and the official reports from the negotiations so far, it is clear that the AEUFTA's investment-related provisions will focus exclusively on market access and investment liberalisation. The AEUFTA will thus not incorporate investment protection obligations and nor will it include an investor-State dispute settlement mechanism. Despite these omissions, the conclusion of the AEUFTA will be significant from the perspective of both negotiating States, including because it reveals the policy and legal constraints guiding the approach of each to the negotiation and conclusion of investment treaties and investment chapters in FTAs. This article first introduces the contours of the bilateral investment relationship between the EU and Australia and then examines why the FTA adopts an exclusively liberalisation-focussed approach, to address whether the exclusion of investment protection and investor-State arbitration from the scope of the FTA is a strategic omission on the part of one or both parties. To consider next whether such omission is a missed opportunity, the article examines the likely focus of the

E. Shirlow (✉)
The Australian National University College of Law, Acton, ACT, Australia
e-mail: esme.shirlow@anu.edu.au

M. Bungenberg, A. Mitchell (eds.), *The Australia-European Union Free Trade Agreement*, Special Issue, https://doi.org/10.1007/978-3-030-91448-6_8

investment-related provisions of the treaty, and what impact the FTA is likely to have vis-à-vis investors and existing investment treaties.

1 Introduction

Negotiations between Australia and the European Union (EU) for a free trade agreement (the AEUFTA) appear to be nearing completion. Based on the EU's negotiating mandate and the official reports from the negotiations so far, it is clear that the AEUFTA's investment-related provisions will focus exclusively on market access and investment liberalisation. The AEUFTA will thus not incorporate investment protection obligations and nor will it include an investor-State dispute settlement mechanism. The AEUFTA is one of the first EU free trade agreement (FTAs) to adopt such a narrowly framed scope vis-à-vis investment, with no indication (as yet) that it will be accompanied by a standalone investment agreement. The negotiations appear to reinforce Australia's largely passive approach to setting the direction of investment negotiations, indicating its willingness to instead be influenced by the negotiating aims of its treaty partner. Despite its omissions and overlaps, the conclusion of the AEUFTA will be significant from the perspective of both negotiating States, including because it reveals the policy and legal constraints on each which guide their approach to the negotiation and conclusion of investment treaties and investment chapters in FTAs. This article will first introduce the contours of the bilateral investment relationship between the EU and Australia (Sect. 2), in order to situate the FTA's relevance to the investment flows between these parties. It will then examine why the FTA adopts an exclusively liberalisation-focussed approach (Sect. 3), to address whether the exclusion of investment protection and investor-State arbitration from the scope of the FTA is a strategic omission on the part of one or both parties. To consider next whether such omission is a missed opportunity, the article will examine what focus the investment-related provisions of the treaty will adopt (Sect. 4), and what impact the FTA is likely to have vis-à-vis investors and existing investment treaties (Sect. 5). A final section will conclude.

2 Investment Relations Between Australia and the EU: Towards an AEUFTA

Globally, the EU is a significant exporter and importer of foreign direct investment (FDI).[1] It is a particularly significant source of foreign investment in Australia: figures indicate that in 2019, for example, investment from the EU into Australia

[1] See, for a recent snapshot of global FDI flows: OECD, 'FDI in Figures: April 2020' (2020) <http://www.oecd.org/investment/FDI-in-Figures-April-2020.pdf>; UNCTAD, 'World Investment Report: 2020' (2020) <https://unctad.org/system/files/official-document/wir2020_en.pdf>.

represented over 35% of Australia's total inbound investment, and Australian investment into the EU over 28% of Australia's total outbound investment.[2] (Of note for both figures is that around 17% of total inbound and outbound investment was linked to the UK,[3] with Australia and the UK announcing a separate in principle agreement on trade and investment in June 2021.[4]) Volumes of portfolio investment between Australia and the EU are also significant.[5]

Reflecting the importance of this two-way investment between the EU and Australia, on 22 April 2015 representatives of the EU and Australia announced that they had concluded negotiations for a Framework Agreement.[6] At the same time, they noted that "[b]ilaterally, we are engaged in an informal process to review each other's policies related to free trade agreements with a view to strengthening our trade and investment relationship".[7] In October 2015, the European Commission

---

[2]Australian Government Department of Foreign Affairs and Trade, 'International Investment in Australia 2019' (2020) 65, 67 <https://www.dfat.gov.au/sites/default/files/international-investment-australia-2019.pdf>. See, also: European Commission, 'Commission Staff Working Document - Impact Assessment Accompanying the Document Recommendation for a Council Decision Authorising the Opening of Negotiations for a Free Trade Agreement with Australia' (2017) 5, 8; Thangavelu and Findlay (2018), pp. 190–192, 202.

[3]Australian Government Department of Foreign Affairs and Trade, 'International Investment in Australia 2019' (2020) 65, 67 <https://www.dfat.gov.au/sites/default/files/international-investment-australia-2019.pdf>. See, also: Messerlin and Parc (2018), p. 47; Drake-Brockman (2018), p. 16.

[4]Department for International Trade, 'Policy Paper: UK-Australia FTA Negotiations: Agreement in Principle" (17 June 2021), <https://www.gov.uk/government/publications/uk-australia-free-trade-agreement-negotiations-agreement-in-principle/uk-australia-fta-negotiations-agreement-in-principle>.

[5]Drake-Brockman (2018), p. 15. See, also: Thangavelu and Findlay (2018), pp. 190–192, 202.

[6]Australia/European Union, 'Towards a Closer Australia-EU Partnership: Joint Declaration of the Australian Foreign Minister and the EU's High Representative for Foreign and Security Policy/Vice President of the Commission' (2015) <https://www.foreignminister.gov.au/minister/julie-bishop/media-release/towards-closer-australia-eu-partnership-joint-declaration-australian-foreign-minister-and-eus-high-representative-foreign-and-security-policyvice-president-commission>. The Framework Agreement was signed in 2017, and provisionally applied from October 2018: Framework Agreement between the European Union and Its Member States, of the One Part, and Australia, of the Other Part (signed 7 August 2017). Under Article 15 of the Agreement, the Parties 'undertake to cooperate in securing the conditions for and promoting increased trade and investment between them', including 'to prevent and remove non-tariff-related obstacles to trade and investment'. Under Article 16, the Parties undertake to 'promote an attractive and stable environment for two-way investment through dialogue, aimed at: (a) enhancing their mutual understanding and cooperation on investment issues; (b) exploring mechanisms to facilitate investment flows; and (c) fostering stable, transparent, non-discriminatory and open rules for investors, without prejudice to the Parties' commitments under preferential trade agreements and other international obligations.'

[7]Australia/European Union, 'Towards a Closer Australia-EU Partnership: Joint Declaration of the Australian Foreign Minister and the EU's High Representative for Foreign and Security Policy/Vice President of the Commission' (2015) <https://www.foreignminister.gov.au/minister/julie-bishop/media-release/towards-closer-australia-eu-partnership-joint-declaration-australian-foreign-minister-and-eus-high-representative-foreign-and-security-policyvice-president-commission>.

published its "Trade for All" communication, in which it indicated that it would "request authorisation to negotiate FTAs with Australia and New Zealand (NZ)".[8] In doing so, it noted that:

> Australia and New Zealand are Europe's close partners, share Europe's values and views on many issues, and play an important role in the Asia-Pacific region and in multilateral settings. Stronger economic ties with these countries will also provide a solid platform for deeper integration with wider Asia-Pacific value chains. Strengthening these relationships should be a priority.[9]

On 15 November 2015, Australia and the EU jointly indicated their agreement to "commence work toward the launch of negotiations for a Free Trade Agreement", noting that they would "aim to achieve a comprehensive and balanced outcome that liberalises trade, promotes productive investment flows and enhances the regulatory environment for business".[10] Subsequently, in January 2016, the European Commission published an "Inception Impact Assessment" on an EU-Australia FTA, noting in respect of Australia that there was "an untapped potential in the areas of trade, investment and economic co-operation".[11] The Assessment noted that one of the key barriers to investments in Australia was that "EU investors face stricter screening thresholds than investors from other countries (e.g. the US, China) that have already concluded FTAs with Australia".[12]

Thereafter, from 11 March to 3 June 2016, the European Commission conducted an open online consultation process concerning "the future trade and economic relationship" between the EU and Australia,[13] to which it received 108 replies.[14] This process asked several questions concerning barriers faced by EU investors in

---

[8]European Commission, 'Communication from the Commission to the European Parliament, the Council, the European Economic and Social Committee and the Committee of the Regions: Trade for All, Towards a More Responsible Trade and Investment Policy', 14 October 2015, 24.

[9]European Commission, 'Communication from the Commission to the European Parliament, the Council, the European Economic and Social Committee and the Committee of the Regions: Trade for All, Towards a More Responsible Trade and Investment Policy', 14 October 2015, 24.

[10]Australia/European Union, 'Joint Statement by President Donald Tusk, President Jean-Claude Juncker and Prime Minister of Australia Malcolm Turnbull' (2015) <https://www.consilium.europa.eu/de/press/press-releases/2015/11/15/pec-tusk-joint-statement-australia/>.

[11]European Commission, 'Inception Impact Assessment: EU-Australia and EU-New Zealand Free Trade Agreements' (2016) 2 <https://ec.europa.eu/smart-regulation/roadmaps/docs/2015_trade_040_aus_nz_trade_agreement_en.pdf>.

[12]European Commission, 'Inception Impact Assessment: EU-Australia and EU-New Zealand Free Trade Agreements' (2016) 2 <https://ec.europa.eu/smart-regulation/roadmaps/docs/2015_trade_040_aus_nz_trade_agreement_en.pdf>.

[13]European Commission, 'Online Public Consultation on the Future of EU-Australia and EU-New Zealand Trade and Economic Relations' (2016) <http://trade.ec.europa.eu/consultations/index.cfm?consul_id=195>.

[14]European Commission, 'Recommendation for a COUNCIL DECISION Authorising the Opening of Negotiations for a Free Trade Agreement with Australia {SWD(2017) 292} {SWD(2017) 293}' 13 September 2017 <https://eur-lex.europa.eu/legal-content/EN/TXT/?uri=COM:2017:472:FIN>.

Australia, eliciting a range of responses related to Australia's foreign investment screening regime, with some respondents also requesting the development of a "sound investment protection regime".[15] The European Commission subsequently sought authorisation from the Council to begin negotiations for an FTA with Australia. It noted that the "main reason for the proposal is to create more favourable conditions for further increasing trade and investment between the EU and Australia".[16] In an Impact Assessment of 13 September 2017 accompanying the request for authorisation, the Commission reported that:

> There is no modern, investment protection for all EU investors. Only five EU Member States have bilateral investment treaties in place with Australia ... Furthermore, the existing BITs that EU Member States have with Australia include investor-state dispute settlement mechanisms, which are not in line with current EU approach.[17]

The Impact Assessment further indicated that one of the goals for the FTA would be to:

> reap the benefits of enhanced trade and investment flows between the EU and Australia ... by reducing barriers for trade and investment ... and by exploring forward-looking regulatory cooperation in appropriately selected areas, such as public procurement, intellectual property investment protection ... [and] provide a new framework with comprehensive, progressive and up-to date set of rules for the EU-Australia ... trade and investment relationships including for the promotion of sustainable development in line with the general EU trade policy objectives.[18]

The Commission thus requested from the Council authorisation to negotiate "an agreement which would cover liberalisation of trade in goods, services, public procurement and foreign direct investment, together with flanking rules dealing, for example, with intellectual property rights".[19] The proposed negotiating directives made no mention of investment protection or investor-State dispute settlement provisions. They also indicated that the focus of the FTA negotiations would be on

---

[15] European Commission, 'Online Public Consultation on the Future of EU-Australia and EU-New Zealand Trade and Economic Relations: Online Contributions – Published Results' (2016) <https://ec.europa.eu/eusurvey/publication/AUZ_NZ>.

[16] European Commission, 'Recommendation for a COUNCIL DECISION Authorising the Opening of Negotiations for a Free Trade Agreement with Australia {SWD(2017) 292} {SWD(2017) 293}' 13 September 2017 <https://eur-lex.europa.eu/legal-content/EN/TXT/?uri=COM:2017:472:FIN>.

[17] European Commission, 'Commission Staff Working Document - Impact Assessment Accompanying the Document Recommendation for a Council Decision Authorising the Opening of Negotiations for a Free Trade Agreement with Australia', Section 1.2.

[18] European Commission, 'Commission Staff Working Document - Impact Assessment Accompanying the Document Recommendation for a Council Decision Authorising the Opening of Negotiations for a Free Trade Agreement with Australia', Section 3.2.

[19] European Commission, 'Recommendation for a COUNCIL DECISION Authorising the Opening of Negotiations for a Free Trade Agreement with Australia {SWD(2017) 292} {SWD(2017) 293}' 13 September 2017 <https://eur-lex.europa.eu/legal-content/EN/TXT/?uri=COM:2017:472:FIN>.

foreign direct investment (leaving out any mention of portfolio investment), specifying that:

> The negotiations should aim at the progressive and reciprocal liberalisation of trade in services and foreign direct investment by eliminating restrictions to market access and national treatment, beyond the Parties' WTO commitments and offers submitted in the context of the negotiations of the Trade in Services Agreement. The Agreement should include rules concerning performance requirements related to foreign direct investment.[20]

On 8 May 2018, the European Council approved negotiating directives for an FTA with Australia for adoption by the Foreign Affairs Council (Trade) on 22 May 2018. These negotiating directives were declassified and released on 25 June 2018.[21] In that document, the Council specified that: "[t]he Agreement should exclusively contain provisions on trade and foreign direct investment related areas applicable between the parties".[22] The mandate nevertheless emphasised that "[t]he Agreement should only include obligations in areas falling under the competence of all applicable authorities and entities of both parties to the Agreement".[23] The Council noted further as follows:

> 3. The Council notes that in the future the Commission intends to recommend draft negotiating directives for FTAs covering exclusive EU competence on the one hand and separate mixed investment agreements on the other, with a view to strengthening the EU's position as a negotiating partner. It is for the Council to decide whether to open negotiations on this basis. It is equally for the Council to decide, on a case-by-case basis, on the splitting of trade agreements. . . .
>
> 4. Negotiating EU-only trade agreements should not lead to a loss of negotiation leverage for the EU to obtain ambitious standalone investment agreements. A first reflection in the Council on the need for investment protection rules with the negotiating partner concerned should take place at the earliest possible stage of the scoping exercise. EU investment agreements, where deemed necessary, should in principle be negotiated in parallel to FTAs.
>
> 5. Regarding future trade negotiations with Australia and New Zealand, the Council notes that the Commission has not presented in these two specific cases recommendations for negotiating directives for investment agreements, alongside the recommendations it has proposed for the negotiation of FTAs. The Council considers that this should not set a precedent for the future.[24]

---

[20] European Commission, 'Recommendation for a COUNCIL DECISION Authorising the Opening of Negotiations for a Free Trade Agreement with Australia {SWD(2017) 292} {SWD(2017) 293}' 13 September 2017 <https://eur-lex.europa.eu/legal-content/EN/TXT/?uri=COM:2017:472:FIN>.

[21] Council of the European Union, 'Negotiating Directives for a Free Trade Agreement with Australia (25 June 2018)' (2018).

[22] Council of the European Union, 'Negotiating Directives for a Free Trade Agreement with Australia (25 June 2018)' (2018).

[23] Council of the European Union, 'Negotiating Directives for a Free Trade Agreement with Australia (25 June 2018)' (2018).

[24] Council of the European Union, 'Draft Council Conclusions on the Negotiation and Conclusion of EU Trade Agreements – Adoption' (2018) 8622/18 <https://data.consilium.europa.eu/doc/document/ST-8622-2018-INIT/en/pdf>.

In June 2018, Australia announced its own objectives for the FTA. Specifically, it announced that it was seeking through the FTA negotiations to: "[i]mprove market access for Australian investment and increase investment into Australia, supporting economic growth [and to] [e]nhance transparency and regulatory frameworks to provide greater certainty for investors."[25] Australia's Department of Foreign Affairs and Trade (DFAT) has also indicated that:

> The EU remains one of our top destinations and sources of investment. We are seeking to improve market access for Australian investment and increase investment into Australia, including through obligations which ensure the free flow of capital related to investments between our economies. We will also seek an undertaking from the EU not to impose residency and/or citizenship requirements on senior representatives of Australian companies established in the EU. Australia will uphold the government's right to regulate for legitimate public purpose and screen investments for national interest. On 22 May, the EU Council authorised the Commission to open trade negotiations with Australia (9102/18). In a separate decision (8622/18), the Council noted that the Commission had not presented a recommendation for a negotiating directive for an investment agreement.[26]

DFAT has also conducted an open consultation process in relation to the AEUFTA (which remains open at the time of writing).[27] Several of the submissions received to date have focussed on investment screening and admission thresholds and other matters of investment liberalisation,[28] with several expressly opposing any inclusion of investor-State dispute settlement (ISDS) provisions in the agreement.[29]

---

[25] Australian Government Department of Foreign Affairs and Trade, 'Australia-European Union Free Trade Agreement: Objectives' (2018) <https://www.dfat.gov.au/trade/agreements/negotiations/aeufta/Pages/australia-european-union-fta-objectives>.

[26] Australian Government Department of Foreign Affairs and Trade, 'Summary of Negotiating Aims and Approach' <https://www.dfat.gov.au/trade/agreements/negotiations/aeufta/Pages/summary-of-negotiating-aims-and-approach>.

[27] Australian Government Department of Foreign Affairs and Trade, 'A-EUFTA Submissions' <https://www.dfat.gov.au/trade/agreements/negotiations/aeufta/submissions/aeufta-submissions>.

[28] ANZ, 'Submission from ANZ: Australia-European Union Free Trade Agreement' (2016) <https://www.dfat.gov.au/sites/default/files/anz-eufta-submission.PDF>; Australian Food & Grocery Council, 'AFGC Submission: Australia European Union Trade Negotiations' (2016); Business Council of Australia, 'Submission – Australia-European Union Free Trade Agreement' (2018) <https://www.dfat.gov.au/sites/default/files/business-council-of-australia-eufta-submission.pdf>.

[29] ACTU, 'ACTU Submission on a Proposed Australia-EU Free Trade Agreement' (2016) <https://www.dfat.gov.au/sites/default/files/australian-council-of-trade-unions-eufta-submission.PDF>; Australian Fair Trade and Investment Network (AFTINET), 'Submission to the Department of Foreign Affairs, Defence and Trade on the Proposed Australia-EU Free Trade Agreement' (2016) <https://www.dfat.gov.au/sites/default/files/australian-fair-trade-and-investment-network-limited-eufta-submission.PDF>; Public Health Association Australia, 'Public Health Association of Australia Submission on the Australian-European Union Free Trade Agreement' (2016) <https://www.dfat.gov.au/sites/default/files/public-health-association-of-australia-eufta-submission.PDF> (also observing that: 'The Investment Court System proposed by the EU for its trade agreement with the US, the Trans-Atlantic Trade and Investment Partnership [TTIP], does not appear to be a viable alternative. This model repeats some of the same flaws as the ISDS mechanisms it is meant to replace, including the potential for high arbitration costs and conflicts of interests.').

Only a handful of submissions have mentioned investment protection and/or ISDS positively: one submission suggested the development of a centre for customs with a forum to resolve customs disputes akin to an ISDS mechanism,[30] with another focussing on the need for provisions in the FTA to protect investments from expropriation and accepting ISDS as a "necessary evil".[31] Two other submissions also expressed support for inclusion of an ISDS mechanism, with one noting that such mechanism should be linked to "[i]nvestment provisions, including market access and post-establishment protections for investors".[32]

Against this background, the AEUFTA negotiations were officially launched on 18 June 2018. The negotiations for each component of the treaty have proceeded "in parallel", forming "part of a single undertaking".[33] At the time of writing, there have been eleven negotiating rounds. The first negotiating round took place from 2 to 6 July 2018 (with 17 working groups) and the second from 19 to 23 November 2018 (involving 16 working groups). The negotiations at the second round were based on several EU text proposals, which have since been publicly released (and which form the focus of Sect. 4 below). Following the second round of negotiations, the parties noted that:

> The discussions on services and investment in this round were based on the EU text proposal. A comprehensive and in depth analysis of the objectives, approach and the substance of the proposal took place. It was agreed to work on the basis of the EU text in most areas. The Australian side will confirm which text proposed by the EU side they can accept and provide detailed alternative proposals ahead of the next round in order to facilitate progress.[34]

The third negotiating round took place from 25 to 29 March 2019, again featuring 16 working groups that worked on the basis of the "textual proposals that had been submitted for all groups".[35] The report from this round of negotiations noted that:

> [b]ased upon the initial EU proposals for texts comprehensively dealing with the liberalisation of services and investment, both sides have been able to achieve consolidated

[30] Export Council of Australia, 'Submission to the Department of Foreign Affairs and Trade on the Proposed Australia-European Union Free Trade Agreement' (2016) <https://www.dfat.gov.au/sites/default/files/export-council-of-australia-eufta-submission.PDF>.

[31] Umair Ghori, 'Protection of Foreign Investor's Investments from Expropriation – The Desired Standards within the Future Australia-EU Free Trade Agreement (AEUFTA)' (2016) <https://www.dfat.gov.au/sites/default/files/dr-umair-ghori-bond-university-eufta-submission.PDF>.

[32] Minerals Council of Australia, 'Australia-EU FTA: Implications for Australia's Mining Industry' (2019) <https://www.dfat.gov.au/sites/default/files/minerals-council-of-australia-eufta-submission.pdf>; Gonzalo Villalta Puig, 'Australia – European Union Free Trade Agreement Submission to the Department of Foreign Affairs and Trade Australian Government' (2016) <https://www.dfat.gov.au/sites/default/files/professor-gonzalo-villalta-puig-eufta-submission.PDF>.

[33] Council of the European Union, 'Negotiating Directives for a Free Trade Agreement with Australia (25 June 2018)' (2018), p. 2.

[34] 'Report of the 2nd Round of Negotiations for a Free Trade Agreement between the European Union and Australia (19–23 November 2018, Canberra)' (2018).

[35] 'Report of the 3rd Round of Negotiations for a Free Trade Agreement between the European Union and Australia (25–29 March 2019, Canberra)' (2019).

texts during this round, containing Australian and EU attributions and substantially reflecting common views in many areas.[36]

The report further noted that, during this round, "[b]oth sides discussed the EU's proposed articles covering a range of goods and investment issues aimed at promoting investment in renewable and clean energy and trade in raw materials needed for green technologies such as batteries".[37] The fourth round of negotiations took place from 1 to 5 July 2019, this time with 18 working groups meeting to discuss a range of "different chapters", including a services and investment liberalisation chapter.[38] During the fifth round of negotiations, from 14 to 18 October 2019, these 18 working groups met again to discuss various textual proposals and comments, including "in relation to investment and cross-border services liberalisation".[39] The sixth negotiating round, involving 22 working groups, met from 10 to 14 February 2020. During this round, discussions on "services and investment ... made continued progress".[40] The seventh negotiating round took place from 4 to 15 May 2020 (involving 23 working groups).[41] The eighth round took place from 14 to 25 September 2020,[42] the ninth from 30 November to 11 December 2020,[43] the tenth from 9 to 19 March 2021,[44] and the eleventh from 1 to 11 June 2021.[45] The parties have noted that "Australia and the EU ... remain on track to achieve a highly ambitious and comprehensive outcome on services and investment".[46]

[36] 'Report of the 3rd Round of Negotiations for a Free Trade Agreement between the European Union and Australia (25–29 March 2019, Canberra)' (2019).

[37] 'Report of the 3rd Round of Negotiations for a Free Trade Agreement between the European Union and Australia (25–29 March 2019, Canberra)' (2019).

[38] 'Report of the 4th Round of Negotiations for a Free Trade Agreement between the European Union and Australia (1–5 July 2019, Brussels)' (2019).

[39] 'Report of the 5th Round of Negotiations for a Free Trade Agreement between the European Union and Australia (14–18 October 2019, Canberra)' (2019).

[40] 'Report of the 6th Round of Negotiations for a Free Trade Agreement between the European Union and Australia (10–14 February 2020, Canberra)' (2020).

[41] 'Report of the 7th Round of Negotiations for a Free Trade Agreement between the European Union and Australia 4 – 15 May 2020' (2020).

[42] 'Report of the 8th Round of Negotiations for a Trade Agreement between the European Union and Australia 14 – 25 September 2020 (Video-Conference)' (2020).

[43] 'Report of the 9th Round of Negotiations for a Trade Agreement between the European Union and Australia 30 November – 11 December 2020 (Video-Conference)' (2020).

[44] 'Report of the 10th Round of Negotiations for a Free Trade Agreement between the European Union and Australia 9 – 19 March 2021' (2021).

[45] 'Report of the 11th Round of Negotiations for a Free Trade Agreement between the European Union and Australia 1 – 11 June 2021' (2021).

[46] 'Report of the 7th Round of Negotiations for a Free Trade Agreement between the European Union and Australia 4 – 15 May 2020' (2020). This article was drafted and finalised prior to any further negotiating rounds being held between the EU and Australia.

3 The Exclusion of Portfolio Investment, Investment Protection, and Investor-State Arbitration from the AEUFTA

As noted above, the EU's negotiating directives for the AEUFTA did not envisage including a dedicated investment protection chapter or associated investor-State dispute settlement (ISDS) provisions. The negotiating mandate instead restricted the investment-related provisions of the FTA to elements of the bilateral investment relationship relevant to FDI, including investment liberalisation. The exclusion of investment protection and ISDS appears to have been predominantly motivated by the EU—rather than Australia's—legal constraints and policy choices. In particular, the negotiating mandate for the AEUFTA was limited to matters within exclusive EU competence, excluding matters of mixed EU/Member State competence which would have required consent to the AEUFTA by both the EU and each Member State prior to ratification.[47] As this Section outlines, this has prompted the exclusion from the FTA of provisions covering portfolio investment, investment promotion, and investor-State dispute settlement. Along with the FTA the EU is currently negotiating with New Zealand, this is the first time an EU negotiating mandate has adopted this approach since the conclusion of the Treaty of Lisbon, which entered into force in December 2009.[48]

The regulation of FDI was designated as an exclusive EU competence in the Lisbon Treaty.[49] The Lisbon Treaty does not define "FDI". Typically, that term has been distinguished from "portfolio investment", with FDI being understood to designate a situation in which an investor acquires a "lasting interest" (usually through shares or other voting rights) in an enterprise, including capacity to exercise influence over the management of that enterprise.[50] The European Commission accepts that FDI differs from portfolio investment, with FDI referring to "any foreign investment which serves to establish lasting and direct links with the undertaking to which capital is made available in order to carry out an economic activity".[51]

---

[47] Drake-Brockman (2018), p. 15.

[48] Drake-Brockman (2018), p. 16.

[49] TFEU, Articles 3(1)(e) and 206. See, further, on the EU and Member State competences vis-a-vis investment prior to the Lisbon Treaty: Moskvan (2017), p. 244; Basedow (2016), pp. 745–748, 755–758; Waibel (2013), p. 4; Meunier (2014), p. 2; Fina and Lentner (2016), p. 425; Shan and Zhang (2010), p. 1050; Soderlund (2007), p. 462; Leal-Arcas (2010), pp. 487, 504–505; Titi (2015), pp. 642–643; Perez de las Heras (2018), pp. 80–81; Hindelang (2015), p. 69; Chaisse (2012), p. 69; Reinisch (2014).

[50] See, for example: OECD, *Benchmark Definition of Foreign Direct Investment* (4th edn, 2010) para. 11; IMF, *Balance of Payments Manual* (5th edn, 1993) para. 362; See, similarly: Meunier (2014), p. 11.

[51] European Commission, 'Communication from the Commission to the Council, the European Parliament, the European Economic and Social Committee and the Committee of the Regions: Towards a Comprehensive European International Investment Policy' (2010) COM(2010)343 2 <https://eur-lex.europa.eu/LexUriServ/LexUriServ.do?uri=COM:2010:0343:FIN:EN:PDF>.

However, the Commission had claimed subsequent to the conclusion of the Lisbon Treaty that "the Union has exclusive competence to conclude agreements covering all matters relating to foreign investment, that is both foreign direct investment and portfolio investment".[52] This was on the basis of a purported implied exclusive competence arising out of Article 63 of the Treaty on the Functioning of the European Union (TFEU). That provision requires that the movement of capital (including portfolio investment) between EU Member States and third countries be free of restrictions.[53] The Commission thus contended that it held an implied exclusive competence in respect of portfolio investment, because Member State action on that topic "may affect common rules or alter their scope".[54] In contrast to the Commission's view, most Member States, and the Council, interpreted the EU's exclusive competence as limited to FDI only.[55] They also queried the EU's competence to negotiate obligations in FTAs concerning expropriation, given that Article 345 of the TFEU provides that "[t]he Treaties shall in no way prejudice the rules in Member States governing the system of property ownership".[56]

These issues were referred to the Court of Justice of the European Union (CJEU) in October 2014, in relation to the conclusion of the EU-Singapore FTA. The Court issued an opinion in May 2017, by which it held that matters related to FDI were within the EU's exclusive competence, whereas matters of portfolio investment were a shared competence.[57] It also held that the EU had competence to negotiate treaties

---

[52] European Commission, 'Proposal for a Regulation of the European Parliament and of the Council Establishing a Framework for Managing Financial Responsibility Linked to Investor-State Dispute Settlement Tribunals Established by International Agreements to Which the European Union Is Party' COM/2012/0335 para. 1.2 <https://eur-lex.europa.eu/legal-content/EN/TXT/?uri=celex%3A52012PC0335>.

[53] European Commission, 'Proposal for a Regulation of the European Parliament and of the Council Establishing a Framework for Managing Financial Responsibility Linked to Investor-State Dispute Settlement Tribunals Established by International Agreements to Which the European Union Is Party' COM/2012/0335 <https://eur-lex.europa.eu/legal-content/EN/TXT/?uri=celex%3A52012PC0335>. See, further: Reinisch (2014), pp. 137–138; Devuyst (2011), p. 655; Kendra and Kozyreff (2013), p. 253.

[54] European Commission, 'Proposal for a Regulation of the European Parliament and of the Council Establishing a Framework for Managing Financial Responsibility Linked to Investor-State Dispute Settlement Tribunals Established by International Agreements to Which the European Union Is Party' COM/2012/0335 para. 1.2 <https://eur-lex.europa.eu/legal-content/EN/TXT/?uri=celex%3A52012PC0335>, referring to Articles 3(2) and 63 TFEU.

[55] See, for example: German Constitutional Court, 2 BvE 2108, 30 June 2009, para. 379 ('Much, however, argues in favour of assuming that the term "foreign direct investment" only encompasses investment which serves to obtain a controlling interest in an enterprise ... The consequence of this would be that exclusive competence only exists for investment of this type whereas investment protection agreements that go beyond this would have to be concluded as mixed agreements.'). See, further: Reinisch (2014), p. 136; Kleimann and Kübek (2016), p. 13; Sharma (2011), pp. 282–283; Meunier (2014), p. 11; Chaisse (2012), pp. 57–58; Bungenberg et al. (2011), p. 2.

[56] See, further: Chaisse (2012), p. 61; Moskvan (2017), p. 255; Kendra and Kozyreff (2013), p. 253; Waibel (2013), pp. 15–16.

[57] *Opinion 2/15 of the Court (Full Court), 16 May 2017* [83].

with expropriation provisions "in so far as they relate to foreign direct investment".[58] It further held that investor-State arbitration—which permits an investor to submit a dispute to arbitration and "removes disputes from the jurisdiction of the courts of the Member States"—could not be established without the consent of EU Member States and so was also a matter of mixed competence.[59] This decision has meant that the EU does not have the competence to negotiate alone all matters that might be included within an investment treaty or an investment chapter in an FTA. As the Court concluded:

> It follows from all the foregoing considerations that the envisaged agreement [the EU/Singapore FTA] falls within the exclusive competence of the European Union, with the exception of the following provisions, which fall within a competence shared between the European Union and the Member States:
> - the provisions of Section A (Investment Protection) of Chapter 9 (Investment) of that agreement, in so far as they relate to non-direct investment between the European Union and the Republic of Singapore;
> - the provisions of Section B (Investor-State Dispute Settlement) of Chapter 9; and
> - the provisions of Chapters 1 (Objectives and General Definitions), 14 (Transparency), 15 (Dispute Settlement between the Parties), 16 (Mediation Mechanism) and 17 (Institutional, General and Final Provisions) of that agreement, in so far as those provisions relate to the provisions of Chapter 9 and to the extent that the latter fall within a competence shared between the European Union and the Member States.[60]

In 2018, an Australian domestic parliamentary review process addressed whether the scope of the AEUFTA negotiations would be impacted by this decision of the CJEU.[61] At the time, DFAT indicated that because FTA negotiations had not yet been launched, and because the EU did not yet have a mandate for such negotiations, "there is currently no draft text" and "the EU has not yet made a proposal to us on investment coverage in the FTA".[62] However, as noted above, subsequent to this decision, the Commission only sought a negotiating mandate in respect of the AEUFTA that covered matters of exclusive EU competence. It thus opted not to negotiate the AEUFTA as a mixed agreement with Member States,[63] likely to avoid the potential delays and complexities that would be associated with seeking the consent of Member States to the FTA on matters of mixed competence.[64] Of course,

[58] *Opinion 2/15 of the Court (Full Court), 16 May 2017* [109].

[59] *Opinion 2/15 of the Court (Full Court), 16 May 2017* [292]–[293].

[60] *Opinion 2/15 of the Court (Full Court), 16 May 2017* [305].

[61] Department of Foreign Affairs and Trade, 'JSCOT Hearing on the Australia-EU Framework Agreement, 7 May 2018: Questions On Notice' (2018) <https://www.aph.gov.au/Parliamentary_Business/Committees/Joint/Treaties/EUFrameworkAgreement/Submissions>.

[62] Department of Foreign Affairs and Trade, 'JSCOT Hearing on the Australia-EU Framework Agreement, 7 May 2018:: Questions On Notice' (2018) <https://www.aph.gov.au/Parliamentary_Business/Committees/Joint/Treaties/EUFrameworkAgreement/Submissions>.

[63] Gantz (2017), p. 381.

[64] On which see, further: Kendra and Kozyreff (2013), pp. 254–255; Devuyst (2011), pp. 643–644; Kleimann and Kübek (2016), p. 11; Gantz (2017), pp. 370–371; Lopez-Rodriguez (2017), p. 163; Reinisch (2014), p. 137; Kerneis (2018), p. 99; Fontanelli and Bianco (2014), p. 230.

the EU could conceivably have sought to negotiate investment protection provisions covering FDI only, whilst leaving portfolio investment to separate Member State negotiation. This would, however, have produced significant complexities.[65] It would also have required the omission of dispute settlement provisions concerning those investment protection provisions. For other FTAs, the restricted competences of the EU have prompted the EU to split the treaties into two parts: a first part covering exclusive EU competences vis-à-vis trade, and a second part covering mixed competences vis-à-vis investment.[66] However, the EU has—thus far at least[67]—not sought a mandate to negotiate two such agreements in the case of Australia. Instead, the AEUFTA negotiating mandate on the EU side was limited solely to matters of investment liberalisation and market access, as exclusive EU competences.

From a policy perspective, the non-inclusion of ISDS in the AEUFTA is in any case consistent with the EU's approach to ISDS reform. The EU is seeking the replacement of investment arbitration with a permanent international investment court mechanism.[68] Australia has not adopted a clear position vis-à-vis the EU's investment court proposal. Indeed, the policy position of the Australian Government vis-à-vis the inclusion of ISDS itself has shifted significantly over the last decade.[69] While the current Liberal Government adopts a case-by-case approach to assessing whether to include ISDS in treaties to which Australia is party, there still remains significant political opposition to the inclusion of ISDS in Australia's treaties.[70] In 2019, for instance, Senator Whish-Wilson (of the Australian Greens) commented on the AEUFTA negotiations as follows:

> It is interesting how we are talking about having a free trade deal with Europe but they do not want an ISDS. Why is that? Why is it that the Europeans are not too keen on ISDS? It is because at least they are progressive and they understand that it has eroded our democracy. Why are we giving corporations a right to second-guess decisions made by parliament that are in the public interest simply because it may not be in their self-interest, in the interest of their profits and their shareholders? You can forget all this rubbish about carve-outs and exceptions. They have been thoroughly debunked. They were written entirely for corporations.[71]

---

[65] Kendra and Kozyreff (2013), pp. 254–255; Reinisch (2014), p. 125.

[66] See, for example: European Commission, 'Key Elements of the EU-Japan Economic Partnership Agreement - Memo' (2018) para. 11 <https://trade.ec.europa.eu/doclib/press/index.cfm?id=1955>.

[67] See, for example: Drake-Brockman (2018), p. 16 (noting an expectation that "in due course", the EU would "achieve a new follow-up FTA negotiating mandate for a supplementary deal with Australia on investment").

[68] European Commission, *Investment in TTIP and Beyond – the Path for Reform: Enhancing the Right to Regulate and Moving from Current Ad Hoc Arbitration towards an Investment Court* (2015) <http://trade.ec.europa.eu/doclib/docs/2015/may/tradoc_153408.PDF>.

[69] See, generally: Dickson-Smith and Mercurio (2018).

[70] See, for example: Trade and Foreign Investment (Protecting the Public Interest) Bill 2014.

[71] Australian Senate, 'Official Hansard: 25 November 2019' p. 4121 (Senator Whish-Wilson).

Australia has omitted ISDS provisions in several treaties, including most prominently in the 2005 Australia-US FTA (AUSFTA).[72] The omission of ISDS from the AUSFTA reflected a view by both negotiating States that ISDS was not needed given "the long-standing economic ties between the United States and Australia, their shared legal traditions, and the confidence of their investors in operating in each others' markets".[73] Perhaps consistent with this approach, the agreement in principle for the UK-Australia FTA indicates that ISDS will be excluded from that agreement. Yet, ISDS is already included in each of Australia's five existing BITs with EU Member States. It is also included in each of Australia's recently concluded FTAs. As Chaisse and Renouf have noted, "[t]his suggests that the existence of an effective domestic judicial system in the other FTA partners will not systematically lead Australia to renounce ISDS."[74] Australia's current approach to ISDS reform appears to favour retention of an arbitration mechanism, albeit with newly concluded treaties modernising both the procedures of investor-State arbitration and the scope of investment protection as compared to earlier treaties. The retention of unmodernised investment treaties between EU Member States and Australia alongside the AEUFTA creates the potential for interactions between these instruments which are returned to in more detail below.

4 The AEUFTA's Coverage of Investment-Related Matters

Neither the EU nor Australia has released a publicly available model investment treaty.[75] This allows each to retain flexibility during negotiations, but makes it difficult to identify the possible starting point of such

[72] Australia-United States Free Trade Agreement (2005) ATS 1 (signed 18 May 2004, entered into force 1 January 2005).

[73] Office of the United States Trade Representative, 'Summary of the U.S.-Australia Free Trade Agreement' <https://ustr.gov/about-us/policy-offices/press-office/fact-sheets/archives/2004/february/summary-us-australia-free-trade-agreement>. See, further: Chaisse and Renouf (2018), pp. 297–298; Dickson-Smith and Mercurio (2018), pp. 223–224; Dodge (2006).

[74] Chaisse and Renouf (2018), p. 298.

[75] Approximately 20 EU Member States have developed a model investment treaty: Calamita (2012), pp. 316–318. The European Parliament in 2011 requested that the Commission develop "a strong EU template for investment agreements, which would also be adjustable according to the level of development of the partner country": European Parliament, 'European International Investment Policy: European Parliament Resolution of 6 April 2011 on the Future European International Investment Policy' (2010/2203(INI)) para, 9. The Commission has resisted developing a model investment treaty, on the basis that a 'one-size-fits-all model . . . would necessarily be neither feasible nor desirable': European Commission, 'Communication from the Commission to the Council, the European Parliament, the European Economic and Social Committee and the Committee of the Regions: Towards a Comprehensive European International Investment Policy' (2010) COM(2010)343 2 <https://eur-lex.europa.eu/LexUriServ/LexUriServ.do?uri=COM:2010:0343:FIN:EN:PDF>.

negotiations.[76] As noted above, however, several of the EU's textual proposals for the AEUFTA have been publicly released. Brief negotiating records of each round of negotiations have also been publicly released. While this has rendered the negotiations more transparent than some, they have still been criticised for their secrecy—particularly in relation to the non-release by Australia of similar negotiating documents.[77] One of the EU's textual proposals, dated 22 October 2018, makes it possible to discern (broadly) the likely contours of the investment-related provisions in the FTA,[78] given the indications in the negotiating records that the negotiations of the investment liberalisation chapter have broadly followed the contours of the EU's textual proposals.

Consistent with the EU's negotiating mandate, the EU's textual proposal on investment focusses on investment liberalisation. It applies to:

> measures of a Party affecting establishment or operation to perform economic activities by: (a) investors of the other Party; (b) covered enterprises; and (c) for the purposes of Article 2.6 [Performance requirements], any enterprise in the territory of the Party which adopts or maintains the measure.[79]

The proposal contains several obligations relevant to investment liberalisation, including provisions regulating market access conditions,[80] national treatment obligations with respect to establishment[81] and operation,[82] most-favoured nation

[76] It also forecloses the benefits to both treaty partners of having developed a model, including the potential for a model to set out a general policy approach to investment liberalisation/protection, garner the support of stakeholders (including from different levels or areas of government), refine textual approaches to key issues, or achieve consistency across treaty commitments. On the potential benefits of developing a model treaty see, further: Calamita (2012), pp. 316–318; Chaisse (2012), p. 63; Dickson-Smith and Mercurio (2018), p. 215.

[77] See, for example: Australian Senate, 'Official Hansard: 25 November 2019', pp. 4120–4122 (Senator Whish-Wilson).

[78] European Union, 'EU-Australia Free Trade Agreement: Investment Liberalisation and Trade in Services' (2018) <https://trade.ec.europa.eu/doclib/docs/2018/december/tradoc_157572.pdf>.

[79] European Union, 'EU-Australia Free Trade Agreement: Investment Liberalisation and Trade in Services' (2018) <https://trade.ec.europa.eu/doclib/docs/2018/december/tradoc_157572.pdf> Article 2.1(1).

[80] European Union, 'EU-Australia Free Trade Agreement: Investment Liberalisation and Trade in Services' (2018) <https://trade.ec.europa.eu/doclib/docs/2018/december/tradoc_157572.pdf> Article 2.2(1).

[81] European Union, 'EU-Australia Free Trade Agreement: Investment Liberalisation and Trade in Services' (2018) <https://trade.ec.europa.eu/doclib/docs/2018/december/tradoc_157572.pdf> Article 2.3(1) ("Each Party shall accord to investors of the other Party and to covered enterprises treatment no less favourable than that it accords, in like situations, to its own investors and to their enterprises, with respect to establishment in its territory.").

[82] European Union, 'EU-Australia Free Trade Agreement: Investment Liberalisation and Trade in Services' (2018) <https://trade.ec.europa.eu/doclib/docs/2018/december/tradoc_157572.pdf> Article 2.3(2) ("Each Party shall accord to investors of the other Party and to covered enterprises treatment no less favourable than that it accords, in like situations, to its own investors and to their enterprises, with respect to operation in its territory.").

(MFN) treatment obligations with respect to operation[83] (with the EU also reserving its right to propose a text on most favoured nation treatment for establishment), and prohibitions on particular performance requirements.[84] The EU's proposed text for the investment chapter also contemplates the potential for the parties to schedule "non-conforming measures and exceptions".[85] The text also contains a denial of benefits provision specifying that:

> A Party may deny the benefits of this Chapter to an investor of the other Party or to a covered enterprise if the denying Party adopts or maintains measures related to the maintenance of international peace and security, including the protection of human rights, which: a. prohibit transactions with that investor or covered enterprise, or b. would be violated or circumvented if the benefits of this Chapter were accorded to that investor or covered enterprise, including where the measures prohibit transactions with a natural or juridical person who owns or controls either of them.[86]

The EU's proposal is specifically adapted to ensure the coverage of a range of government measures in light of the political institutional frameworks of both the EU and Australia. It stipulates, for instance, that the national treatment obligations apply to require:

> (a) with respect to a regional or local level of government of Australia, treatment no less favourable than the most favourable treatment accorded, in like situations, by that level of government to investors of Australia and to their enterprises in its territory.
> (b) with respect to a government of, or in, a Member State of the European Union, treatment no less favourable than the most favourable treatment accorded, in like situations, by that government to investors of that Member State and to their enterprises in its territory.[87]

This reflects the EU's negotiating mandate, which indicated the EU's intention to "ensure that all levels of government, including sub-central authorities and relevant entities, effectively comply with the provisions of the Agreement".[88] As the FTA

---

[83] European Union, 'EU-Australia Free Trade Agreement: Investment Liberalisation and Trade in Services' (2018) <https://trade.ec.europa.eu/doclib/docs/2018/december/tradoc_157572.pdf> Article 2.4(2) ("Each Party shall accord to investors of the other Party and to covered enterprises treatment no less favourable than that it accords, in like situations, to investors of a third country and to their enterprises, with respect to operation in its territory.").

[84] European Union, 'EU-Australia Free Trade Agreement: Investment Liberalisation and Trade in Services' (2018) <https://trade.ec.europa.eu/doclib/docs/2018/december/tradoc_157572.pdf> Article 2.6. See, also, Article 2.5.

[85] European Union, 'EU-Australia Free Trade Agreement: Investment Liberalisation and Trade in Services' (2018) <https://trade.ec.europa.eu/doclib/docs/2018/december/tradoc_157572.pdf> Article 2.7.

[86] European Union, 'EU-Australia Free Trade Agreement: Investment Liberalisation and Trade in Services' (2018) <https://trade.ec.europa.eu/doclib/docs/2018/december/tradoc_157572.pdf> Article 2.8.

[87] European Union, 'EU-Australia Free Trade Agreement: Investment Liberalisation and Trade in Services' (2018) <https://trade.ec.europa.eu/doclib/docs/2018/december/tradoc_157572.pdf> Article 2.3(3).

[88] Council of the European Union, 'Negotiating Directives for a Free Trade Agreement with Australia (25 June 2018)' (2018), p. 2.

does not address ISDS, it has not provided the parties with the opportunity to consider the corollary to such provisions, that is, how investor-State arbitration procedures ought to be managed where a claim is filed against a sub-national government measure. The EU has already produced internal rules on these matters, building on the approach it has taken to these issues under the Energy Charter Treaty.[89] Australia does not have a similar internal procedure, though has sought to exempt certain sub-national government measures from the scope of some (or all) investment treaty obligations in its existing trade and investment treaties.[90] It remains to be seen, in particular, whether Australia will seek to schedule or reserve certain sub-national government measures from the operation of the provisions in the AEUFTA's investment chapter.

Investment screening and admission procedures have also been identified by stakeholders in both the EU and Australia as a major barrier for foreign investment in each territory.[91] It is therefore likely that the future FTA will seek to liberalise the application of such frameworks vis-à-vis investment between Australia and the EU. While screening within the EU was previously exclusively managed by individual Member States,[92] the EU in 2019 adopted a screening framework for FDI from third States.[93] Under the framework, which entered into force in 2020, EU Member States that apply admission requirements must take into account a non-exhaustive list of considerations, including the potential effects of the proposed investment on critical infrastructure and technologies. Australia also has in place screening procedures for foreign investments.[94] Australia's foreign investment

[89] European Commission, 'Proposal for a Regulation of the European Parliament and of the Council Establishing a Framework for Managing Financial Responsibility Linked to Investor-State Dispute Settlement Tribunals Established by International Agreements to Which the European Union Is Party' COM/2012/0335 para. 1.2 <https://eur-lex.europa.eu/legal-content/EN/TXT/?uri=celex%3A52012PC0335>. See, further: McClay (2016), p. 269; Reinisch (2014), pp. 119–120, 133–134; Fina and Lentner (2016), p. 437.

[90] See, for example, the approach adopted in: Comprehensive and Progressive Agreement for Trans-Pacific Partnership. Such approaches carry their own risks, including by creating: negotiating difficulties due to their creation of asymmetrical treaty obligations for central and decentralised States; the risk of piecemeal or even conflicting regulatory regimes at the central and sub-national levels vis-à-vis investment protection, which in turn increase regulatory opacity and compliance costs; and enforcement gaps which remove 'international accountability for local governments at the same time that local governments are increasingly exercising their authority in a way that produces international effects': Meyer (2017), p. 261.

[91] See, for example: European Commission, 'Commission Staff Working Document – Impact Assessment Accompanying the Document Recommendation for a Council Decision Authorising the Opening of Negotiations for a Free Trade Agreement with Australia', p. 8. See, further, Sect. 2 above.

[92] See, further: Meunier (2014), p. 2.

[93] Regulation (EU) 2019/452 of the European Parliament and of the Council of 19 March 2019 Establishing a Framework for the Screening of Foreign Direct Investments into the Union.

[94] The EU and Australia are not alone in imposing screening requirements on foreign investment. At the time of writing, some 29 States had adopted inbound investment screening policies. These have been collated at: UNCTAD, 'Investment Policy Hub' <https://investmentpolicy.unctad.org/

policy is principally set out in the *Foreign Acquisitions and Takeovers Act 1975* (Cth) (FATA) and its implementing regulations, as supplemented by policies developed by the Foreign Investment Review Board. Under the FATA, "significant actions"[95] by foreign individuals[96] related to the acquisition of shareholdings, assets, or Australian land, and actions related to Australian corporations, have to be notified to the Treasurer prior to being carried out.[97] Whether an action is a "significant action" is generally assessed according to whether the investment meets a specified threshold, which will differ depending on the type of investment proposed.

The threshold for screening of inbound foreign investments in Australia is determined by reference to the amount paid for the interest or size of the interest, depending on the act in question.[98] Some investment categories, including investments by State-owned enterprises or investments in certain sectors, must be notified regardless of their value.[99] Australia typically reserves its right to screen inbound investment under its investment and trade treaties, nonetheless undertaking to apply different (more generous) screening thresholds to investments from treaty partners than those applied to other investors under domestic law.[100] As such, it is likely that the EU will seek through the AEUFTA negotiations to benefit from screening thresholds similar to those applied by Australia to investors from States with which it has FTAs. Australia has noted, however, its intent through the negotiations to "uphold the government's right to . . . screen investments for national interest".[101] However, the negotiations will likely produce some undertakings by each party concerning the application of the screening requirements to investors from the other

investment-laws>. Even those States without a dedicated screening law may regulate the admission of investment through other means, including through restrictions on the foreign ownership of assets of certain types (for example, land) or in certain sectors.

[95] Foreign Investment Review Board, 'Significant Actions and Notifiable Actions [GN35]' <https://firb.gov.au/resources/guidance/gn35>.

[96] The Act defines 'foreign person' as: (i) an individual not ordinarily resident in Australia; (ii) a corporation, trustee of a trust or general partner of a limited partnership where an individual not ordinarily resident in Australia, foreign corporation or foreign government (together with its associates) holds an equity interest of at least 20%; (iii) a corporation, trustee of a trust or general partner of a limited partnership in which two or more foreign persons (together with their associates) hold an aggregate equity interest of at least 40%; or (iv) a foreign government or foreign government investor: Foreign Acquisitions and Takeovers Act 1975 (Cth) s 4.

[97] Foreign Acquisitions and Takeovers Act 1975 (Cth) s81.

[98] Foreign Investment Review Board, 'Monetary Thresholds' <https://firb.gov.au/exemptions-thresholds/monetary-thresholds>.

[99] See, for example: Foreign Acquisitions and Takeovers Act 1975 (Cth) s 42 (agribusinesses).

[100] Foreign Investment Review Board, 'Monetary Thresholds' <https://firb.gov.au/exemptions-thresholds/monetary-thresholds>.

[101] Australian Government Department of Foreign Affairs and Trade, 'Summary of Negotiating Aims and Approach' <https://www.dfat.gov.au/trade/agreements/negotiations/aeufta/Pages/summary-of-negotiating-aims-and-approach>.

party, including a potentially altered threshold for screening for investors from the EU into Australia.

The focus of the investment chapter on market access and investment liberalisation means that many of the usual elements of an investment chapter are absent. However, matters relevant to investment liberalisation (and protection) are tangentially also covered in other chapters of the FTA. In respect of trade and sustainable development, for example, the EU is required—when taking actions within the common commercial policy (CCP), to ensure that such action is "conducted in the context of the principles and objectives of the Union's external action".[102] These principles and actions are defined to include promotion of democracy, the rule of law, human rights, sustainable development, and good governance.[103] The EU's negotiating mandate for the AEUFTA thus emphasised that "sustainable development should be taken into account throughout the Agreement, including in the form of a specific chapter on trade and sustainable development, covering both social and environmental issues".[104] To this end, one of the EU's textual proposals tabled for discussion at the third negotiating round addresses the topic of "trade and sustainable development".[105] This proposal indicates an intention on the part of the EU, *inter alia*, to "enhance the integration of sustainable development, notably its labour and environmental dimensions, in the Parties' trade and investment relationship".[106] The proposal contains various specific undertakings, including an obligation on the parties not to "weaken or reduce" environmental and labour protections "in order to encourage trade or investment".[107] It further indicates the EU's expectation that the parties will "recognise the importance of taking urgent action to combat climate change and its impacts", including to "facilitate the removal of obstacles to trade and investment in goods and services of particular relevance for climate change mitigation and adaptation".[108] Australia's recent treaty practice indicates that it may be open to such provisions, particularly as they are flexibly

---

[102] Article 207(1) TFEU.

[103] Article 205 TFEU. See, further: European Commission, 'Communication from the Commission to the European Parliament, the Council, the European Economic and Social Committee and the Committee of the Regions: Trade for All, Towards a More Responsible Trade and Investment Policy', 14 October 2015, para. 4.2.

[104] Council of the European Union, 'Negotiating Directives for a Free Trade Agreement with Australia (25 June 2018)' (2018).

[105] European Union, 'EU-Australia Free Trade Agreement: Trade and Sustainable Development' (2019) <https://trade.ec.europa.eu/doclib/docs/2019/april/tradoc_157865.pdf>.

[106] European Union, 'EU-Australia Free Trade Agreement: Trade and Sustainable Development' (2019) <https://trade.ec.europa.eu/doclib/docs/2019/april/tradoc_157865.pdf> Article X.1(3).

[107] European Union, 'EU-Australia Free Trade Agreement: Trade and Sustainable Development' (2019) <https://trade.ec.europa.eu/doclib/docs/2019/april/tradoc_157865.pdf> Article X.2(3).

[108] European Union, 'EU-Australia Free Trade Agreement: Trade and Sustainable Development' (2019) <https://trade.ec.europa.eu/doclib/docs/2019/april/tradoc_157865.pdf> Article X.5.

worded to largely encourage best efforts approaches.[109] Australia has, for instance, previously indicated specifically in the context of the EU-Australia bilateral relationship that the inclusion of "operative" human rights clauses in a future trade treaty would be "inappropriate".[110]

The FTA's provisions on energy and raw materials may also tangentially address matters relevant to investors in these sectors. The EU's textual proposal in relation to this chapter of the FTA covers a range of matters relevant to the facilitation of investment "in the areas of energy and raw materials".[111] It includes provisions recognising the "sovereign right" of each party:

> to determine whether areas within its territory, as well as in its archipelagic and territorial waters, exclusive economic zone and continental shelf, are available for exploring for and producing energy goods and raw materials.[112]

It also contains provisions restricting the parties' conduct vis-à-vis export pricing, domestic pricing regulation, and exploration and production authorisations. It further contemplates the integration of various environmental objectives with such activities, including to require each party to "ensure that an environmental impact assessment is carried out prior to granting authorisation for a project for the production of energy goods or raw materials, where the project may have a significant impact on the environment".[113] The government procurement chapter may also have implications for investment activities. The EU's proposal in this respect would require each party to accord national treatment vis-à-vis "any government procurement" to "the suppliers of the other Party that have established a commercial presence in its territory through the constitution, acquisition or maintenance of a juridical person".[114] The EU's proposal also addresses discriminatory measures in procurement (above certain stipulated thresholds) by sub-national governments where such procurement "is funded fully or in part by central government entities listed in [an Annex to the chapter]".[115]

---

[109] See, for example: Australia-Hong Kong Free Trade Agreement and associated Investment Agreement (entered into force 17 January 2020).

[110] Markovic (2012) (quoting a 1996 statement of Australia's then-Foreign Minister Alexander Downer).

[111] European Union, 'EU-Australia Free Trade Agreement: Energy and Raw Materials' (2018) <https://trade.ec.europa.eu/doclib/docs/2018/july/tradoc_157188.pdf>.

[112] European Union, 'EU-Australia Free Trade Agreement: Energy and Raw Materials' (2018) <https://trade.ec.europa.eu/doclib/docs/2018/july/tradoc_157188.pdf> Article X.2(1).

[113] European Union, 'EU-Australia Free Trade Agreement: Energy and Raw Materials' (2018) <https://trade.ec.europa.eu/doclib/docs/2018/july/tradoc_157188.pdf> Article X.8(1).

[114] European Union, 'EU-Australia Free Trade Agreement: Public Procurement' (2018) <https://trade.ec.europa.eu/doclib/docs/2018/july/tradoc_157189.pdf> Article X.2(1).

[115] European Union, 'EU-Australia Free Trade Agreement: Public Procurement' (2018) <https://trade.ec.europa.eu/doclib/docs/2018/july/tradoc_157189.pdf> Article X.2(2).

5 Overlaps and Omissions: The AEUFTA's Likely Impact on Existing Investment Treaties

As noted above, five EU Member States have bilateral investment treaties with Australia: the Czech Republic (1994), Hungary (1992), Lithuania (2002), Poland (1992) and Romania (1994).[116] The two-way investment relationship between these States and Australia is not nearly as significant as that between Australia and other EU States, including that between Australia and the Netherlands, Germany and France. Nevertheless, each of these existing treaties contains investment protections and investor-State arbitration provisions. A question therefore arises as to what will happen to these treaties in light of the AEUFTA, and also what their possible interaction may be with that Agreement.

A first question is whether the provisions of the AEUFTA might be used to incorporate protections contained in these other treaties. This is expressly foreclosed by the EU's proposed text for the investment chapter, which provides that "treatment" under the FTA's MFN provision "does not include investor-to-state dispute settlement procedures provided for in other international agreements".[117] It further stipulates that:

> For greater certainty, substantive provisions in other international agreements concluded by a Party with a third country do not in themselves constitute the "treatment" referred to in paragraphs 1 and 2. Measures of a Party pursuant to those provisions [FN9] may constitute such treatment and thus give rise to a breach of this Article. [FN9: For greater certainty, the mere transposition of those provisions into domestic law, to the extent that it is necessary in order to incorporate them into the domestic legal order, does not in itself qualify as a measure.][118]

Australia in its treaty practice has increasingly included clarificatory statements to restrict the scope of MFN provisions, including to foreclose the capacity to use MFN provisions to invoke more favourable dispute settlement provisions from other

---

[116] Agreement between Australia and the Czech Republic on the Reciprocal Promotion and Protection of Investments (entered into force 29 June 1994); Agreement between Australia and the Republic of Hungary on the Reciprocal Promotion and Protection of Investments (entered into force 10 May 1992); Agreement between the Government of Australia and the Government of the Republic of Lithuania on the Promotion and Protection of Investments (entered into force 10 May 2002); Agreement between Australia and the Republic of Poland on the Reciprocal Promotion and Protection of Investments (entered into force 27 March 1992); Agreement between the Government of Australia and the Government of Romania on the Reciprocal Promotion and Protection of Investments (entered into force 22 April 1994).

[117] European Union, 'EU-Australia Free Trade Agreement: Investment Liberalisation and Trade in Services' (2018) <https://trade.ec.europa.eu/doclib/docs/2018/december/tradoc_157572.pdf>, Article 2.4(4).

[118] European Union, 'EU-Australia Free Trade Agreement: Investment Liberalisation and Trade in Services' (2018) <https://trade.ec.europa.eu/doclib/docs/2018/december/tradoc_157572.pdf>, Article 2.4(5).

treaties.[119] It is therefore likely that the AEUFTA will contain a provision to this effect, precluding the capacity for investors (or the States) to circumvent its restricted scope by invoking investment protection or arbitration clauses under the AEUFTA's MFN provision.

A second question is what recourse investors might have to contest the measures of either State as inconsistent with the provisions of the AEUFTA. The AEUFTA will likely include only State-State dispute settlement provisions. Investors may be able to make representations to either the EU or Australia to encourage them to use such provisions to raise issues concerning the other parties' compliance with the provisions of the FTA. Beyond this, few provisions are likely to create particularly useful rights that investors could themselves invoke in international procedures. So too, few provisions are likely to give rise to investor-initiated domestic proceedings. This is both due to the coverage of the investment provisions (focussing on liberalisation, rather than protection), but also due to the practice of both the EU and Australia vis-à-vis the domestic effect of investment and trade agreements.[120] The EU has, for example, "started to insert clauses in about each and every bilateral agreement of the EU and/or the accompanying signing decisions, seeking to deny their applicability or direct effect before domestic courts".[121] As such, investors may have to use other methods to protect their investments. Alternatives to investor-State arbitration or domestic proceedings invoking the AEUFTA itself could include sovereign risk insurance, actions invoking domestic law, or the use of contractual protections.[122] The latter protections frequently channel disputes to commercial arbitration procedures, which themselves may lead to significant unintended consequences that cut against the policies of both the EU and Australia vis-à-vis ISDS reform.[123] The capacity for EU states to conclude ad hoc arbitration agreements having the same content as an investment treaty arbitration clause has moreover been put into doubt by the CJEU in its recent PL Holdings judgment. Investors might alternatively seek to structure their investments through those States in the EU that do have investment treaties with Australia that include investment protection and arbitration provisions. This, again, may produce unintended consequences, particularly as those treaties do not contain many of the modernisations and protections included by these States in newer treaties.

A final question is whether the five investment treaties between EU Member States and Australia will remain in force following the conclusion of the AEUFTA. Again, the impetus for termination of those agreements is likely to arise out of

---

[119] See, for example: Australia – Peru Free Trade Agreement (signed 12 February 2018, entered into force 11 February 2020) Article 8.5(3) ('For greater certainty, the treatment referred to in this Article does not encompass international dispute resolution procedures or mechanisms, such as those included in Section B.').

[120] See, generally: Bronckers (2015), pp. 8–10; Dodge (2006), pp. 24–25; Semertzi (2014).

[121] Bronckers (2015), p. 9.

[122] See, for example: Australian Senate, 'Official Hansard: 25 November 2019', p. 4133 (Senator Patrick); Bronckers (2015), pp. 8–10; Trakman (2014), p. 164.

[123] See, further: Caron and Shirlow (2018); Shirlow (2016).

the operation of the EU's policy and legal framework vis-à-vis investment treaties. The transfer to the EU of some exclusive competences in respect of investment means the loss of those competences by EU Member States.[124] As the CJEU has stated: "[w]hen the European Union negotiates and concludes with a third State an agreement relating to a field in respect of which it has acquired exclusive competence, it takes the place of its Member States".[125] However, under EU law, the EU can authorise Member States to continue to act in areas of EU exclusive competence.[126] To this end, the EU has adopted a Regulation to govern the continued operation of Member State investment treaties in light of the EU's new competence in this area.[127] The Regulation permits each of the existing investment treaties between Australia and EU Member States to remain in force "until a bilateral investment agreement between the Union and the same third country enters into force".[128] The Regulation also permits the Union to:

> assess the bilateral investment agreements ... by evaluating whether one or more of their provisions constitute a serious obstacle to the negotiation or conclusion by the Union of bilateral investment agreements with third countries, with a view to the progressive replacement of the bilateral investment agreements notified pursuant to Article 2.[129]

Given that the EU has not (yet) sought to negotiate an investment agreement with Australia, the five Member State treaties will presumably be permitted (from the EU's perspective) to remain in force for now. Australia and the affected Member States are themselves unlikely to bilaterally seek to terminate those treaties outright, given that their overlap with the AEUFTA is likely to be minimal. Australia has, however, recently embarked upon a process of reviewing its existing BITs, through which it is contemplated a range of policy options to ensure that each of its BITs contains "modern safeguards".[130] It has flagged, in this regard, the possibility for "full renegotiation", "amendment", "termination" or "continuation" of existing BITs, "negotiation and adoption" of either joint or unilateral interpretive notes, or "replacement of a BIT with an FTA chapter that may or may not include ISDS". As this process progresses, the future of Australia's existing BITs with EU Member

---

[124] Article 3(1)(e) TFEU.

[125] *Opinion 2/15 of the Court (Full Court), 16 May 2017* [248].

[126] Article 2(1) TFEU.

[127] Regulation (EU) No 1219/2012 of the European Parliament and of the Council of 12 December 2012 establishing transitional arrangements for bilateral investment agreements between Member States and third countries.

[128] Regulation (EU) No 1219/2012 of the European Parliament and of the Council of 12 December 2012 establishing transitional arrangements for bilateral investment agreements between Member States and third countries, Article 3.

[129] Regulation (EU) No 1219/2012 of the European Parliament and of the Council of 12 December 2012 establishing transitional arrangements for bilateral investment agreements between Member States and third countries, Article 5.

[130] Australian Government Department of Foreign Affairs and Trade, 'Discussion Paper: Review of Australia's Bilateral Investment Treaties' <https://www.dfat.gov.au/trade-and-investment/discussion-paper-review-australias-bilateral-investment-treaties>.

States is likely to become clearer. The existence of these treaties—and the ongoing reform processes in both Australia and the EU—may, for example, give added impetus to the future negotiation of a mixed investment agreement between Australia, the EU and Member States, given that the existing investment treaties do not reflect the recent efforts of either EU States or of Australia to modernise investment protection and arbitration provisions.[131] Indeed, even those politicians within Australia's main opposition party who oppose ISDS have voted in favour of replacing old-style ISDS in existing treaties with modernised ISDS provisions in newly-concluded treaties in an effort to ensure that Australia is better off overall under newly negotiated treaties.[132] There is therefore reason to expect that the five existing investment treaties between EU Member States and Australia will be the subject of modernisation or termination in the future, especially as they create a potential risk of treaty shopping by investors within the EU legal order.

6 Conclusions

The non-inclusion of investment protection and investor-State arbitration provisions in the AEUFTA reflects various complex legal and policy constraints. The majority of these appear to have arisen from the EU side, relating to its legal competences to negotiate investment protection and arbitration provisions. Australia appears (publicly at least) not to be particularly concerned about the restricted focus of the AEUFTA relative to investment. However, parliamentary review of treaties in Australia occurs subsequent to their conclusion—yet prior to their ratification—and thus it is possible that concerns might be raised at a later date about the scope of the AEUFTA, its interaction with Australia's existing investment treaties, and its consistency with Australia's policy goals vis-à-vis investment treaty reform. The above discussion indicates that it is likely that the EU and Australia might in the future seek to negotiate an investment agreement covering the currently omitted matters of investment protection and dispute settlement. Such negotiations are likely to be some way off, and would in any case potentially themselves be further delayed due to the complexities of negotiating such a treaty as a mixed agreement. In the meantime, investors may enjoy some coverage under the provisions of the FTA, including its sector-specific chapters. While the omission from the AEUFTA of investment protection and ISDS (whether in the form of arbitration or a judicial body) therefore appears to have been a strategic exclusion, it is in many ways also a missed opportunity for both sides to solidify and progress their reform agendas.

[131] European Commission, 'Commission Staff Working Document - Impact Assessment Accompanying the Document Recommendation for a Council Decision Authorising the Opening of Negotiations for a Free Trade Agreement with Australia', p. 8.

[132] See, for example: Senate, 'Official Hansard (Tuesday, 26 November 2019)', pp. 4163–4164 (Senator Gallagher).

References

Basedow R (2016) A legal history of the EU's international investment policy. J World Invest Trade 17:743

Bronckers M (2015) Is Investor–State Dispute Settlement (ISDS) superior to litigation before domestic courts?: An EU view on bilateral trade agreements. J Int Econ Law 18:655

Bungenberg M, Griebel J, Hindelang S (2011) Challenges ahead: EU investment protection after the entry into force of the Treaty of Lisbon. Transnatl Dispute Manag 8:2

Calamita NJ (2012) The making of Europe's international investment policy: uncertain first steps. Leg Issues Econ Integrat 39:301

Caron D, Shirlow E (2018) Dissecting backlash: the unarticulated causes of backlash and its unintended consequences. In: Ulfstein G, Føllesdal A (eds) The judicialization of international law – a mixed blessing? Oxford University Press

Chaisse J (2012) Promises and pitfalls of the European Union policy on foreign investment—how will the new EU competence on FDI affect the emerging global regime? J Int Econ Law 15:51–84

Chaisse J, Renouf Y (2018) Investor-state dispute settlement. In: Drake-Brockman J, Messerlin P (eds) Potential benefits of an Australia-EU free trade agreement: key issues and options. University of Adelaide Press <https://www.adelaide.edu.au/press/titles/eu-trade/> (last accessed 9 September 2021)

de las Heras BP (2018) The European Union in international investment governance: a hybrid approach to dispute settlement. Rom J Eur Aff 18:77

Devuyst Y (2011) The European Union's competence in international trade after the Treaty of Lisbon. Ga J Int Comp Law 39:639

Dickson-Smith K, Mercurio B (2018) Australia's position on investor–state dispute settlement: fruit of a poisonous tree or a few rotten apples? Sydn Law Rev

Dodge W (2006) Investor-state dispute settlement between developed countries: reflections on the Australia-United States free trade agreement. Vanderbilt J Transnatl Law 39:1

Drake-Brockman J (2018) An Australian perspective on the Australia-EU free trade agreement. In: Drake-Brockman J, Messerlin P (eds) Potential benefits of an Australia-EU free trade agreement: key issues and options. University of Adelaide Press <https://www.adelaide.edu.au/press/titles/eu-trade/> (last accessed 9 September 2021)

Fina S, Lentner G (2016) The scope of the EU's investment competence after Lisbon. Santa Clara J Int Law 14:419

Fontanelli F, Bianco G (2014) Converging towards NAFTA: an analysis of FTA investment chapters in the European Union and the United States. Stanford J Int Law 50:211

Gantz DA (2017) The CETA ratification Saga: the demise of ISDS in EU trade agreements. Loyola Univ Chic Law J 49:361

Hindelang S (2015) Repellent forces: the CJEU and investor-state dispute settlement. Archiv des Völkerrechts 53:68

Kendra T, Kozyreff L (2013) The future of investment protection in Europe – the EU takes control. Year Book Int Arbitr 3:239

Kerneis P (2018) Limits to European Union negotiating competence. In: Drake-Brockman J, Messerlin P (eds) Potential benefits of an Australia-EU free trade agreement: key issues and options. University of Adelaide Press <https://www.adelaide.edu.au/press/titles/eu-trade/> (last accessed 9 September 2021)

Kleimann D, Kübek G (2016) The signing, provisional application, and conclusion of trade and investment agreements in the EU: the case of CETA and Opinion 2/15. Robert Schuman Centre for Advanced Studies, Global Governance Programme Paper Series

Leal-Arcas R (2010) The European Union's trade and investment policy after the Treaty of Lisbon. J World Invest Trade 11:463

Lopez-Rodriguez AM (2017) Investor-state dispute settlement in the EU: certainties and uncertainties. Houst J Int Law 40:139

Markovic N (2012) “Australia’s Evolving Relationship with the European Union: An Update” <https://parlinfo.aph.gov.au/parlInfo/search/display/display.w3p;query=Id:%22library/prspub/2001025%22> (last accessed 9 September 2021)

McClay S (2016) Can it lead from behind: the European Union’s struggle to catch up in international investment policy making in the wake of the Lisbon Treaty. Tex Int Law J 51:259

Messerlin P, Parc J (2018) A European perspective on the Australia-EU free trade agreement. In: Drake-Brockman J, Messerlin P (eds) Potential benefits of an Australia-EU free trade agreement: key issues and options. University of Adelaide Press <https://www.adelaide.edu.au/press/titles/eu-trade/> (last accessed 9 September 2021)

Meunier S (2014) Integration by stealth: how the European Union gained competence over foreign direct investment. Robert Schuman Centre for Advanced Studies, Global Governance Programme Paper Series

Meyer T (2017) Local liability in international economic law. N C Law Rev 95:261

Moskvan D (2017) The European Union’s competence on foreign investment: new and improved. San Diego Int Law J 18:241

Reinisch A (2014) The EU on the investment path – Quo Vadis Europe? The future of EU BITs and other investment agreements. Santa Clara J Int Law 12

Semertzi A (2014) The preclusion of direct effect in the recently concluded EU free trade agreements. Common Mark Law Rev 51:1125

Shan W, Zhang S (2010) The Treaty of Lisbon: half way toward a common investment policy. Eur J Int Law 21:1049

Sharma A (2011) The entry into force of the Lisbon Treaty: the European Union in retrospect and prospect. Can Yearb Int Law 49:265

Shirlow E (2016) Dawn of a new era? The UNCITRAL rules and UN Convention on transparency in treaty-based investor-state arbitration. ICSID Rev – Foreign Invest Law J 31:622

Soderlund C (2007) Intra-EU BIT investment protection and the EC Treaty. J Invest Arbitr 24:455

Thangavelu S, Findlay C (2018) Foreign investment and innovation. In: Drake-Brockman J, Messerlin P (eds) Potential benefits of an Australia-EU free trade agreement: key issues and options. University of Adelaide Press <https://www.adelaide.edu.au/press/titles/eu-trade/> (last accessed 9 September 2021)

Titi C (2015) International investment law and the European Union: towards a new generation of international investment agreements. Eur J Int Law 26:639

Trakman LE (2014) Investor-state arbitration: evaluating Australia’s evolving position. J World Invest Trade 15:152

Umair Ghori (2016) Umair Ghori - Protection of Foreign Investor’s Investments from Expropriation - The Desired Standards within the Future Australia-EU Free Trade Agreement (AEUFTA) <https://www.dfat.gov.au/sites/default/files/dr-umair-ghori-bond-university-eufta-submission.PDF> (last accessed 9 September 2021)

Waibel M (2013) “Competence Review: Trade and Investment” SSRN <https://papers.ssrn.com/sol3/papers.cfm?abstract_id=2507138> (last accessed 9 September 2021)

Esmé Shirlow is an Associate Professor at the Australian National University’s College of Law. She teaches and researches public international law, international dispute settlement, and international investment law and arbitration. Esmé maintains a practice in these areas, and is admitted as a Solicitor in the Australian Capital Territory. She has been involved as an advisor to parties to investment treaty claims and in proceedings before the International Court of Justice, and has served as an assistant to a number of investment treaty tribunals. Prior to joining the Australian National University, Esmé worked in the Australian Government’s Office of International Law. She completed her PhD as a Dickson Poon Scholar at King’s College London, for which she was awarded the King’s Elsevier Outstanding PhD Thesis Prize. She completed her LL.M. at the University of Cambridge, where she was awarded—among other prizes—the BRD Clarke Prize for Best Overall Performance in the LL.M. and the Clive Parry Prize for Best Result in International Law, as well as the Whewell Scholarship in International Law. Esmé completed her LL.B.(Hons) and a B.A. at the Australian National University.

The Competition Chapter in the EU-Australia FTA

Mareike Fröhlich

Contents

Abstract The chapter deals with the consideration of competition policy in the context of the EU-Australia FTA. It first gives an overview about the reasons for and possible content of competition chapters in general. In the following, the competition chapter of the EU-Australia FTA is analysed and compared with the most common competition rules in FTAs. Moreover, it is put into a broader context by analysing other agreements of the EU and Australia regarding competition issues. Here, especially agreements with the same party, like UK or Canada, are of special interest since they could serve as a model for the future chapter on competition. Finally, conclusions are drawn if the EU-Australia FTA will be another example of the European approach in competition cooperation.

This chapter is based on the doctoral thesis of the author, Wettbewerbsregelungen in Unionsabkommen: Bedeutung und Einfluss für die Entwicklung der internationalen Zusammenarbeit bei Wettbewerbsbeschränkungen mit grenzüberschreitender Regelung, 2021.

M. Fröhlich (✉)
Europa-Institut, Saarland University, Saarbrücken, Germany
e-mail: froehlich@europainstitut.de

M. Bungenberg, A. Mitchell (eds.), *The Australia-European Union Free Trade Agreement*, Special Issue, https://doi.org/10.1007/978-3-030-91448-6_9

1 Introduction

The currently negotiated EU-Australia Free Trade Agreement not only contains classic trade-related chapters, but also deals with other topics. One of the chapters also contains provisions on competition. For some time now, regulations on competition law have been included in FTAs, or countries have concluded either exclusive agreements on cooperation in competition matters or so-called memoranda of understanding (MoU). The EU is the world leader in this area and has concluded up to 62 bilateral agreements of all kinds worldwide.[1] Australia has also concluded similar agreements with numerous countries, but in the past the focus has been mainly on major trading partners or countries in the same region (e.g. Oceania). Both parties have not cooperated bilaterally until 2002 in the field of competition cooperation, since then there has only been one agreement with the EU and its member states on the exchange of information in the area of consumer protection and policy, but this does not contain any competition regulations. However, since both parties are also active in this area, it is not surprising that a chapter on competition issues is to be included in the current FTA.

2 Competition Regulations in FTAs

Since the WTO dropped it of their agenda of WTO-plus topics in 2003, the long-standing mantra that competition law and trade regulations should not be regulated in the same context due to their complexity, lost its grounds in the last decade. Until 2000, FTAs addressed the liberalisation of trade focusing mainly on tariffs reductions and market access.[2] In this respect, international trade law had the function of creating competition in the markets through trade liberalisation, while competition law is intended to secure this competition in the long term. For this purpose, international trade law regulates state restrictions whereas competition law exclusively regulates restrictions between private parties. This context is still true but has changed over times.

2.1 Reasons for the Integration

No single reason can be identified that is responsible for the inclusion of competition law issues in FTAs. On the one hand, it has not yet been possible to codify an international regulatory framework for competition restrictions with international

[1] Compare the list of agreements at European Commission, Bilateral relations on competition issues, https://ec.europa.eu/competition/international/bilateral/ (last accessed 9 September 2021).

[2] Anderson et al. (2018), p. 27.

implications. Such restrictions are still sanctioned by the extraterritorial application of national competition law. However, with today's globalised economy and multinational companies as well as numerous jurisdictions, this finds its limits in the investigation of competition cases and the subsequent enforcement of competition authorities' decisions due to the fact that the states power to regulate and enforce ends at the national border. Various initiatives for international competition rules and/or international cooperation models have been developed since the last century but without success. In addition, WTO regulations and numerous FTAs have reduced trade restrictions. However, this leads to an increasing focus on other forms of restrictions, such as restrictions on competition or strategic competition policy. This has already been shown by the development of the EU internal market, which, in addition to the prohibition of state restrictions through the fundamental freedoms, also made efficient competition law necessary to control private restrictions of competition. For these reasons, nowadays FTAs include chapters or single provisions for regulating restrictions of competition in all its different forms.

There are several reasons to incorporate such chapters in recent FTAs. The restriction of competition with agreements of enterprises or concerted activities of enterprises, the abuse of dominant positions or the merger of companies does not only have effects on the own national market or be "committed by" own national enterprises. Therefore, national states are faced with the challenge to regulate behaviour which was neither activated on their territory nor national enterprises were involved. So far only the extraterritorial application of national law would allow the national authorities to react and regulate since there is a lack of any set of rules on international level. Although different regional and international players, like UNCTAD, OECD, WTO etc., drafted, designed, and proposed rules with different content of substantive and procedural rules, there was no common agreement to adopt such regulations. Until now, the only efficient and to a certain extent successful player is the International Competition Network (ICN) which brings together competition authorities worldwide in a non-formal organisation to cooperate mostly in procedural questions. Although the informality of the network is a benefit for setting up model procedures and rules as well as identifying best practices, at the same time it is a disadvantage for a legal framework since the network lacks binding force. Nevertheless, binding international rules are necessary to regulate the growing international competition due to globalisation. The international trade of goods has led to markets and companies becoming internationalised and they can no longer be considered solely in a national context. Due to multinational companies and increasing international competition, there is an increase in new competition law relevant facts that do not only fall under one jurisdiction. This can lead to different outcomes, resulting in both longer proceedings and legal uncertainties for businesses, and could harm the functions of competition.[3] The

[3]In the case of Microsoft the European and US-American authorities came to different results, cf. U.S. Court of Appeals, US v. Microsoft, (D.C. Cir. 2001), 253 F.3d 34; Europäische Kommission, Microsoft, COMP/C-3/37.792, ABl. L 32 of 6.2.2007.

regulatory function of competition law rules ensures a stable and lasting order that makes the behaviour of market participants and the market itself calculable. The resulting competition is intended to increase consumer welfare.[4] Without regulations for cross-border competition, the gains from trade liberalisation, such as those sought through FTAs, could be diminished. For these good reasons, competition issues are nowadays included in bilateral or regional trade agreements.

More than ¾ of all regional trade agreements include complete chapters on competition issues, sector-specific competition provisions in the chapters about services, telecommunication, intellectual property and government procurement or provisions in the general part explaining as horizontal rules the importance of competition for trade.[5] Besides the inclusion in FTAs, competition issues are regulated either in dedicated competition agreements, such as the EU-USA competition agreements,[6] or in memoranda of understanding between competition authorities which however are not binding since they are not an international treaty under international law. Most of such agreements deal exclusively with procedural rules.

In the context of competition, also state aid and public procurement rules need to be named. The first ones are often also included in the competition chapters, the latter are mostly regulated in own parts. Compared to competition law, both have a strong influence on competition and are capable of distorting it in the long term. For this reason, these topics are also regulated in most legal systems of industrialised nations. In most emerging and developing countries, they are becoming increasingly important and are being implemented there with the support of the OECD, UNCTAD and other organisations. One of the most important differences to competition law is that the legal regulations concerning subsidies and government procurement are directed at the public sector. Competition law, on the contrary, mainly regulates restrictions by private companies or intervenes when the public sector is economically active, i.e. it acts de facto like a private company. The chapter in the EU-Australia FTA chapter will exclusively deal with the distortion of competition through cartels, monopolies or mergers.[7]

2.2 Contents

The contents which can be found in the different FTAs do not vary widely.[8] They focus mainly on basic but important elements, like the commitment to competition regulations, meaning that the contracting parties are urged to adopt efficient

[4]Trebilcock et al. (2013), p. 756 et seq.

[5]Anderson et al. (2018), p. 26.

[6]Agreement between the Government of the United States of America and the Commission of the European Communities regarding the application of their competition laws, OJ 1995 L 95/47.

[7]For state aid provisions in the EU-Australia FTA, see Chap. 5.

[8]Cf. Fröhlich (2018), p. 208 et seq.

competition rules and set up responsible authorities with sufficient resources. Usually, there are no details how such an authority should be organized, so that besides a single authority/agency also a multi-authority approach, which assigns responsibilities to different authorities or establishes sectoral regulation authorities, would be possible. The EU follows a special hierarchy and interplay between the European Commission on EU level and the national authorities in the Member States on national level.

The obligation to adopt and maintain competition laws leaves open what quality the regulations should have. Some just ask for measures, but in most FTAs the anticompetitive behaviour is further defined, as e.g. in all EU FTAs, and includes anticompetitive behaviour, abuses of market power and the newer ones also merger control.[9] In this context, the regulations in the agreements where the EU is one of the contracting parties often reflect the wording of articles 101 and 102 TFEU without a list of specific cases. Rules on merger control are provided only by a handful of countries.[10] Logically, those rules are provided by industrialized countries with a longer experience in competition regulation and a functioning administrative body and procedures. Special rules concerning public enterprises, public monopolies and enterprises with exclusive or special rules are part of most FTAs, so that it is clear that not only private companies are addressees of competition regulations. However, exemptions are provided to guarantee the state obligation to maintain public services. These regulations make it possible, on the one hand, for the activities of the public sector to also fall under competition law and, on the other hand, for a state to fulfil its obligations in the area of services of general interest. They pay tribute to the fact that the state is also economically active. Even though state enterprises are to be found to a greater extent in (former) socialist and communist states, but also in developing and emerging countries, they still play a significant role in industrialised countries despite privatisation efforts. It is surprising that only a few FTAs define more precisely what is meant by services of general interest or to what limited extent exceptions can be permitted.[11]

Competition regulation should respect the fundamental procedural principles of transparency, non-discrimination and fairness, although these are not always found specifically in the competition chapters, but horizontally in the general part of FTAs. This should create confidence and legal certainty in the competent authorities and the efficient application of the respective competition law. In particular, the principle of procedural fairness should not only be applied in judicial proceedings but should ensure that administrative proceedings should already be organised in a consistent,

---

[9] Laprévote et al. (2015), p. 4 et seq.

[10] In 2015, only around 10% of all FTAs also addressed merger control issues, cf. Laprévote et al. (2015), p. 6; Teh (2009), p. 436.

[11] Article 287 para. 2 of the Comprehensive and enhanced Partnership Agreement between the European Union and the European Atomic Energy Community and their Member States, of the one part, and the Republic of Armenia, of the other part, OJ 2008 L 23/4; Article 10 para. 11 of the Free Trade Agreement between the European Union and the Socialist Republic of Viet Nam, OJ 2020 L 186/3.

neutral and comprehensible manner, as well as with appeal procedures. Even if the principle of transparency leaves much room for interpretation, the application of the respective national competition rules should be made comprehensible. New laws or amendments must be published, information must be publicly accessible, and procedural processes must be comprehensible and regulated in terms of time.[12] All this is an expression of the rule of law and reflects the fact that FTAs should not only contain trade regulations, but that they should also be flanked by basic principles of the rule of law.

Almost all FTAs exclude the competition chapter for the dispute settlement mechanism, which is present in the most recent ones. Some agreements provide a mechanism for consultation about the interpretation and application of the rules in the competition chapter. One of the most important reasons for this is that many states have little experience in competition control, as their laws and authorities have only recently been in place. In addition, the states would lose their sovereignty in the area of competition law. In contrast to international trade law or state aid law, which can be dealt with under the WTO dispute settlement mechanism, this does not apply, or only to a very limited extent, to competition laws. Here, states can only be held responsible to the extent that the application of national competition law hinders or complicates international trade.[13] However, since the majority of competition violations are caused by private parties, the state would be held responsible for such actions, which it did not cause or over which it has no influence.[14] Furthermore, it is doubted whether a commercial/trade dispute settlement mechanism has the appropriate rules and expertise for competition law infringements at its disposal.

Nevertheless, it is often affirmed that cooperation and collaboration in competition matters are of great importance. Interestingly, detailed rules on cooperation are mostly found in dedicated competition agreements or in memoranda of understanding and not in FTAs. They vary from general information on the respective competition systems, negative and positive comity to coordination of enforcement actions. For this purpose, in most cases either information is exchanged informally, or formal notifications and consultations are made or mutual assistance is provided. Especially notifications are crucial for a trustful and efficient cooperation and coordination since they enable the other authority to react and support the activities of the other one. In the case of the exchange of information, in principle, a transfer of information, regardless of its nature, is always problematic if the receiving state does not have an equal level of protection. Therefore, explicit regulations are also made as to the extent to which and under what conditions an exchange is possible. This is unproblematic for generally accessible or official information; for confidential information, the consent of the companies concerned must be obtained. In addition, the regulations explain to what extent the receiving authority may use it. Very few

[12] Teh (2009), p. 425.

[13] Panel Report, *Japan-Measures Affecting Consumer Photographic Film and Paper*, WT/DS44/R, adopted 31.03.1998.

[14] Tschaeni and Engammare (2013), p. 58.

agreements also allow the exchange of confidential information, such as the EU-Switzerland Competition Agreement, which enables the authorities to exchange information if both authorities are investigating the same or related conduct or transactions, if the request is complete and in writing, and if the information of concern has been determined with the receiving authority. The regulations on the exchange of information are increasing, as the protection of information is a central aspect of cooperation between authorities, and this is often the only way to successfully investigate cases.[15]

That is why in addition to FTAs, the EU and Australia also use competition agreements and memoranda of understanding to deepen their cooperation with other countries. Logically, both focus on their neighbouring countries and important trading partners. Until now, there is no existing agreement between the two actors in the field of competition enforcement.[16]

3 Chapter "Anticompetitive Conduct, Merger Control and Subsidies" of the EU-Australia FTA

The text is a proposal of the European Union and is subject to possible changes in the course of the negotiations.[17] In the 10th round of negotiations, the possible regulations were further specified and explained, and open questions were clarified.[18] The structure of the regulations is not modelled on the standard EU formulations, but also appears to take into account previous regulations in other Australian agreements. The chapter "Anticompetitive Conduct, Merger Control and Subsidies" consists of 13 articles divided into general provisions and two thematic sections. The first section addresses anticompetitive conduct and merger control whereas the second one deals with subsidies. In the following, I will only refer to the first section.

[15] Capobianco and Nagy (2016), p. 570.

[16] It only exists an agreement for cooperation in consumer policy, An administrative Arrangement for Information Sharing on Consumer Policy and Protection between the Government of Australia and the European Commission, 2002, https://www.accc.gov.au/system/files/Arrangement%20for%20information%20sharing%20on%20consumer%20policy%20%26%20protection%20between%20the%20Government%20of%20Australia%20%26%20the%20European%20Commission.pdf (last accessed 9 September 2021).

[17] EU-Australia FTA, Chapter Anticompetitive Conduct, Merger Control and Subsidies, https://trade.ec.europa.eu/doclib/docs/2019/july/tradoc_158281.pdf (last accessed 9 September 2021).

[18] European Commission, Report of the 10th round of negotiations for a trade agreement between the European Union and Australia, March 2021, EU-Australia trade agreement: report of the 10th round of negotiations (europa.eu) (last accessed 9 September 2021), p. 3.

3.1 General Part

The chapter starts with two general provisions about competition principles and competition neutrality. Article X.1 points out the relationship between "free and undistorted competition" and its possible consequences on trade and investment. It explains that "anticompetitive business practices and state interventions have the potential to distort the proper functioning of markets and undermine the benefits of trade and investment liberalisation". Such formulations are found in various FTAs and can be considered as common expressions to show the importance of competition regulations for the proper functioning of markets and trade flows.

Article X.2 clarifies that the rules of the chapter need to be applied to all enterprises regardless if they are of public or private nature. This article makes clear that there is no difference for public or private enterprises although there are special rules for public ones in the special articles in the following text. It is interesting that such a clause is not used in the introductory parts of the EU FTAs with Canada, Singapore, South Korea or others.

3.2 Specific Rules

After the two introductory articles, section A "Anticompetitive conduct and merger control" starts with Article X.3 about the legislative framework which ask the parties to

> adopt or maintain competition law [...] and addresses, in an effective manner, all of the following practices: (a) horizontal and vertical agreements between enterprises, decisions by associations of enterprises and concerted practices which have as their object or effect the prevention, restriction or distortion of competition; (b) abuses by one or more enterprises of a dominant position; and (c) concentrations between enterprises which would significantly impede effective competition in particular as a result of the creation or strengthening of a dominant position.

This should be applied to all enterprises and no sector of the economy should be excluded. This catalogue includes all anti-competitive practices and addresses all practices which can be considered as a cartel (a) or monopoly (b) topping up with a merger control (c). In contrast to other agreements, Article X.3 does not contain any restriction that such conduct must also affect trade between the two parties or has to be incompatible with the proper functioning of the agreement, in so far as they may affect trade between them. Moreover, there is no clause which explains that the rules in the FTA have no impact on the application of the national competition laws. Since the chapter is still only available as a draft version, these might be included at a later stage of the negotiations. It should be clear for both parties that the rules only apply in case the anti-competitive practices affect the trade between the parties. Although the wording used in the draft version is similar to that of the EU agreements with Canada, Singapore and South Korea, it is not identical in wording. This can be attributed to the stage of development of national competition laws or the degree of cooperation on competition issues to date, as this may have had an impact on the respective regulation in the individual FTAs.

Article X.4 clarifies that undertakings entrusted with the operation of services of general economic interest, i.e. so-called state-owned undertakings or undertakings with special or exclusive rights, are also covered by Section A. However, this is not the case if the fulfilment of the entrusted tasks is legally or factually prevented. In this case, the assignment of tasks must be made in a transparent manner and the regulations may only be deviated from or restricted to the extent that this is absolutely necessary for the fulfilment of the assigned task. Such a rule is common for most competition chapters in FTAs since public enterprises or monopolies are important instruments in the context of the industrial policy of national governments. Most of them are not willing to give up on them. Unfortunately, the draft version lacks a provision to ensure that Article X.4 also applies to markets where the enterprise does not have special or exclusive rights, such as in Article 13.3 EU-Singapore FTA. More specific rules on state monopolies, state-owned enterprises or enterprises with special or exclusive rights can be found in a special chapter.

As all competition chapters of FTAs, the EU-Australian equally includes a rule which deals with the implementation of competition laws. Article X.5 para. 1 states that:

> Each Party shall (establish and) maintain an operationally independent authority which is responsible for and appropriately equipped with the powers and resources necessary to ensure the full application and the effective enforcement of the competition law referred to in Article X.3.

The fact that "establish" was put in brackets leads to the conclusion that this might be deleted in the last version since both parties already have functioning authorities in force. Although this paragraph is maybe of more importance for developing or transition countries, it entails the obligation that the existing authority is independent, has sufficient resources and competences to apply and enforce the rules in Article X.3. Both, the European and Australian competition authorities (respectively the European Commission and the Australian Competition and Consumer Commission) fulfil these requirements. The following Article X.5 para. 2 calls for several procedural rights, such as transparency, procedural fairness including the right of defence as well as the right to be heard and the right to judicial review.

Article X.6 is a commitment to set up or at least promote cooperation in competition policy and enforcement between the two parties. This very general commitment in paragraph 1 is accompanied by the possibility to exchange information but only in the scope of the national confidentiality rules of each party (para. 2) as well as the encouragement to coordinate the enforcement actions when they investigate the same or related conduct or cases. Unfortunately, the FTA lacks more detailed regulations on the cooperation of the competition authorities.

As almost all FTAs, the application of the dispute settlement mechanism of the EU-Australia FTA is excluded in Article X.7. There are no rules for consultations foreseen.

The chapter on competition is quite in line with the trend of such chapters in FTAs in general, but so far does not show any special features compared to other FTAs. Although it can be expected that the parties might take the opportunity to negotiate either a dedicated agreement on competition matters or at least a memorandum of understanding between their competition authorities to safeguard and promote the cooperation in the area of competition. If this is not the case, possibly because such regulations are not used due to lack of application cases, it would be helpful if the chapter, like the other FTAs of the EU that do not refer to a cooperation agreement,[19] would provide regulations on notification, positive comity and consultations. This would enhance the cooperation already without any other agreement.

4 Effects and Consequences of Other Agreements

Both the EU and Australia have concluded further agreements with other states or regions, and the extent to which these have an influence on or serve as a model for the EU-Australia FTA will be shown in the following subsections.

4.1 Agreements of the European Union

As noted above, the EU is a leader in exporting its idea of effective competition law and control. The closer the relationship as a (potential) accession candidate or neighbouring country, the more emphasis is placed on adopting European rules and designs to enable effective cooperation that does not affect bilateral trade. In the framework of free trade agreements, this is also attempted to a lesser extent, but here the EU acts flexibly and tries to reach compromises.[20]

4.1.1 CETA

Since 2017 most parts of the Comprehensive Economic and Trade Agreement between the EU and Canada (CETA) are applied provisionally.[21] The chapter

[19]Like the Free Trade Agreement between the European Unon and the Republic of Singapore, OJ 2019 L 294/3, Trade Agreement between the European Union and its Member States, of the one part, and Colombia and Peru, of the other part, OJ 2012 L 354/3.

[20]Fröhlich (2018), p. 210 et seq.

[21]Comprehensive Economic and Trade Agreement (CETA) between Canada, of the one part, and the European Union and its Member States, of the other part, OJ 2017 L 11/23.

17 deals with competition policy and shows the above said, namely, that the EU is also flexible in its approach concerning the contents. Article 17.1 defines anti-competitive business conduct as "anti-competitive agreements, concerted practices or arrangements by competitors, anti-competitive practices by an enterprise that is dominant in a market, and mergers with substantial anti-competitive effects". The chapter is rather short due to the fact that a dedicated competition agreement is already in force to which Art. 17.2 para. 3 refers, but still the requirements of transparency, non-discrimination and procedural fairness should be applied to all measures taken in the enforcement process.

4.1.2 EU-UK TCA

The Trade and Cooperation Agreement between the EU and UK and Northern Ireland includes in the title XI (level playing field for open and fair competition and sustainable development) the chapter two which deals with competition policy.[22] This chapter differs from other agreements since it tries to reflect the special relationship between the two parties. It must be kept in mind that the UK and the EU still share the same rules, although they are now, after Brexit, interpreted independently by the UK authorities and courts. So far, it is not apparent that the UK intends to drastically change its competition rules in the future. Nevertheless, the definition of anti-competitive behaviour or business practices is not copying the wording of Art. 101 TFEU in Article 2.2 TCA but has the same scope. In para. 3 the parties get the right for exemptions in the case of legitimate public policy objectives, which need to be transparent and proportionate. Besides enforcement principles in Article 2.3, there is a commitment of both parties to cooperate closely and to exchange information if permitted under the parties' laws. For this purpose, the party's competition authorities can enter into a special agreement, which should also consider how confidential information can be exchanged and used.

4.1.3 EU-Switzerland Competition Agreement

In this context, especially the competition agreement with Switzerland could equally be of interest due to its progressive rules on information exchange. Since 2015 the agreement between the European Union and Switzerland for cooperation in competition matters is in force[23] and allows in Article 7 the exchange of information in a

[22] Trade and Cooperation Agreement between the European Union and the European Atomic Energy Community, of the one part, and the United Kingdom of Great Britain and Northern Ireland, of the other part, OJ 2020 L 444/14.

[23] Agreement between the European Union and the Swiss Confederation concerning cooperation on the application of their competition laws, OJ 2014 L 347/3.

graduated manner.[24] Level 1 allows the authorities to discuss orally all information, i.e. also information that is subject to official confidentiality (para. 2). An exchange of documents is possible in stage 2 with the consent of the companies concerned (para. 3). If no consent is given, an exchange is possible at level 3 under certain conditions if the subject of the investigation is the same and the information is already available to the authority (para. 4). The latter is not obliged to pass on the information. Level 5 provides that companies may consent to the disclosure of information resulting from leniency or settlement proceedings (para. 6). These comprehensive and detailed regulations on the exchange of information are new for the EU and can be part of the agreement due to an equal level of protection of the constitutional guarantees of all parties concerned. They could also be used as a model for the exchange of information between the EU and Australia, as an equivalent standard of constitutional protection can be assumed.

4.2 Agreements of Australia

Australia has not been that active in comparison to the EU in concluding dedicated competition agreements or MoU or including competition chapters in FTAs. But they have achieved a harmonization of competition laws with their main trading partner New Zealand, which is often called the Oceania approach. Recently, they concluded a few agreements that could be of interest for the cross-border cooperation in competition policy.

4.2.1 ANZCERTA

One of the most important Australian agreements is probably the Australian-New Zealand Closer Economic Agreement (ANZCERTA), which has existed since 1983 and governs the partnership between the two countries, which is similarly close to that of the member states in the European Union. In the course of harmonizing economic law and the abolishment of antidumping rules between the two countries, the competition regulations of Australia and New Zealand were harmonized in such a way that the New Zealand regulations were adapted to the Australian regulations, although it should be noted that New Zealand was not obliged to do this, unlike the EU candidate countries. However, no supranational competition law was established.[25] Because of the strong and close economic partnership the EU has also established negotiations about a FTA with New Zealand and the competition chapter there has the same wording as the one of the EU-Australia FTA.

[24] Multi-stage modell according to Völcker (2019), para. 104 et seq.

[25] Baetge (2009), p. 412 et seq.

4.2.2 CPTTP

Australia's membership in the Comprehensive and Progressive Agreement for Trans-Pacific Partnership (CPTTP),[26] which Brunei, Canada, Chile, Japan, Malaysia, Mexico, New Zealand, Peru, Singapore and Vietnam have signed, could also have a possible influence on the negotiations of the competition chapter in the future EU-Australia FTA. A competition regime can be found in Chapter 16. It was taken unchanged from the Trans-Pacific Partnership (TPP) agreement, which never entered into force due to the US withdrawal but became part of the CPTTP.[27]

The chapter contains, particularly in Article 16.2, detailed regulations on the procedural fairness in competition law enforcement, such as the possibility to obtain legal assistance and to be able to defend oneself adequately. In addition, the proceedings must be concluded within a certain period and access to information concerning the charge must be guaranteed. It must also be made possible to consult with or reach agreements with the national competition authority on all issues in the investigation proceedings. The burden of proof lies with the competition authority if it finds an infringement. Article 16.7 clarifies that the parties must act in a transparent way and make available to the other party every public information concerning competition laws and policies. In case of any disagreement, the parties should consult each other according to Article 16.8.

Furthermore, the chapter asks in Article 16.3 all parties to adopt and maintain laws which enable private rights of actions. If this is not the case, then at least the person must have the right to ask the competition authorities for investigation. Such a regulation is nowhere included in any of the EU FTAs due to the fact that the EU only slowly implements mechanisms and instruments which can be used by anyone to claim compensation for the infringement of competition laws.[28]

Besides that, there is in Article 16.4 a commitment to cooperation and the possibility to enter into a more detailed cooperation agreement with other competition authorities. In comparison to the EU-FTAs, the CPTTP is very detailed and is not only asking the parties to adopt or maintain laws, measures or actions for due process, but it also gives a detailed framework how these should be designed. This differs strongly from the European approach in competition chapters of their FTAs.

---

[26] Comprehensive and Progressive Agreement for Trans-Pacific Partnership, entered into force for Australia in 2018, https://www.dfat.gov.au/sites/default/files/tpp-11-treaty-text.pdf (last accessed 9 September 2021); Chapter 16 on Competition Policy of the Trans-Pacific Partnership Agreement, https://www.dfat.gov.au/sites/default/files/16-competition-policy.pdf (last accessed 9 September 2021).

[27] Abrenica and Bernabe (2017), p. 165.

[28] Directive 2014/104/EU of the European Parliament and of the Council of 26 November 2014 on certain rules governing actions for damages under national law for infringements of the competition law provisions of the Member States and the European Union, OJ 2014 L 349/1, which needed to be transposed into national law until the end of 2016.

4.2.3 MMAC

The invitation in the CPTTP to conclude cooperation agreements with other contracting parties may have been met by Australia, Canada and Mexico with the Multilateral Mutual Assistance and Cooperation Framework for Competition Authorities (MMAC).[29] This is a competition authority agreement consisting of a memorandum of understanding and a model agreement that also includes the US and the United Kingdom. It is unique in its kind as it is the first multilateral agreement at agency level in the field of competition cooperation. Yet, it is not binding for the parties since it lacks the quality of an international treaty as it is not concluded by the governments of the parties. The framework should engage the parties to more and improved cooperation. The model agreement should be used as a template for future cooperation agreements between the involved agencies in the field of investigations and enforcement.

The MoU allows for exchanges on the development of competition law and experience in competition promotion, the development of regulatory capacity and effectiveness, the study of best practices and cooperation on projects of mutual interest. This should improve the safe and trustful exchange of information, including also confidential ones. According to Article 3.2, this cooperation and assistance shall be implemented particularly in the context of the exchange of information of various kinds and in the coordination of investigative activities (such as voluntary witness interviews). The exchange of information also includes confidential information. Article 4 refers to the model agreement and states that while this is to be largely based on reciprocity, exceptions may be provided for if required by national law. In this regard, the parties are given the flexibility to expand regulations or to make use of existing instruments. The framework MoU should be reviewed every five years. Whether it is open to other parties is not stated in the text but should be possible if all parties give their consent.

The model agreement concretises the scope of assistance in the investigation procedure already mentioned in the MoU. This includes, among other things, the disclosure, forwarding and discussion of investigative information, the questioning of witnesses, the seizure of documents and the carrying out of searches. It is not decisive here whether a conduct is actually qualified as a competition law violation of the answering party. However, if timely and mutual assistance is not possible, this must be justified. Furthermore, the requirements for the request for assistance and its timing are regulated in detail. In addition, the parties guarantee each other that the information will be protected according to the respective national law and will be returned or destroyed after the conclusion of the proceedings. In the case of confidential information, a special standard of protection is applied, stating that disclosure is not excluded if it is necessary for enforcement, is requested by courts and it is

[29] Multilateral Mutual Assistance and Cooperation Framework for Competition Authorities, 2020, https://www.accc.gov.au/system/files/MMAC%20-%20FINAL%20English%20-%202%20September%202020%2811501052.1%29.pdf (last accessed 9 September 2021).

shown that disclosure is permitted by law. This information may only be used in the investigation process.

The MMAC also has very detailed rules on procedures and the exchange of information and thus reflects the so-called NAFTA approach of the USA and Canada,[30] which integrate fewer substantive rules into their agreements, but rather focus on regulating cooperation.

5 Conclusions

The competition chapter in the EU-Australia FTA is a good start for future enhanced cooperation on competition infringements. However, it must be doubted whether the regulations proposed so far are sufficient for this or whether they are not a reason for concluding an official agreement on cooperation in competition matters. In addition, the question arises as to whether adjustments will not be made during further negotiations, as the text proposed so far still resembles an initial draft, not containing any specific provisions reflecting competition between the two parties.

Whether the CPTTP and the MMAC can really act as a model for the further negotiations of the EU-Australia competition chapter is questionable. Both follow the NAFTA-approach that sets different priorities than the EU, which strongly believes in the differentiated definition of anticompetitive behaviour. Nevertheless, CETA between the EU and Canada shows that even countries that predominantly follow the NAFTA approach make concessions, albeit not extensive ones, with regard to substantive rules. Article 17.1, for example, defines more precisely what is meant by anti-competitive business conduct. The existing text in the EU-Australia FTA goes beyond this and can be seen as a compromise between the two parties. This shows that although Australia has concluded some agreements that follow the NAFTA approach, it can still be flexible in its approach. Whether this justifies an independent "Oceania approach" will be shown by future agreements.[31] It is doubtful whether the EU is prepared to include more detailed regulations on cooperation and in particular on procedures, such as in the CPTTP. So far, it has used either dedicated competition agreements or memoranda of understanding for this purpose.

Such agreements are to be recommended, as they give the space to regulate more in detail the specific procedures for investigation and enforcement. In this context the MMAC could be used as an inspiration for a more specific procedural approach. This could be especially advisable since the UK, which as a former Member State of the EU with European oriented competition law, became a member of MMAC but will still be one of the EU's main trading partners. Therefore, a smooth competition cooperation, as exercised in the years of membership, will be in the interest of both.

---

[30] Solano and Sennekamp (2006).

[31] Laprévote et al. (2015), p. 6, who, in relation to ANZCERTA, named Australia's approach in this way, but here identified the duty to harmonise as the distinguishing element.

The EU-UK TCA also includes a chapter on competition issues but without any detailed procedural rules. Nevertheless, it explicitly gives the parties the possibility to enter into a separate agreement on cooperation and coordination on the agency level.

In this context, it will be of great interest to see what will be part of the Australia-UK FTA in the chapter about competition. So far it is mentioned that the chapter will target competition policy and consumer protection by including provisions which maintain competition laws regarding anti-competitive behaviour, anti-competitive practices by undertakings with market power and mergers with substantial effects as well as having competition authorities in force. Moreover, principles on procedural fairness, accompanied by the opportunity to legal representation, and on cooperation and coordination securing the effective enforcement should be reflected in the chapter.[32] There is no explicit proposal of the text available so that it cannot be analysed to which extent these provisions will regulate the competition enforcement between the two parties. However, these agreements could be used as an opportunity at the side of the EU to consider new cooperation and coordination rules, which could be included in new competition agreements to safeguard the cooperation with a former Member State and to open these rules up to new trustful trading partners, like Australia.

Considering this, the exchange of information, especially confidential information, should be more precisely regulated. Another important aspect for successful cooperation would be the inclusion of an obligation to notify any investigations already in the competition chapter. This is the only way to ensure that the other party is informed about any action taken by the competition authorities. Since the exclusion of the dispute settlement mechanism for the competition chapter is standard in most FTAs, the possibility of consultation should nevertheless be considered. This can contribute to the quick resolution of disputes.

In summary, it can be said that cooperation between the EU and Australia, and in future also with New Zealand, is to be welcomed. It can be assumed that the EU-Australia FTA will increase trade and thus also competition, so that this must be protected by accompanying effective competition rules. This can be the basis for trustful cooperation in the future, as both have to face the challenges that arise for competition in a globalised and digitalised world.

References

Abrenica MJV, Bernabe J (2017) Competition chapter in the Trans-Pacific Partnership Agreement: developing a template for a multilateral framework. In: Chaisse J, Gao H, Lo CF (eds) Paradigm shift in international economic law rule-making. Springer, Heidelberg, pp 165–186

[32] Australian Government, Department of Foreign Affairs and Trade, Australia-UK FTA negotiations: agreement in principle, https://www.dfat.gov.au/trade/agreements/negotiations/aukfta/australia-uk-fta-negotiations-agreement-principle#competition (last accessed 9 September 2021).

Anderson RD, Kovacic WE, Müller AC, Sporysheva N (2018) Competition policy, trade and the global economy: existing WTO elements, commitments in regional trade agreements, current challenges and issues for reflection, Staff Working Paper ERSD-2018-12. World Trade Organization, Geneva

Baetge D (2009) Globalisierung des Wettbewerbsrechts. Mohr Siebeck, Tübingen

Capobianco A, Nagy A (2016) Developments in international enforcement co-operation in the competition field. J Eur Compet Law Pract 7(8):566–583

Fröhlich M (2018) The potential influence of free trade agreements as a boost for a multilateral competition law – the special case of SAAs and CEFTA. In: Popović DV (ed) Legal implications of trade liberalization under SAAs and CEFTA. University of Belgrade, Belgrade, pp 203–218

Laprévote FC, Frisch S, Burcu C (2015) Competition policy within the context of free trade agreements. International Centre for Trade and Sustainable Development (ICTSD) and World Economic Forum, Geneva, http://e15initiative.org/wp-content/uploads/2015/09/E15-Competition-Laprevote-Frisch-Can-Final.pdf

Solano O, Sennekamp A (2006) Competition provisions in regional trade agreements, OECD Trade Policy Papers No. 31. OECD Publishing, Paris

Teh R (2009) Competition provisions in regional trade agreements. In: Estevadeordal A, Suominen K, Teh R (eds) Regional rules in the global trading system. Cambridge University Press, Cambridge, pp 418–491

Trebilcock M, Howse R, Eliason A (2013) The regulation of international trade. Routledge, Abingdon, Oxfordshire, pp 756–780

Tschaeni H, Engammare V (2013) The relationship between trade and competition in free trade agreements: developments since the 1990s and challenges. In: Herrmann C, Krajewski M, Terhechte J (eds) European yearbook of international economic law, vol 5. Springer, Heidelberg, pp 39–69

Völcker S (2019) in: Wettbewerbsrecht und seine internationale Durchsetzung: Kartellbehörden in Drittstaaten und ihre Beziehungen zur Europäischen Kommission. In: Körber T, Schweitzer H, Zimmer D (eds) Immenga/Mestmäcker Wettbewerbsrecht, Band 1. EU Kommentar zum Europäischen Kartellrecht, vol 6. Beck, München

Mareike Fröhlich is a research associate at the Europa-Institut of Saarland University and specialized in European and International Economic Law. She studied law at the Rhenish Friedrich Wilhelm University of Bonn (German: Rheinische Friedrich-Wilhelms-Universität Bonn) and graduated in 2005. She holds a LL.M. in European and International Law of the Europa-Institut of Saarland University. She did her legal clerkship at the Land Rheinland-Pfalz and is a fully qualified lawyer. In 2021, she defended her doctoral thesis at Saarland University in the field of European and International Competition Law. She coordinates as a research associate several European and international projects.

European Trade Policy and the Regulation of Subsidies: What Can We Expect from the EU-Australia FTA?

Philipp Reinhold

Contents

Abstract Subsidies play an important role in the European Union's trade policy. This concerns both the use of autonomous instruments and the many bilateral and multilateral trade negotiations. Currently, the creation of a new regulation is being discussed, on the basis of which the European Commission could act against foreign subsidies that distort the internal market. At the same time, the EU is trying to agree on more far-reaching subsidy rules in its bilateral trade agreements and continues to advocate a reform of subsidy rules at the WTO level. Overall, the EU's aim is to create a level playing field for the provision of subsidies. For Australian trade policy, the regulation of subsidies has been less important so far. Nevertheless, there are reasons for including more far-reaching subsidy rules in a free trade agreement between the EU and Australia ("EU-Australia FTA"). On the one hand, they can serve as a template for further agreements and as a political signal with regard to multilateral reforms of WTO subsidy law. On the other hand, Australia can use the opportunity to negotiate provisions that make it easier for Australian companies to deal with a new EU subsidy regime.

P. Reinhold (✉)
Saarland University, Saarbrücken, Germany
e-mail: reinhold@europainstitut.de

M. Bungenberg, A. Mitchell (eds.), *The Australia-European Union Free Trade Agreement*, Special Issue, https://doi.org/10.1007/978-3-030-91448-6_10

1 Introduction

The regulation of subsidies represents a controversial area of international trade law and policy. Every state provides subsidies to a different extent and for different reasons. At the same time, subsidies can have an impact on international economic relations, which is why they were the subject of intergovernmental negotiations early on.[1] The WTO Agreement on Subsidies and Countervailing Measures ("ASCM") is the most comprehensive attempt to date to reach a multilateral compromise on the regulation of subsidies. However, WTO rules reflect the state of the world economy in 1994, which is why many see them as in need of reform. So far, this has not happened. The WTO is in crisis, with members unable to agree on any significant reform steps and the dispute settlement mechanism being blocked by the US.

As a result of the ongoing stalemate in negotiations at the WTO level, but also due to the dissatisfaction of some members with the existing WTO law, states have increasingly started to negotiate trade agreements outside the WTO framework.[2] On the one hand, these agreements contain rules that reflect WTO law. On the other hand, states agree on provisions that deviate from WTO law and lead to deeper market integration ("WTO+").[3] As a result, new rules for world trade emerge that exist in parallel to thc WTO legal order, including in the area of subsidies.[4]

Both the European Union and Australia have already concluded a number of FTAs and have thereby in many cases agreed on regulations that go beyond existing WTO law. In this context, many of the EU's new FTAs contain provisions on subsidies that differ from the ASCM rules. For Australia, subsidies have not played a comparable role in this context so far. Against this background, the aim of this chapter is to consider what role subsidies could play in an EU-Australia FTA. It will be argued that the EU has a strong interest in incorporating more extensive subsidy rules into an EU-Australia FTA, but that Australia also has some incentive to do so, at least with regard to the EU's proposed new subsidy instrument.

In a first step, it will be shown how subsidies have become an important issue in EU trade policy (Sect. 2). This will be contrasted with the limited importance of subsidies within Australian trade policy to date (Sect. 3). In a second step, possible interests and incentives in negotiations on subsidy rules will be examined (Sect. 4). The chapter concludes with an outlook on the ongoing negotiations (Sect. 5).

---

[1] Viner (1923), pp. 166–191.

[2] Griller et al. (2017), pp. 4–5; Mattoo et al. (2020), p. 3.

[3] The term "WTO+" refers to deeper integration in areas covered by the WTO, see WTO (2011), p. 11.

[4] See e.g. Rubini (2020), pp. 427–461.

2 Regulation of Subsidies as an Objective of European Trade Policy

Subsidy rules are of particular importance for the EU. Free trade in the internal market and the resulting cross-border competition are protected by European state aid law against selective favouritism by Member States, which would otherwise lead to market access restrictions, subsidy races and an impairment of the equal opportunities of competing companies.[5] State aid law is part of the European competition rules, which the European treaties declare to be a constitutive element of the internal market.[6]

While this unique system of state aid regulation contributes to effective competition between European companies, it has at the same time negative consequences in external relations with third countries. While state aid law in the internal market ensures a level playing field in competition, in international trade it represents a self-restriction, as the member states of the European Union cannot support their companies in international competition if this violates Article 107 TFEU. As a result, European companies are at risk of being disadvantaged compared to foreign companies that receive extensive state support.[7]

Nevertheless, unlike the US, the EU has traditionally not been a driver of international subsidy regulation. One reason for this lies in European agricultural policy, which has traditionally been strongly protectionist and still includes a high level of subsidies.[8] The former EC therefore argued for an exclusion of the agricultural sector in the ASCM negotiations and, apart from that, has also advocated for the integration of exemptions in relation to other subsidies.[9]

In the meantime, however, the regulation of subsidies became an important aspect of EU's trade policy: On the one hand, a closer convergence of the current subsidy rules to the model of European state aid law is seen as an important element for the creation of a level playing field in the context of the EU's recent FTAs (Sect. 2.1). This has been described as the "exportation of state aid law".[10] On the other hand, the EU has recently seen a greater need to protect European companies against the effects of foreign subsidies as part of its autonomous trade policy. In this context, the European Commission has recently proposed a new instrument to regulate foreign subsidies (Sect. 2.2).

---

[5] Monopolkommission, Hauptgutachten XXIII: Wettbewerb 2020, paragraph 743 and 861. An English translation of the chapter on Chinese state capitalism can be found under https://monopolkommission.de/images/HG23/Main_Report_XXIII_Chinese_state_capitalism.pdf (last accessed 9 September 2021).

[6] See Article 3 (3) TEU as well as Protocol (No 27) on the internal market and competition OJ 2008 C 115/309.

[7] See on this already Ehlermann (1994), pp. 1219–1221.

[8] On EU agricultural policy see Feindt (2018), pp. 115–133.

[9] E.g. Croome (1994), pp. 58–66, 171–177 and 261–263.

[10] Ehlermann (1994), pp. 1219–1221. See also Neumann (2019).

2.1 *Exportation of European State Aid Law Through FTAs*

While a preference for multilateral agreements prevailed in European trade policy for a long time, a change in strategy has taken place since 2005, with greater emphasis being placed on the conclusion of individual, more comprehensive trade agreements.[11] Until then, the EU had unsuccessfully tried to negotiate an alignment of the ASCM with its own state aid law within the framework of the WTO.[12] The new trade agenda aims to take the EU "further and faster in promoting openness and integration, by tackling issues which are not ready for multilateral discussion and by preparing the ground for the next level of multilateral liberalisation".[13] One objective in this context is the integration of more far-reaching competition rules along the lines of European competition law, i.e. also in the area of subsidies.[14]

Many of the EU's more recent agreements contain a separate chapter on "Competition" which, in addition to antitrust and merger regulations, also includes subsidy provisions.[15] Others provide for a separate chapter on subsidies.[16] The subsidy rules contained in these chapters are based on the ASCM as a common basis between the EU and its trading partners. However, many agreements contain provisions that go beyond these rules and can therefore be referred to as WTO+.

In some cases, the EU and its trading partners have agreed that a subsidy under Article 1.1 ASCM should cover not only goods but also services.[17] In addition, the category of prohibited subsidies was expanded to include forms of unlimited debt coverage, as well as aid to insolvent or ailing companies without the existence of a viable restructuring plan.[18] Regulations can also be identified that oblige the EU and its contractual partner to prevent the misuse of subsidies.[19] At the same time, many

---

[11] Bungenberg (2016), pp. 96–99; Griller et al. (2017), p. 5.

[12] Coppens (2014), pp. 35–38.

[13] European Commission, Communication from the Commission to the Council, the European Parliament, the European Economic and Social Committee and the Committee of the Regions, Global Europe: Competing in the World – A Contribution to the EU's Growth and Jobs Strategy, COM(2006) 567 final, p. 8. The agreements can be found at https://ec.europa.eu/trade/policy/countries-and-regions/negotiations-and-agreements/ (last accessed 9 September 2021).

[14] European Commission, Global Europe: Competing in the World – A Contribution to the EU's Growth and Jobs Strategy, COM(2006) 567 final, p. 7; Trade for all – Towards a more responsible trade and investment policy, COM(2015) 497 final, p. 10.

[15] E.g. Chapter 11 EU-Korea FTA; Chapter 11 EU-Singapore FTA; Chapter 10 EU-Vietnam FTA; Chapter 12 New EU-Mexico Agreement (Agreement in Principle), https://trade.ec.europa.eu/doclib/docs/2018/april/tradoc_156791.pdf (last accessed 9 September 2021).

[16] E.g. Chapter 12 EU-Japan EPA; Chapter 7 CETA; Chapter 11 New EU-Mercosur Agreement, (Agreement in Principle), https://trade.ec.europa.eu/doclib/docs/2019/june/tradoc_157964.pdf (last accessed 9 September 2021).

[17] Article 11.5 (1) EU-Singapore FTA; Article 12.2 (b) EU-Japan EPA; Article 10.5 (1) EU-Vietnam FTA; New EU-Mexico agreement (Agreement in Principle), p. 13.

[18] Article 11.11 EU-Korea FTA; Article 11.7 (2) EU-Singapore FTA; Article 12.7 EU-Japan EPA; Article 10.9 EU-Vietnam FTA; New EU-Mexico Agreement (Agreement in Principle), p. 13.

[19] Article 12.9 EU-Japan EPA.

agreements contain provisions on legitimate reasons for granting subsidies. Different approaches can be found in this context: In some cases, the subsidy rules are linked to the exceptions in Article XX GATT and Article XIV GATS.[20] In addition, there are many individual exceptions, e.g. for the cultural industry[21] or for services of general interest[22] or for exceptional occurrences such as natural disasters[23] or financial crisis.[24] Annex 11-A of the free trade agreement between the EU and Singapore ("EU-Singapore FTA") contains a broad catalogue of exemptions very similar to those in European state aid law.[25]

The enforcement of subsidy rules is often subject to a separate consultation procedure, which replaces the general state-to-state dispute settlement mechanism.[26] At the same time, the chapters contain review clauses that provide for future adjustments after a fixed period of time.[27] In addition, political agreements can be found in which the EU and its trading partner undertake to promote further development of subsidy rules at the WTO level.[28] In principle, the bilateral agreements

---

[20] Article 12.9 EU-Japan EPA.

[21] Article 7.7 CETA.

[22] Article 12.3 (2) EU-Japan EPA; Article 10.5 (4) EU-Vietnam FTA.

[23] Article 12.3 (3) EU-Japan EPA.

[24] Article 12.3 (6) EU-Japan EPA.

[25] See paragraph 2 of Annex 11-A (Principles Applicable To Other Subsidies):

> Notwithstanding paragraph 1, the following subsidies may be granted by a Party where they are necessary to achieve an objective of public interest, and where the amounts of the subsidies involved are limited to the minimum needed to achieve that objective and their effect on the trade of the other Party is limited:
>
> (a) subsidies that have a social character and that are granted to individual consumers, provided that such subsidies are granted without discrimination regarding the origin of the products concerned;
> (b) subsidies to make good the damage caused by natural disasters or exceptional occurrences;
> (c) subsidies to promote the economic development of areas in which the standard of living is abnormally low or in which there is serious underemployment;
> (d) subsidies to remedy a serious disturbance in the economy of one of the Parties;
> (e) subsidies to facilitate the development of certain economic activities or the development of certain economic areas, where such aid does not affect the conditions of trade of either Party or competition between the Parties (1);
> (f) subsidies to companies entrusted with the operation of clearly defined services of general economic interest, provided that such subsidies are limited to the cost of providing such services;
> (g) subsidies to promote culture and heritage conservation, where those subsidies do not affect conditions of trade of either Party and competition between the Parties; and
> (h) subsidies to promote the execution of an important project of regional or bilateral interest.

[26] Article 12.6 EU-Japan EPA; Article 7.3 and 7.4 CETA; Article 10.8 EU-Vietnam FTA.

[27] Article 11.14 EU-Korea FTA; Article 10.10 EU-Vietnam FTA; Article 11.8 (2) and 11.10 EU-Singapore FTA.

[28] Article 11.15 (2) EU-Korea FTA.

shall not affect the rights and obligations of the Parties under the ASCM or Article XV GATS.[29] But it can be assumed that the bilateral subsidy rules will have an impact on WTO law. This probably applies in particular to the special transparency obligations contained in all recent agreements of the EU.[30]

All in all, it becomes clear that the controversial and highly political issue of subsidies is being addressed through individual forms of political convergence. This may result in new rules for WTO law in the long run, or FTA rules will become more prominent for solving trade disputes in the future if the WTO fails to evolve.

In addition to the FTAs mentioned above, the EU has, on the one hand, concluded a large number of association agreements that provide for greater integration, also politically. On the other hand, it has recently concluded a trade and cooperation agreement with the United Kingdom ("EU-UK TCA") that regulates their common trade relations after the UK's withdrawal from the EU and the single market. Association agreements, regularly contain the obligation of the partner state to introduce a state aid system along the lines of Article 107 TFEU.[31] Usually, this corresponds to an adoption of the *aquis communitaire* as a precondition for closer ties with and possibly later accession to the EU.[32] The EU-UK TCA represents the opposite case of a detachment from the political as well as economic system of the EU. Due to the long-standing membership in the single market and the danger of fierce competition in the future, the EU pushed in the negotiations for the agreement of a comprehensive subsidy system *sui generis* which is very closely aligned with Article 107 TFEU.[33] It forms part of the chapter on a "level playing field" which intends to ensure "fair competition" in the future.[34]

In summary, it becomes clear that the EU has already achieved a greater alignment of international subsidy rules with European state aid law by concluding various forms of agreements. These rules are open to development and could become an alternative to the WTO subsidy system in the event of stronger efforts for effective enforcement in the future.

2.2 *Unilateral Protection Against Foreign Subsidies*

In addition to bilateral and multilateral trade negotiations, the EU is also pursuing stronger protection of European companies with its recently announced open,

---

[29] Article 11.13 EU-Korea FTA; Article 12.4 EU-Japan EPA; Article 10.6 EU-Vietnam FTA; Article 11.6 EU-Singapore FTA.

[30] Article 11.12 EU-Korea FTA; Article 12.5 EU-Japan EPA; Article 7.2 CETA; Article 10.7 EU-Vietnam FTA; Article 11.9 EU-Singapore FTA.

[31] E.g. Article 71 EU-Albania SAA; Article 267 EU-Ukraine AA.

[32] See Neale-Besson (2016), paras. 1.438–1.565.

[33] See on the subsidy control system of the EU-UK TCA e.g. Kotsonis (2021), pp. 15–29.

[34] Article 355 (1), 363–375 EU-UK TCA.

sustainable and assertive EU trade strategy.[35] On the one hand, this includes stronger enforcement of international trade rules, for which a new post of "Chief Trade Enforcement Officer (CTEO)" has been created.[36] On the other hand, the EU shall "develop its tools to confront new challenges and protect European companies and citizens from unfair trading practices, both internally and externally".[37] In particular, the rise of China and the pressure exerted by Chinese state capitalism on European companies have led to a number of reform ideas in this context.[38]

One recent reform proposal ties in with the fact that European state aid law only applies to member states. The resulting unequal treatment vis-à-vis foreign subsidies cannot be compensated for by other legal instruments, such as EU anti-subsidy law.[39] Against this background, the European Commission published a White Paper "on levelling the playing field as regards foreign subsidies" in 2020 ("White Paper").[40] The White Paper contained proposals for three sub-instruments which, individually or together, would provide protection against competition-distorting foreign subsidies: a general *ex officio* control of harmful subsidies, a specific control of subsidies which have an impact on corporate mergers and a control of subsidies which affect public procurement.

On 5 May 2021, the Commission presented a legislative proposal following consultations with industry associations and the academia.[41] The proposal is closely

---

[35] European Commission, Communication from the Commission to the European Parliament, the Council, the European Economic and Social Committee and the Committee of the Regions, Trade Policy Review - An Open, Sustainable and Assertive Trade Policy, COM(2021) 66 final, pp. 4–5.

[36] European Commission, Press release: European Commission appoints its first Chief Trade Enforcement Officer, 24 July 2020, IP/20/1409.

[37] European Commission, Communication from the Commission to the European Parliament, the Council, the European Economic and Social Committee and the Committee of the Regions, Trade Policy Review - An Open, Sustainable and Assertive Trade Policy, COM(2021) 66 final, pp. 19–21.

[38] See e.g. BDI, Grundsatzpapier China. Partner und systemischer Wettbewerber – Wie gehen wir mit Chinas staatlich gelenkter Volkswirtschaft um?, January 2019, https://bdi.eu/publikation/news/china-partner-und-systemischer-wettbewerber/ (last accessed 9 September 2021); Bertelsmann Stiftung, Beyond investment screening. Expanding Europe's toolbox to address economic risks from Chinese state capitalism, October 2019, https://www.bertelsmann-stiftung.de/fileadmin/files/BSt/Publikationen/GrauePublikationen/DA_Studie_ExpandEurope_2019.pdf (last accessed 9 September 2021); Business Europe, The EU and China – Addressing the Systemic Challenge, January 2020, https://www.businesseurope.eu/sites/buseur/files/media/reports_and_studies/the_eu_and_china_full_february_2020_version_for_screen.pdf (last accessed 9 September 2021); Permanent Representation of the Netherlands to the European Union, Non-paper – Strengthening the level playing field on the internal market, 9 December 2019, https://www.permanentrepresentations.nl/documents/publications/2019/12/09/non-paper-on-level-playing-field (last accessed 9 September 2021); Monopolkommission (2020), pp. 242–377. See also Kühling et al. (2020), pp. 403–417.

[39] Kühling et al. (2020), pp. 405–409.

[40] European Commission, White Paper on levelling the playing field as regards foreign subsidies, COM(2020) 253 final.

[41] European Commission, Proposal for a Regulation of the European Parliament and of the Council on foreign subsidies distorting the internal market, COM(2021) 223 final.

aligned with the White Paper and combines all three sub-instruments. It would create a completely new legal regime on the basis of which the European Commission can investigate foreign subsidies and impose remedies. According to the proposal, the rules would be applicable to any company doing business in the internal market. Therefore, if the Council and European Parliament agree on the creation of this new instrument, it would most likely also cover Australian companies operating in the domestic market and receiving subsidies at the same time.

3 The Role of Subsidies in Australian Trade Policy

Compared to the EU, subsidies play a much smaller role in Australian trade policy. First of all, this concerns the use of trade defence instruments. Australia is one of the WTO members that make more frequent use of trade defence measures, but not as often as the EU and not nearly as often as the US.[42] As of 31 December 2020, 11 definitive countervailing measures and 68 anti-dumping measures were in force.[43] By comparison, there were 18 countervailing measures and 101 anti-dumping measures in force in the EU at the same time.[44]

The different importance of subsidies in trade policy becomes even more apparent in the context of contractual trade relations. Like the EU, Australia is increasingly concluding comprehensive FTAs, including areas such as investment, services and competition.[45] However, subsidies have not played a particularly important role within these agreements so far. None of the agreements contains a separate subsidy chapter. There are also no subsidy rules in chapters on competition.[46] In the majority of cases, the agreements only confirm the ASCM rules and the possibility to use

[42] WTO, Trade Policy Review Body, Trade Policy Review Report by the Secretariat – Australia, WT/TPR/S/396, paragraph 3.56. See also https://www.wto.org/english/tratop_e/scm_e/CV_MeasuresByRepMem.pdf (last accessed 9 September 2021).

[43] WTO, Committee on Subsidies and Countervailing Measures, Semi-Annual Report Under Article 25.1 of the Agreement – Australia, G/SCM/N/371/AUS, p. 8; Committee on Anti-Dumping Practices, Semi-Annual Report Under Article 16.4 of the Agreement – Australia, G/ADP/N/350/AUS, pp. 21–25.

[44] European Commission, Anti-Dumping, Anti-Subsidy, Safeguards – Trade Statistics covering the full year 2020, December 2020, p. 2, https://trade.ec.europa.eu/doclib/docs/2021/february/tradoc_159452.pdf (last accessed 9 September 2021).

[45] The agreements can be found at https://www.dfat.gov.au/trade/agreements/trade-agreements (last accessed 9 September 2021).

[46] See Chapter 12 Singapore-Australia FTA; Chapter 14 Australia-United States FTA; Chapter 12 Thailand-Australia FTA; Chapter 14 Australia-Chile FTA; Chapter 14 ASEAN-Australia--New Zealand FTA; Chapter 14 Malaysia-Australia FTA; Chapter 14 Korea-Australia FTA; Chapter 15 Japan-Australia EPA; Chapter 16 CPTPP; Chapter 15 Australia-Hong Kong FTA; Chapter 15 Peru-Australia FTA; Chapter 16 Indonesia-Australia CEPA.

countervailing duties.[47] Sometimes, this is supplemented by an agreement on joint action against export subsidies in the field of agriculture and/or a commitment that both sides will refrain from imposing or maintaining export subsidies on a reciprocal basis.[48]

In individual cases, however, Australia has also agreed to subsidy rules that go beyond the current status of the ASCM: The first example concerns the Australia-New Zealand Closer Economic Relations Trade Agreement ("ANZCERTA"). Under this agreement Australia agreed with New Zealand in 1988 "to avoid the adoption of industry specific measures (bounties, subsidies and other financial support) which have adverse effects on competition between industries in the Free Trade Area".[49] Furthermore, in the event that one of the two countries nevertheless considers that it must undertake such a measure, e.g. for reasons of "overriding national interest", both countries agreed to "seek and take into account the opinion of the other country before making its final decision".

The second example concerns the Japan-Australia Economic Partnership Agreement ("Japan-Australia EPA") and the Regional Comprehensive Economic Partnership ("RCEP"). In both cases, Australia and its trading partners agreed to review the treatment of subsidies in relation to trade in services, taking into account the development of multilateral disciplines under Article XV of the GATS, and to enter into a consultations if either party considered that its interests had been adversely affected by a subsidy from the other party.[50] With Japan, Australia has in addition also agreed on a consultation mechanism concerning the impact of subsidies in the area of investments.[51] However, in all cases the application of the general dispute settlement procedure is excluded.

Finally, Australia is a party to the Comprehensive and Progressive Agreement for Trans-Pacific Partnership ("CPTPP"), which contains a separate chapter on state-owned enterprises ("SOEs").[52] In this chapter, the Parties have agreed on a new concept of so-called "non-commercial assistance". This term covers direct transfers of funds or potential direct transfers of funds or liabilities that are exclusively or

---

[47] See Article 2 of Chapter 2 Singapore-Australia FTA; Article 207 and 208 Thailand-Australia-FTA; Article 8.2 Australia-Chile FTA; Article 7.3 Malaysia-Australia FTA; Article 6.8 Korea-Australia FTA; Article 2.12 Japan-Australia EPA; Article 7.10 China-Australia FTA; Article 2.11 Australia-Hong Kong FTA; Article 5.9 Peru-Australia FTA; Art. 2.14 Indonesia-Australia CEPA; Article 7.1 and 7.2 Pacific Agreement on Closer Economic Relation Plus.

[48] See Article 13 of Chapter 2 Singapore-Australia FTA; Art. 3.3 Australia-United States FTA; Article 3.13 Australia-Chile FTA; Article 3 of Chapter 2 ASEAN-Australia-New Zealand FTA; Article 2.7 Japan-Australia EPA; Article 2.21 CPTPP; Article 2.17 Peru-Australia FTA; Article 2.7 Indonesia-Australia CEPA; Article 2.13 RCEP.

[49] See Agreed Minute on Industry Assistance, paragraph 3, https://www.dfat.gov.au/sites/default/files/285.pdf (last accessed 9 September 2021). See also Department of Foreign Affairs and Trade, Closer Economic Relations Background Guide to the Australia New Zealand Economic Relationship, p. 10, https://www.dfat.gov.au/sites/default/files/cer.pdf (last accessed 9 September 2021).

[50] Article. 9.11 Japan-Australia EPA; Article 8.22 RCEP.

[51] See Annex 11 of the Japan-Australia EPA.

[52] Chapter 17 CPTPP.

predominantly granted to SOEs.[53] In line with the concept of anti-dumping or anti-subsidy law, no party shall cause adverse effects or injury through the use of such forms of support in its home market, but also in foreign markets.[54] The provisions can be made subject of a dispute settlement procedure.

4 Possible Interests and Incentives in Negotiations on Subsidy Rules

The EU and Australian negotiations start from the ASCM as the basic consensus on subsidy regulation in international trade. The question will be whether or which individual provisions both sides will include in a future FTA.

According to the negotiation directives by the Council of the European Union, "[t]he Agreement should contain robust and binding provisions on subsidies, in line with the EU standards and principles on State aids".[55] This is reflected in the EU's proposal for the negotiations with Australia: According to the proposal, provisions on subsidies are to be included together with antitrust and merger rules in a separate competition chapter.[56] It includes an extension of the concept of subsidies to services, which is in line with the previous approach of the EU.[57] This would mean that another WTO member would in principle accept the application of the ASCM to services. The same passage also contains a placeholder for a common definition of the term "public body". This also ties in with recent reform discussions at WTO level.[58] Further, the proposal provides for a variety of provisions already included in other FTAs such as the extension of prohibited subsidies to unlimited or unconditional guarantees and financing of insolvent or distressed companies,[59] as well as a transparency obligation. The latter could also be fulfilled by notification under Article 25.1 ASCM.[60] The use of the general dispute resolution mechanism would presumably be replaced by a consultation procedure.[61]

The crucial question is: How likely is an agreement on the above-mentioned or even further WTO+ rules? The impact assessment prepared by the European Commission for the negotiations did not identify subsidies as a problem, apart from

---

[53] Article 17.1 CPTPP.

[54] Articles 17.6, 17.7 and 17.8 CPTPP.

[55] Council of the European Union, Negotiating directives for a Free Trade Agreement with Australia, 7663/18 ADD 1 DCL 1, p. 16.

[56] The proposal can be found at https://trade.ec.europa.eu/doclib/docs/2019/july/tradoc_158281.pdf (last accessed 9 September 2021).

[57] See Article X.8 (1) of the proposal.

[58] See for the discussions e.g. Ding (2014), pp. 167–189; Chiang (2018), pp. 845–886.

[59] Article X.12 of the proposal.

[60] Article X.10 of the proposal.

[61] Article X.11 of the proposal.

individual export subsidies, which are, however, already covered under the ASCM.[62] So why should ambitious agreements on subsidies be expected?

In the following, two recent developments will be highlighted that could potentially influence subsidy negotiations and make new rules seem useful: On the one hand, individual subsidy rules between the EU and Australia could support the development of a reformed international subsidy regime, which seem necessary in particular vis-à-vis the effects of state capitalist systems on international trade (Sect. 4.1). On the other hand, within the framework of the EU-Australia FTA, there is the possibility to agree on individual provisions for the future application of the proposed new subsidy instrument of the EU (Sect. 4.2).

4.1 Reform of International Subsidy Law in the Competition of Systems

The world trading system and its rules have traditionally been shaped by the idea of liberal trade between market economies. Against this background, China had to make a number of concessions when it joined the WTO and it was hoped that the country would develop into a market economy in the long run. Instead, China became an economic superpower and is openly challenging the world trading system through its state capitalism.[63] Not only does the Chinese state actively intervene in international competition in many ways, but the Chinese model is simultaneously being spread worldwide through large-scale economic projects such as the Belt and Road Initiative (BRI) and a complementary web of trade and investment agreements.[64] In this context, the question is already being asked whether the existing economic system will ultimately be replaced by a new Chinese economic order.[65]

From the EU's point of view, the strong influence of the state on the economic framework and the political control of corporate decisions leads to a variety of significant distortions that harm European companies and that are not compatible with free and fair trade.[66] In particular, the massive provision of subsidies to SOEs is

[62] European Commission, Commission Staff Working Document, Impact Assessment, Recommendation for a Council Decision authorising the opening of negotiations for a Free Trade Agreement with Australia, SWD(2017) 293 final, p. 63.

[63] See e.g. Wu (2016); Shaffer and Gao (2020).

[64] Shaffer and Gao (2020), pp. 614–627.

[65] Shaffer and Gao (2020).

[66] See on the market distortions identified by the EU in particular European Commission, Commission staff working document on significant distortions in the economy of the People's Republic of China for the purposes of trade defence investigations, 20 December 2017, SWD(2017) 483 final/2, https://trade.ec.europa.eu/doclib/docs/2017/december/tradoc_156474.pdf (last accessed 9 September 2021).

seen as a significant problem by the EU and European business.[67] On the one hand, this concerns the direct provision of subsidies. On the other hand, in the course of the various economic projects of the Chinese state, so-called "transnational subsidies" are granted in third countries, for example through the creation of special economic zones.[68]

The EU addresses these distortions through its autonomous trade policy by conducting a large number of anti-dumping and anti-subsidy proceedings.[69] The European Commission now also extends the latter to cases of transnational subsidies, although it is not clear whether such types of subsidies are covered by the ASCM.[70] Apart from that, the proposal for a new subsidy instrument is also closely linked to Chinese state capitalism.[71]

At the same time, the EU is seeking allies to tighten subsidy rules at the WTO level. The EU's proposals include increasing transparency through more effective enforcement of the notification requirement, better capture of SOEs as subsidy recipients and providers, and stricter rules against particularly harmful industrial subsidies, for example, unlimited guarantees, subsidies given to an insolvent or ailing enterprise with no credible restructuring plan or dual pricing.[72] The strongest signal in this regard recently came from a joint statement by the EU, the US and Japan, which called for a reform of the ASCM.[73] In this statement, the three states argue, among other things, in favour of expanding the category of prohibited subsidies, adapting the concept of "public body", introducing the possibility of counter-notification and taking market distortions into account in the subsidy assessment.

Australia is not similarly affected by industrial subsidies, which is why some are critical of former Trade Minister Simon Birmingham's plans to join EU reform

---

[67] Business Europe, The EU and China – Addressing the Systemic Challenge, January 2020, pp. 106–109.

[68] Crochet and Hegde (2020), pp. 843–845.

[69] European Commission, Trade Defence Statistics covering the full year 2020, https://trade.ec.europa.eu/doclib/docs/2021/february/tradoc_159452.pdf (last accessed 9 September 2021).

[70] Crochet and Hegde (2020), pp. 845–855.

[71] European Commission, Proposal for a Regulation of the European Parliament and of the Council on foreign subsidies distorting the internal market, COM(2021) 223 final, p. 2 fn. 8.

[72] European Commission, WTO modernisation - Introduction to future EU proposals, Concept paper, pp. 3–5 https://trade.ec.europa.eu/doclib/docs/2018/september/tradoc_157331.pdf (last accessed 9 September 2021).

[73] Joint Statement of the Trilateral Meeting of the Trade Ministers of Japan, the United States and the European Union, 14 January 2020, https://trade.ec.europa.eu/doclib/docs/2020/january/tradoc_158567.pdf (last accessed 9 September 2021). China is not openly mentioned, but is the primary target. See for the role of China in this context Gerstel D, Trade Trilateral Targets China's Industrial Subsidies, 22 January 2020, https://www.csis.org/analysis/trade-trilateral-targets-chinas-industrial-subsidies (last accessed 9 September 2021).

efforts with the US and Japan.[74] The majority of Australia's exports include raw materials and semi-processed products.[75] There is also the fear of further deterioration of the relationship with China. Currently, Australia is experiencing significant conflicts with China in political and economic terms.[76] In this context, the Chinese government has recently imposed high anti-dumping and countervailing duties on Australian exports of barley and wine, which Australia intends to challenge in WTO dispute settlement proceedings.[77]

For the EU, Australia's support would be important, also because of its role in the Pacific region. Agreeing on reformed subsidy rules in a bilateral agreement could be seen as an important signal in this regard. Moreover, common rules can serve as a template for further trade negotiations. Australia and the EU have the opportunity to further develop international subsidy law according to market economy principles, both by broadening the scope of application and by creating common standards for exemptions in key areas such as environmental protection and research and development.

A reform of international subsidy rules would also be of interest to Australia. Even though Chinese subsidies do not appear to be of great importance in trade relations between China and Australia at present, this does not mean that Australian companies cannot in principle be injured by foreign subsidies. The WTO dispute settlement proceedings between Australia and Indonesia over dumping measures against the Indonesian paper industry can serve as an example in this respect.[78] In this case, the Australian Anti-Dumping Commission ("ADC") found a number of market interventions by the Indonesian state, in particular through a number of subsidies.[79] Against this background, it rejected the exporters' domestic prices, claiming a "particular market situation".[80] In the original proceedings, the ADC

[74] Kehoe J, Australia urged to fight China's industrial subsidies. Financial Review, 27 June 2020, https://www.afr.com/policy/foreign-affairs/australia-urged-to-fight-china-s-industrial-subsidies-20200727-p55frm (last accessed 9 September 2021).

[75] See https://www.dfat.gov.au/sites/default/files/trade-investment-glance-2020.pdf (last accessed 9 September 2021).

[76] See Ferguson and Lim (2021).

[77] Van Leeuwen H and Greber J, Australia on cusp of taking on China at WTO over punitive wine tariffs, Financial Review, first published May 28 2021, updated 30 May 2021, https://www.afr.com/world/europe/china-to-vigorously-defend-against-australia-s-wto-push-on-barley-20210528-p57w8g (last accessed 9 September 2021).

[78] Report of the Panel, *Australia – Anti-Dumping Measures on A4 Copy Paper*, WT/DS529/R, adopted 27 January 2020.

[79] Report of the Panel, *Australia – Anti-Dumping Measures on A4 Copy Paper*, WT/DS529/R, adopted 27 January 2020, paragraphs 7.9–7.14. See also Anti-Dumping Commission, Report No. 341, alleged dumping of A4 copy paper exported from the Federative Republic of Brazil, the People's Republic of China, the Republic of Indonesia, and the Kingdom of Thailand and alleged subsidization of A4 copy paper exported from the People's Republic of China and the Republic of Indonesia (17 March 2017, published 19 April 2017), paragraph 6.5.

[80] See for the discussions on the interpretation of the term "particular market situation" in this case Zhou and Peng (2021).

also identified subsidies granted by the Chinese state, for example.[81] The vast majority of countervailing duties in force at the end of 2020 were directed against Chinese exporters.[82]

Overall, Australia will have to decide in principle whether it will participate in stronger action against significant market distortions in international trade or whether it fears retaliation against its own export industry as a result, which outweighs the benefits of participation. In any case, Australia can act as a rule maker in an agreement with the EU and thus contribute to the proliferation of new subsidy rules. These may consist of an extension of the scope or exemptions for important areas such as climate protection and technological development. Conversely, the EU can help to ensure that new concepts such as specific subsidy rules for SOEs, as agreed within the CPTPP, become more widespread.

4.2 Procedural Facilitation with Regard to the EU's New Subsidy Instrument

Another reason for individual subsidy rules in an EU-Australia FTA could be the proposed new subsidy instrument of the EU. Once the Council and the European Parliament agree on the implementation of a new instrument, Australian companies active in the internal market will most likely be covered by the new regulation. Apart from the burden of additional *ex officio* subsidy investigations, this would in particular delay corporate mergers. The FTA negotiations provide a good opportunity for arrangements that would make it easier for Australian businesses and the Australian state to deal with the proposed regulation. Conversely, it must not be forgotten that the European Commission has only limited capacities and that procedural regulations in particular could lead to a relief.

Article 40(7) of the Commission's proposal states:

> An investigation pursuant to this Regulation shall not be carried out and measures shall not be imposed or maintained where such investigation or measures would be contrary to the Union's obligations emanating from any relevant international agreement it has entered into.

In addition, the Commission may, in accordance with Articles 42 and 44 of the proposal, adopt implementing acts and thereby make adjustments which may concern both the procedure and the scope of application.

---

[81] See e.g. Anti-Dumping Commission, Report No. 341, alleged dumping of A4 copy paper exported from the Federative Republic of Brazil, the People's Republic of China, the Republic of Indonesia, and the Kingdom of Thailand and alleged subsidization of A4 copy paper exported from the People's Republic of China and the Republic of Indonesia (17 March 2017, published 19 April 2017), appendix 3.

[82] WTO, Committee on Subsidies and Countervailing Measures, Semi-Annual Report Under Article 25.1 of the Agreement – Australia, G/SCM/N/371/AUS, p. 8.

Against this background, agreements could be made in an EU-Australia FTA that would allow for faster and more efficient handling of the individual procedures. Exemptions from application would also be conceivable. In the past, for example, it has been suggested that under certain circumstances the Commission could issue a recognition decision which would contain the binding statement that by entering into an international agreement between the EU and a third country or by unilateral measures adopted by the third country itself, a system of subsidy control has been created which can be regarded as comparable to the state aid control system of the EU.[83]

Individual agreements that are to be regarded as *lex specialis* vis-à-vis the autonomous trade measures of the contracting parties are nothing new. In the area of trade defence instruments, both the EU and Australia have in the past agreed on procedural or substantive adaptations of WTO rules in FTAs.[84] The special feature in this case is that the new subsidy instrument has not yet come into being. However, this is not problematic. The regulations could be conditional. Another option would be to agree on a general review clause, which would result in negotiations on bilateral provisions if the new instrument is adopted.

5 Outlook

At the time of writing, the negotiations between the EU and Australia are ongoing. An agreement in principle has not yet been reached. However, it can be assumed that sooner or later a trade agreement will be concluded that will certainly also contain some form of subsidy rules. What concrete form these will take is still open and will possibly also depend on further developments in world trade and world trade law. What seems to be certain so far is only that regulations on subsidies and SOEs will be merged into a separate chapter on competition.[85]

For the EU further convergence of subsidy rules would be an expression of a level playing field and an important signal for multilateral and further bilateral negotiations in the field of subsidies. Australia may also have an interest in reforming international subsidy law due to a growing importance of foreign subsidies. Moreover, as the EU has recently emphasised its strategic independence and wants to assert its own interests more strongly, it would make sense for Australia to respond to this with common regulations. Whether common procedural or substantive rules on a new subsidy instrument will be included in an agreement remains to be seen.

[83] Kühling et al. (2020), p. 415.

[84] See e.g. Ahn and Shin (2011), pp. 434–438; Prusa (2020), pp. 321–342.

[85] European Commission, Report of the 10th round of negotiations for a trade agreement between the European Union and Australia, 9 – 19 March 2021, p. 3, https://trade.ec.europa.eu/doclib/docs/2021/march/tradoc_159518.pdf (last accessed 9 September 2021).

Although this would be useful for Australia in particular, the EU seems to be setting the negotiating framework for subsidies with its proposal.

Overall, subsidy rules are only one element of the comprehensive negotiations and does not seem to be a pressing issue in EU-Australia trade. However, they will continue to form an important part of international trade rules in the future. With no reform of the ASCM yet in sight, while climate change, digitalisation and a competition of systems are already shaping international trade in significant ways, both countries should not miss the opportunity to engage in the further development of international subsidy law.

References

Ahn D, Shin W (2011) Analysis of anti-dumping use in free trade agreements. J World Trade 45(2): 431–456

Bungenberg M (2016) EU-Freihandelsabkommen in der Entwicklung. In: Müller-Graff PC (ed) Europäische Union und USA – Europas nordatlantische Aufgaben. Baden-Baden, pp 91–106

Chiang T (2018) Chinese state-owned enterprises and WTO's anti-subsidy regime. Georgetown J Int Law 49(2):845–886

Coppens D (2014) WTO disciplines on subsidies and countervailing measures. Balancing policy space and legal constraints. Cambridge University Press, Cambridge

Crochet V, Hegde V (2020) China's 'Going Global' Policy: transnational production subsidies under the WTO SCM agreement. J Int Econ Law 23(4):841–863

Croome J (1994) Reshaping the world trading system: a history of the Uruguay Round. Kluwer Law International, Alphen aan den Rijn

Ding R (2014) Public body's or not: Chinese state-owned enterprise. J World Trade 48(1):167–189

Ehlermann CD (1994) State aid control in the European Union: success or failure? Fordham Int Law J 18(4):1212–1229

Feindt PH (2018) EU agricultural policy. In: Heinelt H, Münch S (eds) Handbook of European policies. Edward Elgar Publishing, Cheltenham/Northampton, pp 115–133

Ferguson V, Lim DJ (2021) Economic power and vulnerability in Sino-Australian relations. In: Ferguson V, Jaivin L, Strange S (eds) China stories yearbook 2020: crisis. ANU Press, Acton

Griller S, Obwexer W, Vranes E (2017) Mega-regional agreements: new orientations for EU external relations? In: Griller S, Obwexer W, Vranes E (eds) Mega-regional trade agreements: CETA, TTIP, and TiSA – new orientations for EU external economic relations. Oxford University Press, Oxford

Kotsonis T (2021) The squaring of the circle: subsidy control under the UK-EU trade and cooperation agreement. Eur State Aid Law Q 20(1):15–29

Kühling J, Reinhold P, Weck T (2020) State capitalism and level playing field: the need for a 'Third Country State Aid Instrument' to restore a level playing field in the EU's internal market. Eur State Aid Law Q 19(4):403–417

Mattoo A, Rocha N, Ruta M (2020) Overview: the evolution of deep trade agreements. In: Mattoo A, Rocha N, Ruta M (eds) Handbook of deep trade agreements. World Bank, Washington D.C., pp 1–43

Monopolkommission (2020) Hauptgutachten XXIII: Wettbewerb 2020. Nomos, Baden-Baden

Neale-Besson I (2016) External aspects of State aid policy part 2: accession. In: Pesaresi N et al (eds) EU competition law, vol. IV: state aid, Book One, 2nd edn. Claeys & Casteels, Deventer/ Leuven, pp 141–186

Neumann F (2019) Export des europäischen Beihilfenrechts. Eine Analyse der Europäisierung des internationalen Subventionsrechts durch bilaterale Handelsabkommen. Springer, Wiesbaden
Prusa T (2020) Anti-dumping and countervailing duties. In: Mattoo A, Rocha N, Ruta M (eds) Handbook of deep trade agreements. Washington D.C., pp 320–342
Rubini L (2020) Subsidies. In: Mattoo A, Rocha N, Ruta M (eds) Handbook of deep trade agreements. Washington D.C., pp 427–461
Shaffer G, Gao H (2020) A new Chinese economic order? J Int Econ Law 23(3):607–635
Viner J (1923) Dumping: a problem in international trade. University of Chicago Press, Chicago
WTO (2011) World Trade Report, The WTO and preferential trade agreements: from co-existence to coherence. Geneva
Wu M (2016) The "China, Inc." challenge to global trade governance. Harv Int Law J 57(2): 261–342
Zhou W, Peng D (2021) Australia–anti-dumping measures on A4 copy paper. Am J Int Law 115(1): 94–101

Philipp Reinhold is a Research Associate at the Chair of Public Law, Public International Law and European Law and the Europa-Institut, Saarland University, Germany. He studied law at the University of Bonn and the Université de Lausanne. He is a member of the IILCC Study Group on the reform of investor-State dispute settlement and was, as a staff member of the German Monopolies Commission, involved in the drafting of Chapter IV ("Chinese State Capitalism: A challenge for the European market economy") of the Biennial Report XXIII ("Wettbewerb 2020").

The manufacturer's authorised representative in the EU is Springer
Nature Customer Service Centre GmbH, Europaplatz 3, 69115 Heidelberg,
Germany. If you have any concerns regarding our products, please
contact ProductSafety@springernature.com

Printed and bound by CPI Group (UK) Ltd, Croydon, CR0 4YY
30/09/2026
02225706-0003